Catholic Intellectual Life in America

MAKERS OF THE CATHOLIC COMMUNITY

The Bicentennial History of the Catholic Church in America
Authorized by the National Conference of Catholic Bishops

Gerald P. Fogarty, S.J., ed. *Patterns of Episcopal Leadership*

Joseph P. Chinnici. O.F.M. *Living Stones: The History and Structure of Catholic Spiritual Life in the United States*

Margaret Mary Reher. *Catholic Intellectual Life in America: A Historical Study of Persons and Movements*

Dolores Liptak, R.S.M. *Immigrants and Their Church*

David O'Brien. *Public Catholicism*

Karen Kennelly, C.S.J., ed. *American Catholic Women: A Historical Exploration*

Catholic Intellectual Life in America

A Historical Study of Persons and Movements

Margaret Mary Reher

The Bicentennial History of the Catholic Church in America
Authorized by the National Conference of Catholic Bishops
Christopher J. Kauffman, General Editor

MACMILLAN PUBLISHING COMPANY
NEW YORK

Collier Macmillan Publishers
LONDON

Macmillan Publishing Company
866 Third Avenue, New York, NY 10022

Collier Macmillan Canada, Inc.

Library of Congress Catalog Card Number: 88-18106

Printed in the United States of America

printing number
1 2 3 4 5 6 7 8 9 10

Library of Congress Cataloging-in-Publication Data

Reher, Margaret Mary, 1930–
    Catholic intellectual life in America : a history of persons and
movements / Margaret Mary Reher.
        p.   cm. — (The Bicentennial history of the Catholic Church in
America)
    Includes index.
    ISBN 0-02-925902-9
    1. Catholics—United States—Intellectual life. 2. Catholic
Church—United States—Membership. 3. Catholic Church—Education—
United States—History. 4. United States—Church history.
I. Title. II. Series.
BX1407.I5R44 1989
282'.73—dc19   88-18106
                                                              CIP

In loving memory of my parents,
unflinching models of the best in American Catholicism

Contents

General Editor's Preface

The Second Vatican Council developed a new apologetic, a fresh articulation of faith suitable to the diverse peoples of the world. The Council also marked the turn from the atemporal transcendental character of the neoscholastic theological synthesis to a historical approach to the role of culture in the development of dogma, an approach influenced by the historical-literary methodology fostered by Catholic biblical exegetes. Implicit in the Council Fathers' call to discern the "signs of the times" is the need of the historian to provide a lens to improve our vision of the signs of past times. New models of the church, such as the "pilgrim people" or the "people of God," stressed not the institutional structures but rather the people's religious experiences.

Concurrent with these general trends in apologetics, systematic theology, and ecclesiology was the dramatic rise in consciousness of the ethnic particularities throughout the world. Just as the movements in the Catholic church were based upon a dynamic of historical consciousness, so the rise in ethnic awareness was steeped in the historical dynamic of national and regional identities.

Of all the students of American Catholicism, James Hennesey, S.J., stands out for his singular contribution to the dialogue between theologians and historians. In several studies he has focused on the role of the Christian historian in the process of discerning the authentic tradition of the church. To sharpen our focus on that tradition he juxtaposes a quotation from John Henry Newman with a text from the conciliar decree on Divine Revelation.

Newman in 1859:

> I think I am right in saying that the tradition of the Apostles, committed to the whole Church in its various constituents and functions *per modum unius* [as one unit], manifests itself variously at various times, sometimes

by the mouth of the episcopacy, sometimes by the doctors, sometimes by the people, sometimes by liturgies, rites, ceremonies and customs, by events, disputes, movements, and all those other phenomena which are comprised under the name of history. It follows that none of these channels of tradition may be treated with disrespect; granting at the same time fully that the gift of discerning, discriminating, defining, promulgating, and enforcing any portion of that tradition resides solely in the Ecclesia Docens [the teaching Church].

The Council Fathers in 1965:

What was handed on by the apostles [the tradition] comprises everything that serves to make the People of God live their lives in holiness and increase their faith. In this way the Church in her doctrine, life and worship, perpetuates and transmits to every generation all that she herself is, all that she believes.

Of course this implied religious task of the church historian must be grounded in the rigorous principles and scholarly methodology of the profession. Writing religious history is by its very nature different from writing, say, economic history. Both must avoid a priori reasoning and evaluate the sources of their discipline with a precise analysis. Just as the economic historian must be conscious of the biases embedded in her or his social-class perspective, so the church historian must explore her or his place at the intersection of faith and culture. Without such a hermeneutical exercise of self-exploration one can neither adequately struggle against biases nor develop clear principles for understanding the past. During several group meetings with the six primary contributors to this work such a hermeneutical process developed. Since all of us have been influenced by recent trends in ecclesiology and historiography, each has a sense of her or his place at the intersection of faith and culture. Though some focus on the institutional church and others analyze the movement of peoples, all are professionally trained historians and are sensitive to Newman's notion of the diverse manifestations of tradition.

We conceived this topical approach of the six-volume history as the most effective means of dealing with an enormous amount of material. In a sense this project was an attempt to weave the American fabric of tradition into distinctive patterns. Although I designed the overall project, each of the primary contributors, either author or editor-author, was responsible for the particular design of his or her book. We seven historians met several times over a three-year period. In this case the term "community of scholars" is no exaggeration; a remarkable climate of honesty, candor, civility, and humor prevailed in our discussions. Though each volume stands on its own, the six achieve an unusual unity. There is a common beginning in most of the books. Commemorating the bicentennial of the appointment of John Carroll, each of the books opens during the federal period when Catholics achieved some semblance of ecclesiastical organization. We anticipate that a fresh synthesis of colonial Catholic history will be published at the quincentennial in 1992 of Columbus's arrival in the New World.

Throughout these volumes one reads about the persistent need for Catholics to forge their religious identities within the ethos of the new nation. In its origins the nation tended toward enlightenment and toleration; Catholics in Maryland and Pennsylvania reflected an open cosmopolitanism symbolized by the leadership of John Carroll. There was a conscious effort to embrace religious liberty and pluralism as positive factors; a denominational civility characterized the era. Subsequently, periodic outbursts of militant anti-Catholicism and nativism during the periods of immigration led Catholics to identify their loyalty to the United States in terms of good citizenship, but they retreated from the culture into ethnic enclaves; these were the preservationists who nurtured their particular Old World cultures in defense against this hostility. Isaac Hecker and the Americanists, such as John Ireland, forged a transformationist identity, one that was derived from the Carroll era and was based upon the spiritual compatibility of Catholicism and American culture.

Preservationist and transformationist are more appropriate concepts than ideological terms such as conservative and liberal because they are rooted in the religious and social contexts. Though today the lines are blurred between these identities, they are still viable conceptually. Today's preservationists are defensive against what they perceive as the antireligious tendencies of the culture and are searching for a wholeness in their view of the past. Transformationists tend to mediate religion in the terms of the culture and, like Isaac Hecker, see the movement of the Spirit not in opposition to modern society but within strands of the larger national ethos.

The "Romanness" of the American Catholic identity has seldom been a problem. During periods of conflict and controversy leaders in both camps have appealed to Rome as symbolic of their general loyalty to the papacy. American notions of religious liberty, denominationalism, pluralism, and voluntarism were not legitimated by Rome until the Second Vatican Council. While many Americans have consistently held that this attitude by the Vatican represents the inherent conflict between Roman authority and American democracy, Catholics have tended to consider the assumption that there is such a conflict to be another malicious manifestation of the anti-Catholic animus. While very loyal to Rome, Catholics have shared with other Americans a pragmatic sense, a sense that Martin E. Marty refers to as a kind of experimentalism. While Catholics articulated a loyalty to Rome as the center of their changeless religion, paradoxically many had derived from their American experience a spirituality and a religious worldview that accept change as a fact of life. Marty quotes Jacques Maritain on American experimentalism: "Americans seem to be in their own land as pilgrims, prodded by a dream! They are always on the move—available for new tasks, prepared for the possible loss of what they have. They are not settled, installed. . . . In this sense of becoming and impermanence one may discern a feeling of evangelical origin which has been projected into temporal activity." In a sense this Catholic insistence on changeless faith, while their religious behavior is protean, allowed many leaders to hold to an Americanist vision and even a modernist methodology (applied not to Scripture but to evangelization) after the condemnations of Americanism and modernism.

Catholic identities derived from race, gender, and non-European ethnic groups are distinctive from the Roman, transformationist, and preservationist identities. Black Catholics were so marginalized that there was no sizable number of black clergy until the mid-twentieth century. The general periodization, particularly "immigrant church," is simply meaningless to their experience. The racism of the vast majority of people was reflected in the church. Many black Catholics now identify with Afro-American culture and the exodus experience basic to liberation theology. French Canadians and many Hispanic people also have developed their distinctive identities. Their non-European origins marginalized them in a church dominated by assimilationists of the more affluent classes. As with the black Catholics, their identities are deeply influenced by their historically rooted outsider status.

These six volumes struggled against exclusivism based on race, ethnicity, and gender. While chapters in these books deal with race and major non-European ethnic groups, an entire volume focuses on gender. I consulted with several Catholic feminists before deciding on a separate book on women in the Catholic community. Some might ask why not each of the other five books deals with this subject. Because there are so few secondary works on Catholic women and because not each historian could do ground-breaking research in women's studies, it became evident that an entire book should be devoted to this topic. As a consequence of a corollary decision, specialists in particular areas wrote separate chapters in the book because one author could not do justice to a general history of Catholic women. Of course, many Catholic women were drawn into the issues discussed in the other five volumes, but many behaved in a countercultural manner and opposed the dominant ecclesiastical identity represented by the conventional notion of the "ideal Catholic woman." In the shadow of patriarchy many women formed spiritual identities that did not fit religious and social categories.

Dolores Liptak, R.S.M., and Karen Kennelly, C.S.J., help us to understand the varieties of ethnic and female identities; David O'Brien and Gerald P. Fogarty, S.J., elaborate on the public forms of Catholicism and episcopal leadership; Margaret Mary Reher and Joseph P. Chinnici, O.F.M., locate various Catholic identities on the intellectual, spiritual, and devotional planes.

These six historians have been sensitive to regional variations, to differing contexts of urban development, and to the need to expand beyond the boundary of the stated theme of each volume into such frontiers as the micro-history of neighborhoods and parishes, the rural Catholic experience, meanings of the Catholic rites of passage and of Catholic "habits of the heart." The design of the project and the bicentennial deadlines limited the historians' range to the broad national contours of their topics. Though there is unavoidable overlapping in the treatment of persons and movements, the particular points of view preclude redundancy. More significantly, these books focus on the distinctive character of the American aspect of the Catholic community and represent various blends of original research and a unique rendering of topics derived from secondary literature.

From design to production I have had the good fortune to work with excellent historians and other fine people. To Justus George Lawler, the literary editor, to Charles Buggé, our liaison with the United States Catholic Conference, to Elly Dickason and Charles E. Smith of Macmillan Publishing Company, to Virgil C. Dechant and the late John M. Murphy of the Knights of Columbus, to Archbishop William D. Borders of Baltimore and Archbishop Oscar H. Lipscomb of Mobile, chairmen of the bicentennial committees of the National Conference of Catholic Bishops, and to John Bowen, S.S., Sulpician archivist and consultant, I am exceedingly grateful for their participation in making this six-volume set an appropriate tribute to John Carroll and to all those people who formed the Catholic tradition in the United States. I am particularly indebted to the inspiration of John Tracy Ellis in this the fifty-first year of his priesthood. May we always cherish his tradition of scholarship, honesty, and civility.

                                          Christopher J. Kauffman

Acknowledgments

The National Conference of Catholic Bishops in 1981 established an ad hoc committee to plan for an appropriate observance of the 200th anniversary of the appointment in 1789 of John Carroll of Baltimore as the first Roman Catholic bishop for the United States of America. It was quickly determined that an important component of that observance should be a serious and substantial effort to shed added light on the growth and development of the Catholic church in Carroll's native land for these two hundred years. A subcommittee for publications was formed and the six volumes, *Makers of the Catholic Community*, are the result of its initiatives.

Grateful acknowledgment is made to the Knights of Columbus and their Supreme Knight, Virgil C. Dechant, who provided a generous grant that underwrote the scholarly efforts necessary to such a venture. For more than a century the work of the Knights of Columbus has epitomized much of the Catholic life that fills these volumes just as their presence and spirit have given discernible form to the faith and external witness of the Catholic church in the United States.

The Order has a rich tradition of fostering historical studies. In 1921 the Fourth Degree established the K of C Historical Commission. It presented its awards to Samuel Flagg Bemis and Allan Nevins, historians who later became notable figures. The commission also sponsored the publication of the K of C Racial Contribution Series: W. E. B. DuBois, *The Gift of the Black Folk*; George W. Cohen, *The Jews in the Making of America*; and Frederick F. Schrader, *The Germans in the Making of America*. Coincidentally, these books were also published by Macmillan. The K of C microfilm collection of the manuscripts of the Vatican archives, which resides at Saint Louis University, is a remarkable testimony to the Knights' promotion of scholarship. In 1982 a scholarly history of the Order, *Faith and Fraternalism*, by Christopher J. Kauffman, was published, a book that has been widely noted as a solid contribution to social and religious history. Hence, *Makers of the Catholic Community* is a significant mark on the long continuum of the Knights' role in historical scholarship.

For six years the NCCB Ad Hoc Committee for the Bicentennial of the U.S. Hierarchy has given consistent and affirmative support for this series, and the Subcommittee for Publications has provided the technical insights and guidance that were necessary to the finished work. All who have thus contributed time and talent deserve recognition and gratitude. The members of the committee were: Archbishop William D. Borders, chairman; Archbishops Eugene A. Marino, S.S.J., Theodore E. McCarrick, and Robert F. Sanchez; and Bishops John S. Cummins, F. Joseph Gossman, Raymond W. Lucker, and Sylvester W. Treinen. The staff consisted of Rev. Robert Lynch and Mr. Richard Hirsch. Members of the subcommittee were: Rev. William A. Au, Ph.D.; Msgr. John Tracy Ellis, Ph.D.; Sister Alice Gallin, O.S.U., Ph.D.; Msgr. James Gaffey, Ph.D.; Rev. James Hennesey, S.J., Ph.D.; and Msgr. Francis J. Lally.

Most Reverend Oscar H. Lipscomb
Chairman, Subcommittee for Publications

Foreword

In his classic essay on the nature of historiography, H. Stuart Hughes elaborates on the historian's roles as scientist and artist. With a skeptical eye the historian collects and analyzes the data, knowing full well that the entire story cannot be told with precise accuracy. As an artist with a seasoned sense of intuition regarding the vagaries of human nature the historian also composes the canvas of the past, frames events in perspective, and, conscious of the need for restraint and balance, strives to achieve unity.

Margaret Reher has rendered the story of the religious thought of the American Catholic tradition with the rigor of the scientist and the sensitivity of the artist. Determined to avoid the hazards of writing intellectual history as if it were devoid of social meaning, Dr. Reher has thoroughly developed the religious and social backgrounds that form a perspective for her presentation of the major figures and movements in the intellectual life of the Catholic community in the United States.

In the religious history of the American Catholic people, intellectual leaders have tended to be transformationists rather than preservationists, that is, they viewed the American experience as having had a positive transformationist effect upon Catholicism, and the Catholic faith as having had a similar impact upon American culture. Such men as John Carroll, John England, Isaac Hecker, John Lancaster Spalding, and John Keane did not fall in with the tendency to preserve European forms of Catholicism as if American culture were inherently in opposition to the traditions of the faith. Instead, they attempted to develop an apologetic, the means of passing on the faith, suitable to the evolution of modern American culture. At the dawn of the twentieth century there was a strong intellectual ferment, symbolized by the publication of the *New York Review* and dedicated to exploring the relationship between religion and culture. However, within a matter of a few years the antimodernist forces within the church had succeeded in their effort to terminate the movement for fashioning a new apologetic. What might have been a turning point in the history of Catholicism was a failure; the church was afraid to turn, and the preservationists won the day.

As Dr. Reher points out, despite the religious separatism of the postmodernist period, there was a gradual movement toward a realignment of Catholicism and modern culture, a movement that reached almost revolutionary proportions in the Second Vatican Council. As we attempt to sort these experiences of the past twenty years, we rely upon historians to articulate the story of American Catholic intellectual life. Dr. Reher has provided such articulation with scientific precision and artistic sensitivity.

Christopher J. Kauffman

Preface

In May of 1955, Monsignor John Tracy Ellis delivered an address to the Catholic Commission on Intellectual and Cultural Affairs. It was entitled "American Catholics and the Intellectual Life," and in it the distinguished church historian offered a rigorous analysis of the roots of his subjects' failure to produce a vital intellectual tradition. He acknowledged that the ancestors of many American Catholics were poor, illiterate immigrants, often the victims of a deep anti-Catholicism that pervades the annals of American history. Those factors, Ellis continued, no longer excuse Catholics for their failure to exert a significant influence on the culture of their country. He placed the blame squarely on the shoulders of his coreligionists. Americans in general are anti-intellectual, Ellis observed, but Catholics in undue proportion value material gains over those of the mind. Part of the problem the lecturer traced to Catholic institutions of higher learning. They had failed to articulate their goals clearly. Many were more concerned with apologetics than with liberal learning. Consequently, their graduates often failed to grasp the connection between the pursuit of an intellectual vocation and their daily lives. In particular Ellis deplored the multiplicity of Catholic graduate schools that were in competition with each other. This had the debilitating effect of diluting the pool of scholars available to staff and maintain superior institutions.[1] Everything that the Monsignor said, however, had already been articulated earlier by other Catholic critics.

Archbishop John Carroll, whose elevation to the American Catholic bishopric in 1789 this volume commemorates, was the first to offer criticism about Catholic higher education. He was the guiding force behind the foundation of Georgetown College, now Georgetown University. Theoretically, this institution was intended as a nursery of the higher life that would produce an intellectual Catholic elite. In fact, however, Carroll complained that the college's constitutions were "not calculated for the meridian of America." Though the students were thoroughly catechized, they were not given sufficient "acquaintance with the manners & language of the world."[2] When, in 1799, the Sulpicians opened Saint Mary College in nearby Baltimore, the rivalry between Catholic institutions began.[3] The process of establishing colleges accelerated as the country expanded and the children of immigrants added mightily to the numbers of American Catholics. By 1876 there were seventy-four Catholic colleges in the United States chartered to grant degrees. In the view of the Catholic convert Bishop Thomas A. Becker of Wilmington, Delaware, not one of these "small fry" colleges (as he called them) was deserving of the name *university* in the European tradition.[4] Concurrently, the distinguished layman John Gilmary Shea, founder of American Catholic historiography, complained about American Catholics' underevaluation of literary culture and the failure of wealthy Catholics to endow their own institutions.[5] In 1893, another lay Catholic intellectual, Maurice Francis Egan, professor of English at the University of Notre Dame, addressed the audience at the Columbian Catholic Congress held in Chicago. Egan avoided carping criticism of American Catholic colleges but made several recommendations to improve their quality. They needed to broaden their curricula and clarify their goals; they needed to be truly liberal and not apologetic. "We cannot reasonably close our eyes to the facts," he said, "that we need a system of discipline which will lay more stress on the honor of the youth [in our charge] and less on the subtle distinction between venial and mortal sin." Unless the colleges and universities employed more qualified lay professors, institutions completely controlled by "ecclesiastics" could not thoroughly do their work or obtain their proper effect on society in America.[6]

Almost three decades later, George Shuster—another layman, former professor from the same department and university as Egan, and editor of the liberal weekly *The Commonweal*—made similar observations. To the rhetorical question, "Have We Any [American Catholic] Scholars?" he flatly responded in the negative.[7]

A few names, Bishop John Lancaster Spalding of Peoria and Orestes A. Brownson, the latter a layman and editor successively of the *Boston Quarterly Review* and *Brownson's Quarterly Review*, could be added to this list of distinguished and loving critics of their coreligionists' cultural standards. Collectively, however, they represented a minority opinion.

What made Monsignor Ellis's exposition so remarkable, aside from its lucidity, was the response it provoked. His lecture was published four months later in the journal *Thought* in the midst of a decade when thinking Catholics were becoming increasingly self-critical.[8]

Although, as Ellis recalls, some members of the hierarchy were annoyed by his article, most Catholics agreed with his assessment. They had become leaders in business, politics and in most other fields, with the exception of intellectual activities.[9]

The essay set off a spate of literature, and "the great debate" was launched. Three years later, an associate professor of sociology at Fordham University, Thomas F. O'Dea, published the results of his study in *American Catholic Dilemma: An Inquiry into the Intellectual Life*. After having examined the data, O'Dea agreed with Ellis's conclusions. He indicated that the causes of his coreligionists' poor representation in intellectual matters were an abstract formalism in education that led to boredom and a weakness in their educational institutions, which were clerically dominated, moralistic, and authoritarian. Finally, a defensiveness still lingered in the collective consciousness of Catholics from bygone days of prejudice and even persecution.[10] A chorus of voices rose within the ranks. Monsignor Joseph Fenton of The Catholic University and Jesuit Robert I. Gannon of Fordham University were among those who disagreed with the critics, but, for the first time, such opinion was in the minority.

In 1965, Philip Gleason, professor of history at the University of Notre Dame, pointed to the difficulty in conceptualizing the problem of American Catholics' anti-intellectualism. He suggested that the term be abandoned because it was too laden with emotion and seemed to lead nowhere. He cited the fact that three recent commentators, Andrew Greeley, John D. Donovan, and James W. Trent, intelligent and highly trained, had examined the status of American Catholic intellectuals and reached widely divergent conclusions. Gleason accurately observed that the "American Catholic mentality," real culprit though it might be, had been shaped by the fundamental "social and cultural conditions of the past," which could not be dismissed.[11]

The debate continues to the present, and most scholars agree that the current status of American Catholic intellectual life has improved since Ellis first addressed the question. They differ on the degree of that improvement.[12] However, it is not the purpose of this study to resolve the dispute. Rather, it is to look at the "condition of the past," in Professor Gleason's words, and to examine the contributions of those American Catholics who did value the intellectual life. The major figures who will be discussed all had a love of learning and all, in a particular way, attempted to respond to the intellectual climate of the day. All were loyal sons of the Catholic church—laymen, priests, and members of the hierarchy. It will not be argued that these figures were typical of the person in the church pew; intellectual leaders rarely are. Yet, each had a vision of the role that the Catholic church should play in American sociey. No doubt some creative thinkers have been omitted. In a short work that spans two hundred years, omission is inevitable, even necessary. However, scholars are generally in agreement about the contribution to Catholic thought of those who have been selected.

John Carroll and Charles Carroll, heirs of the Enlightenment, contributed richly to the young Catholic church and the new republic of the United States of America as church and state began to formalize themselves in the late eighteenth century. Irish immigrant bishop John England shared their appreciation of constitutionality and creatively drafted a constitution for his own diocese of Charleston, South Carolina. The Yankee converts Orestes A. Brownson and Isaac Hecker, lifetime friends, illustrate the diversity of positions within the romantic movement of the mid–nineteenth century. Bishop John Lancaster Spalding, a champion of culture, was primarily responsible for the foundation of the Catholic University of America toward the end of the nineteenth century. The Americanist and modernist crises at the turn of the twentieth century should give comfort and warning to contemporary readers. They document the deep divisions that often exist within the Catholic church. The Americanizers stoutly defended fin de siècle liberalism and the scientific impulse. In their efforts to embrace new avenues of thought, they uncritically accepted America's expansionism and materialism. The reaction against modernism, on the other hand, shut down the *New York Review* (1905–1908), the most scholarly undertaking ever produced by American Catholics up to that time. In his desire to protect orthodoxy, Pope Pius X's global condemnation of modernism stifled creative scholarship in the church. The *Catholic Encyclopedia* survived the postmodernist era because of the prudence of its editors and authors. It stands as a monument to early-twentieth-century American Catholic scholarship and creativity. The neo-Thomistic revival of the post-Depression era has had some harsh critics. It did, however, help American Catholics establish a common identity in a country that still looked upon them with suspicion. The 1950s were a turning point in American Catholic consciousness as scholars began to question their role in the larger American society; the 1960s were revolutionary both for the nation and for the American Catholic community.

As a cradle Catholic who experienced the years before Vatican II and emerged as a trained historian after the council, I have grappled with my own biases and particular intellectual tradition in preparing this study. There is always a great risk involved in writing about events of the recent past. Since the mandate for this project was to tell the story of American Catholic intellectual leadership from 1789 to the present, that risk had to be taken. The enviable task of uncovering the history of our female intellectual leaders, a trove buried beneath the stones of patriarchy, has been left to my colleagues. Primary sources have not been neglected, but the insights and interpretations of previous scholars have been invaluable as well.

Most authors confess that the most pleasant aspect of their work lies in thanking all those who have contributed to its production. In the present case, the enormous number of individuals who have had a hand in this project make the task almost impossible. They know who they are, and they are aware of my gratitude to them. The administrators, library staff, faculty secretaries, and students of Cabrini College deserve special recognition for their generous support, encouragement, and patience throughout this project. Without the careful editing of Christopher Kauffman who, as Tertullian said of Marcion, "did his exegesis with a knife," this manuscript would have remained unfinished. James Hennesey, S.J., graciously read large segments of the original text and final draft and made many helpful comments and corrections. My colleague Margaret McGuinness carefully read and criticized the final draft. Joseph Casino, archivist of the Ryan Memorial Library Archives and Historical Collection housed at Saint Charles Borromeo Seminary, Philadelphia, generously aided and facilitated my research. In the final month spent completing this book, my mother died. My two sisters, my nephew, my nieces, and their families gave me loving support during that period and continue to do so. Last but by no means least, I owe a deep debt of gratitude to my dear friends Marie Kelly and Anita Johnson. Marie tirelessly and patiently checked and rechecked my endnotes for accuracy. It was Anita's magic fingers that commanded her word processor to meet my deadline. God bless all my generous colleagues, family, and friends.

CHAPTER
1
Enlightenment and Episcopal Leadership, 1780–1830

The year 1789 is an important date both in the history of the United States and in the annals of the American Catholic church. That year George Washington had been unanimously elected to the presidency of the infant republic; John Carroll had been appointed as its first Catholic bishop. This was historical coincidence. Nonetheless, there is a parallel between the two events. When Washington took office, the federal Constitution was an untested piece of paper. As Carroll began his episcopacy, the organization of the Catholic church in America was but a blueprint in his mind.[1]

It is this blueprint, as well as its subsequent execution and elaboration by Catholic thinkers, that is the focus of this study. Since no idea develops in a vacuum, attention will be paid to intellectual movements and events that affected the Catholic church as it struggled to adapt to as well as shape its environment. Among these movements, the most salient was the Enlightenment.

To define the philosophy of the Enlightenment is a difficult task. The term denotes the widely shared intellectual currents peculiar to the eighteenth century. Enlightenment expressed independence from the past, an aggressive self-reliance, and an appreciation of the new intellectual methods available. It was a thorough attempt to reconstruct Western societies' traditional ideas and institutions. The rallying cry of the Enlightenment was "Have the courage to use your own understanding." This extended into the area of religion. Not doubt but dogma became the intellect's most dreaded foe. Out of this thinking came demands for freedom of conscience and religious toleration. John Locke (1632–1704) was one of the towering figures of the Enlightenment. Despite his plea for the union of diverse theologies within the Christian church, he excluded that possibility for Catholicism. He thought its "superstition and dogmatism" were incurable.

The Enlightenment, in both its European and American manifestations, is generally considered uniquely Protestant—"two faces of the same happy history, whose great milestone was the rational and Protestant Revolution of 1688," as one historian wrote.[2]

However, scholars have recently isolated a group of European Catholic thinkers who attempted to bridge the gap between Roman Catholicism and the intellectual forces of the Enlightenment.[3] They rejected the ecclesiology of post-Tridentine Catholicism, which included the ideal of union of church and state and the belief that error had no rights. Three of these thinkers will be considered briefly because of their influence on the thought of John Carroll and other Americans.

Arthur O'Leary (1729–1802), Joseph Berington (1743–1827), and John Fletcher (1766–1845) were from the British Isles. As such, they inherited a minority status within an established church. They were heirs of a tradition that had already rejected the idea that the religion of the subject was necessarily that of the king. They also had a strong tradition of respect for constitutional forms of government. This background enabled them to deal with the problem of accepting religious pluralism without acknowledging doctrinal indifference.

Fletcher distinguished between an admissible and an inadmissible form of Catholic intolerance. He defended a refusal to mix belief with error as a prudential practical caution against error's contagion. This, he asserted, was the only kind of intolerance taught by the church. He argued that the church's jurisdiction is in the spiritual realm and has no authority over life, liberty, or property.

O'Leary also argued that the right to life, liberty, and property were natural rights, neither to be reversed by religion nor destroyed by civil rulers. Religion and conscience were anterior to any social contract. He argued against the position advanced by John Calvin and Cardinal Robert Bellarmine in favor of state regulation of religion. Faith, O'Leary held, was a gift of God and not at government disposal.[4]

Under the influence of Locke, Berington wrote that no religion should be established by law. He considered state policy and the concerns of conscience separate. To be a good subject, all that is necessary is to comply with the laws of the land. For Berington, religious toleration was not a concession but a human right. For a time, John

Carroll considered Berington one of the ablest Catholic authors of his day.[5]

Fletcher, O'Leary, and Berington were able to develop a theoretical and integrated approach to the Enlightenment and Catholicism, but were denied the chance to see their theories put into practice. This opportunity was given instead to their coreligionists on the other side of the ocean, among whom were the cousins John and Charles Carroll.

During his sixteen years in Europe, Charles Carroll, John's wealthy cousin and later signer of the Declaration of Independence, had come into contact with the new natural-law trend articulated by Locke and with Montesquieu's theory of republicanism.[6] He also studied the Aristotelian-Thomistic natural-law tradition advanced by the Catholic Jesuit theologians Robert Bellarmine and Francesco Suarez. Now the young Marylander studied the *Mathematics* of Newton and devoured the works of other seventeenth- and eighteenth-century Enlightenment figures. He pondered the implications of their ideas about the origins of civil society and of government as arising from the people.[7] His incipient revolutionary mentality was being formed through exposure to both Protestant and Catholic explorations of the intellectual and cultural climate. In a letter written to his father from Paris in 1759, the twenty-two-year-old Carroll made clear his belief that he could be both a complete gentleman and a good Christian, the latter being the more important; that he performed his religious duties and that he loved God, though less than the deity deserved or the young man wished. Some years later, when Carroll suspected that one of his English Protestant friends was trying to convert him, he retorted that he had "too much sincerity & too much pride" to honor and humor "the prejudices of fools or be on a footing with Knaves." Nonetheless, Carroll declared himself a warm friend of toleration and decried what he called the "intolerating thirst of ye Church of Rome." He stood staunchly for a separation of religion, Protestant or Catholic, from politics.[8]

Every cultured gentleman of the late eighteenth century was expected to study law, and Charles Carroll was no exception. He pored over ancient Roman law and French civil law, and he went to London so that he could study English law firsthand. But there he became thoroughly disillusioned, for all he saw was greed and corruption where he expected to find a balanced, representative government. Before he left London, Carroll had determined that the colonies had to cut the umbilical cord from such an unfit mother.[9] With an optimism typical of Enlightenment thinking, he envisioned a civilization directed by a law of progress and destined to be carried forth by the New World, not the Old.

When Carroll returned home to Maryland, he was admitted to the very exclusive Homony Club, an association of young and wealthy Maryland intellectuals. There, any discussion of religion or politics was off limits, and he enjoyed the friendship of a tolerant and broadly humanistic group of friends.

While he had been abroad, Charles Carroll had been in a position to travel quite freely. His cousin John Carroll's opportunity came in 1771, after his religious profession in Liège. A wealthy English Catholic, Lord Stourton, in his quest for a traveling companion for his eighteen-year-old son, Charles Philip, prevailed upon Carroll's Jesuit superior to allow him to accompany the young man on a grand tour of the Continent that lasted almost two years.[10] One impressive experience was his first encounter with a system of general, free, and compulsory education in Protestant German Baden Dourlach. He never forgot it, and later the cause of education became one of his passions.[11] Another experience, one of a far less benign character, also made a deep impression on the sensitive Jesuit. By the time that he and his protégé reached Rome, a growing hostility against the Jesuit order, begun in Portugal, had reached a fevered pitch. Both pilgrims had to enter the Eternal City incognito.[12]

As he watched from the New World, Charles Carroll angrily denounced the "warfare" launched in Europe against the Society of Jesus because of its real or imagined political power. This does not imply that Carroll never criticized the Jesuits. As an Enlightenment thinker, he held in acute disdain the "blind obedience" required by the Jesuit rule.[13] Even his cousin John, despite his deep loyalty, complained about the limited education he had received at the Jesuit scholasticate. He wrote that little Greek and even less Hebrew were taught, and Latin elegance went uncultivated. Modern authors in science and language were not available in the library, and there were precious few books in English. The net result was that "genius and talent were cramped, & a habit of inapplication was acquired, which few escaped."[14]

The Carroll cousins could brook private criticism but not public humiliation of the Jesuits. When the Society of Jesus was suppressed in 1773 by the Franciscan Pope Clement XIV, both Carrolls were pained.[15] John felt that "an immediate death" would be the greatest blessing he could receive from God. Leaving England, he set sail for America after an absence of twenty-five years; there he could be near those he loved and escape the "reaches of scandal and defamation."[16] The former Jesuit arrived home in 1774, too late to see the excitement stirred up by his cousin Charles. The royal governor, Robert Eden, had imposed a schedule of fees—a euphemism for taxes—on his subjects; Charles Carroll believed that Eden had overstepped his power. In defense of the governor's action, the distinguished Tory lawyer

Daniel Dulany published an essay in the *Maryland Gazette*.[17] This took the form of a dialogue between a dull-witted "First Citizen" who opposed the measure and an enlightened defender, "Second Citizen." Carroll entered the fray. Using the pseudonym "First Citizen," he charged that his views had been so misrepresented that they were scarcely recognizable.

As a result of the "First Citizen" debate, Charles Carroll, probably the wealthiest man in the colonies, was drawn into a network of political involvements as the colonies grew more restive under what they perceived as abuses of their political rights. He joined the association to resist the tax on tea. He and like-minded colonists held that the ancient charters, based on English common law, had granted that taxes be levied by representatives of the colonists themselves, not by the Parliament of England. Subsequently Carroll was appointed to the committee on Non-Importation, then to the important Committee on Correspondence. He became a delegate to the Maryland convention. In many minds, it was justice that the colonies were seeking, not independence. But not in the mind of Charles Carroll. He had long been convinced of the need to sever ties with England. One biographer has claimed that Carroll's views were more radical than those of Benjamin Franklin and other patriots in the decade immediately preceding the Revolution.[18]

In 1784, John Carroll was appointed by Rome as superior of the missions in the thirteen United States of North America. His career in this capacity was barely launched when he suffered a painful public embarrassment, which came from the hands of a close relative and friend, Charles Wharton.[19] The native Maryland ex-Jesuit had left the Catholic church for the Anglican communion while he had been serving as a chaplain in Worcester, England. He had returned home a month before his cousin John Carroll's appointment. Shortly after, Wharton's "Letter to the Roman Catholics of Worcester" was reprinted in Philadelphia. The convert claimed that the letter was simply intended as an explanation to his former congregation about his election of Anglicanism. But since the tract had been printed on both sides of the Atlantic, John Carroll felt compelled to respond. He embarked upon his most ambitious literary project and wrote a 115-page pamphlet complete with 117 footnotes. At the outset, Carroll made it clear that he would not have taken up his pen if the congregation at Worcester alone had been involved. However, since this had not been the case, he felt the need to "enlighten the understanding of his own flock."

Wharton had one advantage over Carroll: he had composed his letter in Europe, where scholarly books were available. Carroll scoured the library at Annapolis with little success in an effort to track down

the sources that Wharton had misrepresented. In addition, Carroll
was forced to compose his essay, entitled "An Address to the Roman
Catholics of the United States of America by a Catholic Clergyman,"
amid pressing responsibilities and, in his words, "almost without any
materials but those which my memory suggested."[20] In the face of
these obstacles, Carroll demonstrated a remarkable grasp of the great
theologians of antiquity as well as of the works of contemporary Protestant and Catholic authors. Historians have judged that Carroll
emerged from this episode as a skilled apologist who stood squarely
in the Enlightenment tradition, especially in respect to his positions
on freedom of inquiry, on the locus of infallibility, and on the doctrine
extra ecclesiam, nulla salus.[21]

Regarding freedom of inquiry, Wharton had charged that Catholics
were excommunicated if they read heretical books. Carroll insisted
that "rational investigation is as open to catholics, as to any other
set of men." He asserted that the former chaplain himself knew that
Catholics read "protestant authors without hesitation or reproof."
Carroll explicitly extended that intellectual freedom to include theological opinion in the context of his discussion on infallibility. Whereas
Wharton argued that Catholic theologians could not agree whether
the locus of infallibility resided in the pope, in a general council, or
in the pope together with council received by the church, Carroll responded that the third position was not mere theological opinion but
constant teaching. Unquestionably, infallibility resided in "the body
of bishops united and agreeing with their head, the bishop of Rome."
He did admit that some divines held that the pope was infallible even
outside a council—but "with this opinion faith has no concern, every
one being at liberty to adopt or reject it, as the reason for or against
may affect him." Carroll's collegial view of infallibility as well as his
opinion on the personal infallibility of the pope reflected a tradition
that endured well into the nineteenth century.

To Wharton's contention that Catholics believed that Protestants
were damned, Carroll made a forceful rejoinder. He wrote that Catholics "not only *may,* but *are obligated* to believe that *out of our communion* salvation may be obtained." Carroll based his argument on
Saint Augustine, Saint Thomas Aquinas, and others who held that
people could be saved without baptism.[22]

In this context, it has been shown that Carroll went beyond the
position of other Catholic Enlightenment apologists who focused on
the sacrament of baptism as the common basis of all Christian traditions.[23] He was, however, typical in his focus on individual faith
and the particular appropriation of truth. He accepted religious pluralism, not as a necessary concession, but as a positive good. He never,
however, blurred the line between religious toleration and religious

indifference.[24] He believed that if his young republic "had the wisdom
and temper to preserve [civil and religious liberty], America may come
to exhibit a proof to the world, that general and equal toleration, is
the most effectual method to bring all denominations of Christians
to a unity of faith." Carroll worried in print that his cousin's letter
had "scattered the seeds of religious animosity."[25]

John Carroll was a Federalist in politics and reflected in his church
polity that party's suspicion of the democratic element. He betrayed
an elitist strain in 1791, when he told one congregation composed of
poor Irish and prominent French, that the "best pew shall be reserved
for the [French] consul." In the early years of his administration, Carroll had promised the lay trustees a role in choosing their own pastors
at the time when canonical parishes would be established. By 1814,
the year before he died, Carroll had explicitly repudiated any form
of "ecclesiastical democracy." Before his death, he confessed that the
opinion of the laity would never weigh with him "so much as a straw,
in determining things, belonging of right to Episcopal or pastoral
matters." Yet, he continued, "in all other matters I deem it prudent
to act concurrently with the [lay] Trustees." In light of this sentiment,
what the aging archbishop wrote next comes as a bit of a surprise.
He advised Enoch Fenwick, pastor of the Pro-Cathedral, as well as
Carroll's secretary, to assemble the board of trustees, confident that
they would acknowledge their "incompetency to chuse an Organist
and leave it to your choice. Be ready to recommend the one whom
you prefer & obtain their approbation."[26]

It was the subject of lay prerogatives that caused John Carroll to
have second thoughts about the English apologist, Joseph Berington.
In his early struggle with the trustees of Saint Peter's in New York,
Carroll learned that Berington countenanced the nomination by the
laity of their own pastors. Carroll judged that the practice would be
"fatal" if allowed in his own country.

Originally, Carroll had high praise for Berington's *State and Be-
haviour of the English Catholics* and quoted from it freely in his
controversy with Wharton. Carroll had appreciated the Englishman's
enlightened position on religious toleration, a sentiment that the
American had long shared. In a letter complimenting Berington on
his apologetic work, Carroll made his own position clear: a "reasonable system of universal Forbearance, and charity amongst Christians
of every denomination . . . giving an open Field to the Display of Truth
and fair argument may greatly contribute to bring mankind to a unity
of Opinion on matters of Religious Concern." In Carroll's view, the
two greatest obstacles to a reunion of other Christian groups with
Catholics were insistence on "the Latin Tongue in the publick Liturgy"
and imprecision about "the Extent and Boundaries of the Spiritual

Jurisdiction of the Holy See," and he asked Berington to examine both questions. Carroll expressed the conviction that use of the vernacular "ought not only to be sollicited, but *insisted on*, as essential to the Service of God & Benefit of Mankind." To cling to a dead language could be chalked up to "chimerical Fears of Innovation or to Indolence."

Berington circulated Carroll's opinion on vernacular usage as a fait accompli. In a subsequent letter, Carroll said, "I am able to do not more than express my Wishes, and enforce on my Brethren my own Sentiment;" most of these agreed that a change was needed in America. In two additional letters to different correspondents Carroll again turned to the topic. In the first he suggested that he would not have cooperation from the American clergy even if he were so rash as to introduce the vernacular "upon my own authority." In the other he insisted that any change of discipline had to be authorized by "the Holy See and the first Pastors of the Church."[27]

This was Carroll's last private statement on the subject, but it may not be the whole story. Evidence has been presented suggesting that Carroll did allow the vernacular to be used in portions of the rites of sacraments after his episcopal consecration in 1790.[28]

For close to two decades Carroll watched Berington's work with apprehension.[29] He believed that the Englishman's treatment of papal power as not of supernatural but merely human origin was indicative of "the leveling spirit of the times." He lamented to his English friend Charles Plowden, a former Jesuit, that Berington's works brought "disrespect, I had almost said, hatred . . . agst. the Holy See." In the same letter Carroll denounced Berington's campaign against clerical celibacy.[30]

When Berington resurrected the story of the medieval star-crossed lovers, Abelard and Eloise, Carroll was dismayed.[31] He was sorry, as he told Plowden, to see Berington, "a man who manages his pen so well," run after "fleeting and dishonourable applause" by treating such an "indelicate subject."[32] Abelard, the gifted philosopher and famous teacher at Paris, had seduced his brilliant and beautiful protégée Eloise, who was less than half her teacher's age.[33] The romantics have it that Abelard spoke more of love than of philosophy to Eloise.[34] John Carroll adopted a *cherchez la femme* interpretation of the celebrated romance that immortalized the couple. Carroll judged Eloise's youthful conduct "imprudent." "In her later years," he wrote, "I hope she made reparation."[35] Carroll remained silent about the conduct of Abelard, a cleric in minor orders when the affair began. History reports that the philosopher was castrated by the girl's family, in revenge for the dishonor Abelard had brought to Eloise.[36]

Carroll may not have been in sympathy with Eloise's side of the story, but he was not a misogynist. He conducted a long correspondence with Johanna Barry and her husband James, wealthy Irish Catholic immigrants who resided in the federal district. Both were Carroll's personal friends. The bishop came to "venerate and love" Johanna, a devoted wife, mother, and unsung benefactress to those suffering from "wretchedness or disease."[37]

The friendship between Carroll and Mrs. William Magee Seton, better known as Elizabeth Ann Bayley Seton, is a more familiar story.[38] Carroll had taken a personal interest in the cultured young widow, a convert to Catholicism, and her five small children. When they moved from New York to Baltimore, Seton opened a small school. Later, she became convinced that she had a call to religious life and a few women joined her. In 1809, Bishop Carroll accepted the vows of the pioneer "Sisters of Charity of Saint Joseph," as the first American sisterhood was originally called.[39] In 1975, Elizabeth Seton became the first declared saint in the United States; in time, her Sisters of Charity became a widespread teaching order.

John Carroll was comfortable when dealing with women in traditional roles of wife and mother or religious sister. When a woman crossed over the boundary into supposedly masculine territory, he had some reservations. "Female missioners are not much to my taste!" Carroll told Plowden in 1788, after he learned of the work of one Donna Maria Antonia de San José de la Paz. She was having remarkable success in promoting the *Spiritual Exercises* of Ignatius Loyola in South America. Carroll recognized his own bias. As he told Plowden, "I hope, I shall not be blind to the wonderful works of God, if he chuse [sic] to make use of such instruments for the salvation of the world." Carroll's subsequent discussions "of that extraordinary woman," Donna Maria Antonia, are quite laudatory. He considered her an instrument of divine providence, as she continued the retreat work initially inspired by the Jesuits. Although providence had ordained "the destruction of the Society," Carroll wrote, that same "mysterious" providence, through Donna Maria Antonia, continued to produce good religious results "from the past services, & practices introduced by the Society."

The *Spiritual Exercises* of Saint Ignatius had been a formative factor in John Carroll's spiritual development as they were in the lives of all the young Catholic gentry who had been educated at Saint Omer in French Flanders and other Jesuit institutions.[40] Both John Carroll and Charles Carroll were Saint Omer alumni. The annual retreat of these students, sometimes conducted from the perspective of spiritual combat in defense of the faith, emphasized a prayerful, personal grasp of Christian virtue.[41] Another staple of their spiritual regimen was the classic *Introduction to the Devout Life* of Saint Francis de Sales, which presented a compelling analysis of the spiritual transformation required of a Christian gentleman. It was one of John Carroll's favorites and was read by all Jesuit masters and some pupils.[42] Another popular French author, Jean Croiset, drew upon scripture, literature, and what has been called "his own sophisticated insights into the Christian gentleman's secular world." In his eighteen-volume *l'Année chrétienne*, Croiset presented an integrated view of secular society with the spiritual values of the Christian gentry's code. Charles Carroll while a student in Europe bought a complete set of *l'Année* for his family's library in Maryland.[43]

Another aid to spiritual development promoted by the Jesuits was membership in the Sodality of the Blessed Virgin Mary. It fostered the personal piety of students as well as their cultural development. John Carroll had served as the prefect of the Marian Society in Bruges in 1773 shortly before he returned to America.[44]

The general piety of the Anglo-American Catholic people reflected that of English Catholics. A favorite spiritual writer was John Gother, a convert from Protestantism, who wrote manuals of prayer and instruction. His emphasis was practical and ethical and his focus was the life of Christ. Gother's work has been called "subtly undenominational," suited to promote amity with other Christians.

Gother's disciple, Richard Challoner, who became vicar apostolic of the London District, with technical jurisdiction over colonial Catholics, supplanted the master as an American favorite. Challoner was a prolific writer; he composed prayers, meditations, and catechisms. His 1740 classic *Garden of the Soul* became synonymous with eighteenth-century Anglo-American Catholicism.[45] It emphasized a life of conformity to the gospel in a deep and personal relationship with Jesus, and it was suited to all walks of life. By 1818 twenty-five editions of fifteen of Challoner's works were published in the United States.[46] The bishop's works, sober in tone, stood in marked contrast to the enthusiasm of the Evangelical revivals that burst onto the colonial scene in the first half of the eighteenth century and erupted periodically.

The religious instruction of the illiterate population was taken seriously by priests and the landed gentry, who held indentured servants and slaves. The truth of this claim is attested to by the numerous catechisms that circulated in Maryland and were used for elementary religious instruction.[47] For almost a century, colonial Catholics depended primarily on England for their religious books. The first Catholic book published in the colonies was a translation of the Frenchman François Fénelon's *Dissertation on Pure Love*. It was printed in 1738 by a Protestant, Andrew Bradford in Philadelphia.[48] The first original Catholic prayerbook, *The Manual of Prayers*, was compiled by Robert

Molyneux and published in 1774. Molyneux, a Jesuit, had taken charge of Saint Joseph's church in Philadelphia the year before. He was a well-educated Englishman, judged superior to John Carroll in learning; he was characterized by Carroll as a "good natured creature, fat as a porpoise," with a "natural talent for elegant life and manners."[49] It is believed that Molyneux had a hand in the literature published by Christopher Talbot, the first Catholic publisher in the city. In 1784 Talbot put out a reprint of Jesuit Joseph Reeves' *New History of the Old and New Testament.*[50] Two years later Talbot published Molyneux's funeral oration for Ferdinand Farmer, which had been carried in all the Pennsylvania newspapers and translated into German.[51]

Farmer, whose German surname was Steinmeyer, caused by his death a tragic loss to the entire Philadelphia community. He was highly respected by Catholics and Protestants and was active in civic affairs. He was a member of the board of trustees of the University of Pennsylvania and of the famous Philosophical Society of Philadelphia. In 1781 he and Molyneux purchased a house from Quakers and began the first parochial school in the United States.[52]

Not all émigré clerics were of Farmer's caliber. Consequently, Carroll tried to exercise caution in granting faculties to them, but pressing pastoral needs led him to make decisions he later regretted. In some instances, he misjudged an individual's true character. One classic case involved an Irishman, Patrick Smyth. Smyth came to Maryland in 1787, well recommended by his ecclesiastical superior in Ireland. Carroll himself interviewed the priest and found him perfectly satisfactory. He assigned the newcomer to Fredricktown to replace an ailing pastor, a former Jesuit. Later a dispute arose over a small amount of money Smyth claimed the sick priest owed him. The Irishman asked to be reimbursed by the local procurator general, who refused on the ground that it was a private matter. Smyth began to circulate rumors that he was ill treated at the hands of the former Jesuits and was returning home. When Carroll caught wind of the story and confronted Smyth, the Irishman feigned shock and claimed that he was leaving America because he was homesick. He told Carroll, with whom he lived for a month immediately before he set sail, that he had been treated with "as much generosity & attention, as if he had been an old & intimate acquaintance & friend."

But Smyth's warmth was disingenuous. He had scarcely landed on Irish soil when he had *The Present State of the Catholic Mission*, a scurrilous attack on the church in America, published in Dublin in 1788. Carroll was dismayed by his former guest's "treachery & falsehood."[53] Smyth, described by one of his contemporaries as "restless as a wave," had filled his account with historical inaccuracies and innuendo.[54] He dragged out the old anti-Jesuit canards and added a few of his own. Maryland, where the Jesuits had labored for over two hundred years, was depicted as a spiritual wasteland. The priests were described as power-hungry, money-grabbing sloths who lived lavishly while the poor were neglected. This was more than Carroll's sense of fair play could abide. He had to set the record straight for the European audience lest Smyth's calumny deter "some good & virtuous Priests" who might be thinking about coming to labor in America. First Carroll undercut Smyth's pretension at historical accuracy by pointing out that he never even visited the areas on which he was reporting. To the Irishman's claim that the former Jesuits lived in three splendid manors on the Potomac, Carroll countered that one house was ordinary, another was in ruins and scarcely afforded shelter from inclement weather. In terms of size, the third dwelling was more like the cell the Shunammite woman prepared for the Hebrew prophet Elias. Carroll did not deal with the issue Smyth had raised about slaveholding, but he did defend the Jesuits' treatment of their slaves. He claimed that their slaves "work less and are much better fed, lodged and clothed, than laboring men in almost any part of Europe . . . a *priest's negro* is almost proverbial for one, who is allowed to act without control." Carroll praised the zeal of the English Jesuits who had planted Catholicism in Maryland and attributed Smyth's animus to the traditional hostility that existed between the Irish and the English. As it happened, Carroll's reply was never published. The archbishop of Dublin, John Troy, assured Carroll that he and the other Irish bishop would prevent circulation of Smyth's pamphlet, which should not be dignified with a response.[55]

Carroll took up his pen not only to defend the church in America from the accusations of discontented clergymen but to defend Catholics' status as loyal citizens of the young republic. During the years 1786 and 1787 the *Columbian*, a Philadelphia magazine, published several letters objecting to religious liberty for Catholics. Carroll sent off a letter to the editor in which he claimed that it was the spirit of Christianity that led the federal government to ban intolerance from its system. He protested the fact that some states still barred Catholics from posts in their governments. He insisted that the "freedom and independence acquired by the united efforts, and cemented with the mingled blood of Protestant and Catholic fellow-citizens, should be equally enjoyed by all."[56]

Several years later Carroll felt compelled to write a letter to the editor of the *United States Gazette* published in New York. The *Gazette* had carried an article opposing Catholics as officeholders, in anticipation of the debate over ratification of the federal Constitution. Carroll, whose brother Daniel later became one of the signers of the Constitution, confessed that he always suffered hurt feelings when

Catholics were excluded from political office.[57] Now the *Gazette* argued that the United States was founded to preserve Protestantism, and that everything of worth in the arts, science, and government flowed from Protestantism. Under the pseudonym "Pacificus," Carroll penned a spirited rejoinder. Again he reminded his audience that Catholics' "blood flowed as freely [in proportion to their numbers]" and that Catholics "opened their purses as freely in the cause of liberty and independence, as any other citizen, [but still they] are most unjustly excluded from the advantages they contributed to establish." What kind of system of polity is it, Carroll added rhetorically, that is calculated "for the express purpose of divesting of rights legally acquired [by] those citizens, who are not only unoffending, but whose conduct has been highly meritorious?" In his conclusion, Carroll made it clear that he was not simply defending the rights of Catholics, but that for the "preservation of her liberties and her government," the United States must be attached to all its citizens' "political happiness, to the security of their persons and their property, which is independent of religious doctrines, and not restrained by any."[58]

Historians point out the fact that here Carroll went on record for the separation of church and state at a time when most Europeans and some Americans thought that the basis of social unity depended on the acceptance of one state-sponsored religion.[59] They also note that it fell to Carroll's brother, Daniel, to help shape the 1791 amendment to the federal Constitution that prohibits Congress from making any law respecting an establishment of religion.[60] For men of the Enlightenment like the Carroll brothers and their signer-cousin, Charles, religion and piety were closely identified with morality, doing good to one's neighbor, and living a virtuous life. Social and political unity depended upon the republican virtue of the people and their zest for the common good.[61]

At times, events shook the convictions of both John and Charles Carroll about the rule of reason in human affairs. In July of 1789, Charles worried that the Confederation would break down and that Great Britain would attempt a reconquest.[62] John realized that it would take more than the work of the brilliant controversialist John Fletcher to effect a reunion of Christendom. Carroll had the Englishmans' *Reflections on the Spirit of Religious Controversy*, which he himself read four times, reprinted in America. Though Carroll told a friend that the book made a "deep impression here . . . alas, it is not conviction alone that will produce conversion. The heart stands more in need of reformation, than the understanding of the light of truth." Carroll did not close his reflection with that gloomy assessment, but expressed the hope that "divine providence, at its own time, will . . . fulfill God's design of mercy in the western world."[63]

In 1789, the papal bull *Ex Hac Apostolicae* was signed by Pope Pius VI, and John Carroll made history as the first Catholic bishop of the United States. Before he had an opportunity to travel to Europe for episcopal consecration, the French Revolution had erupted. John Carroll's cousin Charles Carroll was enthusiastic about the turn of events in a country for which he felt a particular attachment. He was pleased when the titles and distinctions of the French nobility fell. He was subsequently horrified when the head of King Louis XVI rolled from the guillotine in 1793.[64] John Carroll was equally appalled by the "furious democracy" run amok. It colored his attitude toward "ecclesiastical democracy."

French anticlericalism reached a fevered pitch. In its wake, John Carroll told his friend Plowden of a surprising offer he had received from the superior general of the Sulpicians. Writing from Paris in 1790, M. Jacques-Andre Emery informed Carroll that the Sulpicians were anxious to ensure the preservation of their institute and hoped to establish a seminary in America. The revolution frustrated the Sulpicians' apostolate, the training and education of future priests. Emery promised to send a learned faculty and students and to provide for the erection of a seminary building gratis.[65]

When the newly consecrated bishop returned home in 1791, four Sulpician priests and five seminarians had already arrived in his episcopal see in Baltimore. The stage was set for what would be a long and complex saga involving Carroll, the Sulpicians, and the former Jesuits of Georgetown.

Carroll had scarcely returned to America when a pet project of his was published by Matthew Carey's press on December 1, 1790. Three years before, Carey, a Philadelphia publisher, had sought Carroll's advice about putting out an English edition of the Catholic Challoner's Douai-Rheims version of the Bible. Carroll enthusiastically supported the plan: he promoted the project from the pulpit, sought out subscribers among priests and people, acted as a collection agent, and occasionally acted as Carey's consultant on troublesome texts.[66] Carey collated eighteen different editions of the sacred Scriptures before the project was completed.[67] He is credited with having published the first American Catholic Bible.[68] One of the remarkable things about the Carey Bible is that the publisher had arrived in the United States almost penniless, just three years before he began plans for the project.

Matthew Carey was a Dublin-born, Jesuit-trained firebrand who had been apprenticed to a printer as a youth of fifteen.[69] Four years later he published *The Urgent Necessity for a Repeal of the Penal Code against Roman Catholics*. Its controversial nature forced him to flee to France where he continued his apprenticeship in Benjamin Franklin's print shop. It was probably Franklin who introduced Carey to the Marquis de Lafayette. When Carey felt it was safe to return to Ireland, he continued his inflammatory rhetoric against Parliament. He soon became convinced that prudence dictated flight rather than fight. In 1784, Carey escaped to the United States disguised as a woman.[70]

The Irish immigrant decided to try his fortune in Philadelphia. It was the largest, richest, most culturally diverse city in the United States. It boasted iron works, flour mills, shipyards, and a variety of shops where merchants sold everything from shoes to candles. There were artisans who crafted cabinets and smithed silver. Benjamin Franklin had long established himself as the city's most famous printer.[71] If it is proper at all to speak of a cultural capital in the nascent republic, the title has to go to Philadelphia.[72] It supported "mutual improvement" clubs to facilitate the exchange of ideas. One such, the Junto club, promoted a public lending library.

The Quakers led the way in fostering practical education for boys and girls that was free for families too poor to pay. The idea spread, and, by the 1750s, Philadelphia had schools staffed by blacks for black children. Franklin and others established a public hospital and fire brigades and had the streets paved, swept, and patrolled for safety after dark.[73]

An additional and very strong attraction the City of Brotherly Love held for Carey was the large number of Irish Catholics who had settled there. His reputation as a patriot preceded him, and the twenty-four-year-old Carey was received warmly by his former compatriots. When he had been in the country scarcely two months, Carey received a surprise visit from Lafayette. He was even more startled when the Frenchman gave the would-be publisher four hundred dollars. Though it was intended as a gift, Carey treated it as a loan and was finally able to repay it almost four decades later.[74]

Carey launched a career in publishing that has earned for him a qualified designation as Philadelphia's first Catholic intellectual.[75] He set standards for newspaper journalism and magazine publication, and eventually he made Philadelphia the book capital of the United States. Always interested in politics, Carey published almost verbatim—with the help of a retentive memory and a crude form of shorthand—an address delivered by the leader of the Pennsylvania Bar, Jared Ingersoll.[76] The readership appreciated the novelty in the *Pennsylvania Herald*, and other editors copied Carey's approach. He really made his mark, however, with *The American Museum or Repository of Ancient and Modern Fugitive Pieces, etc., Prose and Poetical.*[77]

The *Museum*, begun in 1787, is considered the first successful literary undertaking of its kind in the United States and a "thoroughly American" phenomenon. Carey dedicated the first volume of the *Mu-*

seum to John Carroll, who in turn solicited subscribers, among them Charles Carroll.[78] When the publication first appeared, Philadelphia was the capital of the young nation, and a copy of the *Museum* fell into the hands of George Washington. The President wrote a glowing letter to the editor, which Carey published in subsequent issues. It read in part: "The work is not only eminently calculated to disseminate political, agricultural, philosophical and other valuable information . . . I will venture to pronounce, as my sentiment that a more useful literary plan has never been undertaken in America." Washington complimented Carey on his taste and sense of propriety, and hoped that the journal would enjoy wide readership "to preserve the liberty, stimulate the industry, and meliorate the morals of an enlightened and free people." Carey returned the compliment and dedicated the fourth volume to the president, "the most zealous and successful defender of the one [liberty], and the most perfect model of the other [virtue]."[79] Part of the historical value of the *Museum* is that it gives an insight into the political, moral, and general mood of the period. Since it was intended for both general and specialized readership, articles range from those contributed by Benjamin Franklin on food to those on medicine by Doctor Benjamin Rush. The articles generally sustained a high quality, but the *Museum* fell victim to new postal rates in 1792.[80] Before its demise, the *Museum* was praised by the governors of Pennsylvania and Virginia and by Ezra Stiles, President of Yale University. A European visitor considered the journal equal to the best published on the continent.[81]

Carey was an egalitarian in a period when that view was debatable. He was always a champion of the disadvantaged, and this concern included the status of women. He took the *Boston Pilot* to task for an article that Carey thought called for a "highly improper degree of subordination . . . on the part of the wife." Among the *Pilot*'s injunctions regarding husbands was this counsel: "If he be abusive!! never retort! and never prevail over him to humble him!!" [Carey printed the quote in italics.] Carey editorialized tartly that these were "admirable rules for a bound servant or slave!" The publicist cared about other aspects of women's lives as well. He espoused the cause of underpaid female garment workers and wrote on the "pernicious effects of the use of corsets."[82]

It has been remarked that Carey was not a Catholic publisher, but rather a publisher who was a Catholic.[83] His mind was too expansive and his sense of business too acute to restrict himself to a Catholic market alone, as his less successful friend and competitor, Bernard Dornin, had done.[84] Carey was a humanitarian as well as the most influential Roman Catholic in Philadelphia when he and two others began the first nonsectarian Sunday school in America. In 1791 Benjamin Rush, Protestant Episcopal Bishop William White, and Carey opened a Sunday school to provide for the educational needs of the children of laborers and mechanics. Since the youngsters were often apprenticed, their opportunities for learning were almost nil. The pupils were taught to cipher and to read and write using the Bible or other moral tracts as a text.[85]

Carey freely associated with Protestants, but he would quickly pick up his pen if either his own Catholicism or that of his coreligionists was under fire. In that respect he was very much like John Carroll, whose "Pacificus" apologetic Carey reprinted in the *Museum.*

Carey's flirtation with local lay Catholic trusteeism problems contributed to the restrained tone of his obituary notice published in Philadelphia's *Catholic Herald* on September 16, 1839. It stated tersely, "There are few to whom his public acts of philanthropy and benevolence did not introduce him. His death will be felt and mourned by many to whom his kindness extended patronage and protection." Edgar Allan Poe, Carey's personal friend, put the publicist's passing into better perspective. The poet claimed that "the strictest scrutiny [of Carey's life] can detect nothing derogatory to the character of 'the noblest work of God, an honest man'."[86]

Carey's early episcopal collaborator, John Carroll, had died in 1815. A contemporary witness of the aftermath of his demise reported: "All Baltimore honored Carroll's memory. The public papers were bordered in black . . . as when Washington died."[87] Apparently there was some talk at the time about a full-length biography to be written about the venerable prelate. Reportedly, however, there was not much enthusiasm for printing it, even among wealthy Catholics like Charles Carroll.[88] Subsequent historians have filled the void with enthusiasm, making John Carroll *the* American Catholic about whom the most has been written.

For all the praise that historians have justifiably bestowed upon John Carroll, he has not been without his critics. As prototype founder of a Catholic college, he has been accused of fostering an anti-intellectual attitude in higher education.[89] The same charge has been leveled against Americans in general and Catholics in particular. Pioneer founders of colleges under denominational auspices had an eye to the preparation of their future ministers. This has been judged too vocationally restrictive and not calculated to incite a love of learning for its own sake. One Carroll defender has pointed out that the epithet "anti-intellectual" ill suits John Carroll.[90] All that has been said about his personal culture demonstrates that. It had been argued that it was "intellectually very defensible" for Carroll to regard Georgetown College primarily as a force in creating an American priesthood. The difficulties he encountered with some European priests and the problems they created justified his desire for a native clergy. Of even greater importance, Catholics cannot worship or have access to most sacraments without priests, who were painfully scarce in Carroll's era and beyond.[91]

Carroll's staunchest supporters try to explain rather than defend his attitude toward slavery. It has been shown that colonial and post-revolutionary Catholics of Maryland were social conformists.[92] This included the landed gentry's position on the South's "peculiar institution." Blacks may have fared somewhat better under Catholic ownership than other slaves did. This assumption is based on the attention given to their matrimonial rights and duties and to their religious instruction.[93] John Carroll reminded his flock of the duties masters had to catechize their servants. He was horrified when he discovered that the black youth at Jesuit-owned Bohemia Manor were both inadequately housed and almost ignorant of the rudiments of Catholicism. He had agreed with John Thayer, America's first Yankee convert from Boston, that he, too, was uneasy "at many things I see, and know, relating to the treatment & manners of the Negroes." In a sentence he later deleted, Carroll was clearly also bothered by Thayer's implied censure of the "many very learned & holy priests, our Predecessors in this country" who owned slaves. Carroll did tell Thayer, "I do the best I can to correct the evils I see; and then recur to those principles, which, I suppose, influenced the many eminent & holy missioners in S. America & Asia, where slavery equally exists."[94]

Charles Carroll has also received a great deal of historical attention, not all of it flattering. He has been praised as a patriot, but not always as a Catholic. One biographer has sardonically remarked that his religious beliefs and practices have been "pawed over."[95] Without falling victim to that accusation, the historian may find that there is one aspect of Charles Carroll's religious thought deserving of attention. It is a classic illustration of his Enlightenment mentality. Carroll believed that anyone who had the leisure and the means of examining the orthodoxy of his or her religious position had a duty to do so. Early instructions or habits could not be a substitute for the intellectual conviction that one held the truth. To that end, and with help from cousin John, the gentleman of Carrollton began a rigorous course of theological investigation that lasted three years.[96] His episcopal cousin thought frankly that Charles might spend his time more profitably in another pursuit and that a study of Protestantism led to the conclusion that there is "little more of divinity in Christianity" than in Plato or Confucius.[97] Nonetheless, he cooperated in the project. To the orthodox list of books that he submitted Charles added works by Presbyterians, Deists, Muslims, and a variety of other sources as he pursued his do-it-yourself course on comparative religions. Apparently

his investigations satisfied him intellectually, for he remained a sacramental Catholic to the end. It has been well documented that Carroll
was a philanthropist with schools and colleges his most frequent ben-
eficiaries. A large part of the "charity account" he kept in his ledgers
went for gifts and annuities for different servants and to the poor
around him.[98]

Charles and John Carroll, as heirs to the Enlightenment, completely accepted the American experience and the position of the
Catholic church within it. Charles Carroll had the good fortune to
outlive all the other signers of the Declaration of Independence and
became a legend in his own time. John Carroll received an encomium
almost two centuries after his death that might most have pleased
the architect of American Catholicism. A sympathetic Protestant historian wrote simply but eloquently that John Carroll's "argument for
disestablished and non-imperial faith inside a pluralist republic is
his special legacy."[99]

The bishop who personified the Enlightenment vision of the Carrolls was appointed to the see of Charleston, South Carolina, in 1820.
When the talented young John England came to his new diocese, he
was faced with two immediate problems, trusteeism and nativism.[100]
The evangelical fervor excited by the revivalism of the Second Great
Awakening of the 1820s precipitated an outbreak of nativism, with
Catholic immigrants as the special target. The evangelicals wanted
to expose the dangers of popery without being accused of mixing religion and politics. England believed that the greatest danger posed
by the would-be saints was a failure in separation of church and
state.[101] His own experience convinced him that union of the two had
proved disastrous in Great Britain.

His experiences in Ireland had not left England totally unprepared
for the new world. It is true that he was not used to being part of a
Catholic minority, but he was no stranger to religious discrimination.
He was heir to a strong and growing Irish tradition of separation
between church and state. With the Carrolls and many others of his
day he shared the Enlightenment mentality.[102] In Ireland, he had come
under the influence of Arthur O'Leary and was a friend of the Irish
Catholic patriot and antivetoist, Daniel O'Connell. In the United
States, England distinguished himself as "the first theoretician in the
American Catholic Church on Church-State questions."[103]

One of the goals England attempted to accomplish was to prove
to the American majority that Catholicism and republicanism were
compatible. To that end he established a weekly, the *U.S. Catholic
Miscellany*, the first Catholic diocesan newspaper that survived for
any length of time.[104] England had acquired considerable journalistic

experience in Ireland, where he had published pieces in the *Religious Repository* before he assumed responsibility for the Cork *Mercantile Chronicle*, organ of the liberal party.[105] The first issue of England's pioneer American journal, dedicated solely to the defense of Catholic doctrine, appeared on July 5, 1822.[106]

The aim, as the editorial policy stated, was to present "a simple explanation and temperate maintenance of doctrines of the Catholic Church . . . [with the] hope that many sensible persons will be astonished at finding they have imputed to Catholics doctrines which the Catholic Church had formally condemned, and imagined they were contradicting Catholics, when they held Catholics doctrines themselves."[107] The bishop of Charleston, with only five thousand Catholics scattered throughout the vast diocese, intended that the *Miscellany* would be the national organ of the American Catholic Church. He had agents spread along the entire Eastern seacoast and into Quebec and Nova Scotia. However, there was always a struggle to keep the journal afloat. As England's reputation as a progressive grew, his weekly circulated beyond his diocese, but he received little support from the other members of the hierarchy. Because he was frequently outspoken about affairs beyond his own jurisdiction, the bishops of Philadelphia and New York were particularly resentful. Some members of the clergy actively prevented news from reaching the *Miscellany*.[108]

The mainstay of the operation was England's devoted sister Johanna who had accompanied him to Charleston. She poured her time and her money into the *Miscellany* and kept a check on her brother's outspokenness and imprudence. In controversies, he was not above direct personal attack and vituperation.[109] Johanna's untimely death in 1827 was a deep personal loss to her brother.[110]

Whatever irenic hope England may have harbored as he launched his journalistic venture was quickly dissipated. The climate of his literary world was imbued with prejudice and misrepresentation. The *Miscellany* soon became a vehicle of controversy.[111] England had been in the country only a few years when he wrote to a friend, "I am convinced from what I have read—& from conversing with our many litterati here that it is only by rectifying the gross misrepresentations of history that the prejudices of America can be encroached upon."[112]

Three years later, England attempted to analyze the causes of anti-Catholicism, and he was one of the first American Catholic apologists to do so. Taking his cue from the works of Joseph Fletcher, who was called the prototype if not the source of England's essays, he pinpointed five reasons for Protestant prejudice. They were: family loyalties; respect for teachers who instill anti-Roman sentiments; flagrant misuses of history, of sciences, and of belle lettres. Of the quintet, England underlined historical inaccuracies as the chief culprit. As a result of this investigation, the bishop of Charleston concluded that it was morally, even almost physically impossible, for any American Protestant to be free of violent prejudice during the revolutionary period.[113]

During his own lifetime, England repeatedly employed his pen in order to set straight the historical record. His greatest contribution to apologetics is his carefully reasoned "Calumnies of J. Blanco White."[114] Joseph White, the subject of this writing, was a Spanish priest of Irish descent who fled to England in the wake of Napoleon's conquest. Shortly after, he joined the Anglican Church. In 1825 he published *The Practical and Internal Evidences*, which among other accusations charged that Catholics were a danger to the liberty and existence of Protestants. It has been suggested that White's immediate purpose was to defeat a Catholic emancipation bill presented to Parliament that year.[115] The following year, *Internal Evidences* was published in Washington, D.C., with the endorsement of James Kemp, bishop of the Episcopal Church in Maryland and some thirty clerics and laity of various denominations. Perhaps the timing was coincidental, but the American edition appeared just one month before the October election in Maryland and could have cast suspicion on Catholics running for office.

Internal Evidences was the most powerful attack upon the Catholic Church since Wharton's "Address." John England proved as equal to the task of unmasking historical inaccuracies as John Carroll had in the earlier conflict. For a year and a half, England rigorously examined White's claims. He addressed *Internal Evidences'* personal, political, dogmatic, and historical sections. He faulted White's misuse of history and attacked the crux of White's argument that Catholics could not be trustworthy citizens. The Anglican educed four reasons for his contention: papal temporal power, Catholic intolerance of error, the papal dispensing power, and exclusive salvation within the Catholic church. In his response, England made a distinction between matters of faith and those of opinion. According to him, the temporal power of the pope is a concession made by princes.[116] Later, in another context, England stated more forcefully that Cardinal Robert Bellarmine's position that "God gave to the Pope as much temporal power as was necessary for guarding the faith" was so much "specious sophistry [that] was rejected . . . by the great bulk of Catholic princes, clergy, and people."[117] To White's second contention, that no Catholic can in conscience tolerate error, England used the American experience as an example. In a Protestant country, perforce, legislation must be restricted to the temporal realm. Like Matthew Carey, England accused Protestants of intolerance. He continued his defense by insisting that there is no doctrine that justifies religious persecution.

The Inquisition, a favorite theme of anti-Catholic polemics, was a political institution. As for the pope's power of granting dispensation, England countered that it was exercised when sufficient reason warranted and only in the areas of general ecclesiastical law. The pope had no authority for excusing "the observance of the natural law, or of the divine law." Therefore the pope cannot interfere with a nation's political process nor exempt Catholics from the duties of citizenship. To underscore the point, England gave as example the fidelity of Irish Catholics during years of persecution. He followed the same approach John Carroll had used to counter the claim of exclusive salvation— he proved from public documents that the sects to which his opponents belonged held an even more strict interpretation than that of the Catholic church.

"The Calumnies of J. Blanco White" touched upon most of the points at issue between Catholics and Anglicans and is considered John England's most powerful apologetic work. He has been praised for evincing ". . . deep historical knowledge, expert casuistry and magnificence eloquence." If he was not able to check prejudice, yet he did make some of the church's opponents more cautious in their accusations.[118]

England's ardent republicanism has been widely recognized. He returned to the theme on numerous occasions in order to defend Catholics against the claims that "Republicanism and Catholicism bear no affinity in any one single relation, nor can they ever cordially unite in character." To answer that charge, the bishop of Charleston demonstrated a good sense of American colonial Catholic history. He called upon the example of John Carroll, who was "notorious for his love of Republican institutions." He underlined the patriotism of Charles Carroll and that expressed in the congratulatory address Catholics had presented to George Washington upon his election in 1789.[119]

Like Carroll, England set himself the task of demonstrating the compatibility of Catholicism and republicanism. England, however, probed more deeply into the attendant theological problems. On the theoretical level, he frequently cited the theologian Bellarmine, who favored a form of government combining the best elements of monarchy, aristocracy, and democracy. England believed that Bellarmine's theory most closely approximated American republicanism.[120] In the pages of the *Miscellany*, England outlined Bellarmine's plan. The ruling body would be composed of a president with overall authority and governors of states or provinces who would supervise these as their own, yet who would owe obedience to the authority of the chief *princeps*. No office of government would be hereditary. This plan, England concluded triumphantly, came from the pen of a Jesuit cardinal "who attempted to push the [temporal] power of the Popes to the greatest length of any author with whose work we have met." Further, England claimed that the vital principles of true republicanism had been preserved by the Catholic church. Not quite accurately, he cited the government of monastic orders as an example. He also pointed to various models of republics that were Catholic: the Swiss cantons, Venice, San Marino, and Genoa.

England concluded by arguing that the difference between a properly regulated republic and despotism is a well-known constitution. In it, the general will is expressed; each individual knows his rights, each officer his power, "and all the members of the community being fully aware of the extent of jurisdiction and the limits of obedience, there can be no mistake." He drew a parallel with the Catholic church throughout the world. "There is, in every separate community where it is properly organized, a constitution." It should be noted, however, that the enlightened bishop included only men in his organizational plans.[121]

England never blurred the distinction between the church's constitution, a purely spiritual reality, and a political constitution of human origins. Although he delineated the essential differences, it has been shown that he frequently compared similarities.[122] He used metaphors drawn from American government to explain the workings of God in relationship with society. God and Christ are "supreme legislators"; the pope is an ecclesiastical president, not a monarch. The church is similar to the supreme court, with the bible its constitutional guide. Church doctrines are additional laws the court uses; a papal legate is the pope's ambassador; a council is the church's congress, and bishops its congressmen.

Understandably, the bishop's Protestant contemporaries were incredulous about his claim that the Catholic church was the great patron of democratic republics. Some Catholics were, too. Archbishop Ambrose Maréchal, John Carroll's second successor, had wanted a French-speaking English bishop for Charleston when the diocese was created, not one who was Irish- or French-born. He did not want factionalism to increase in the young American church. He feared that Hibernian or Gallican hierarchs would retard the Americanization process of the immigrants. Despite his respect for the young nation, Maréchal was always suspicious of England's republican tendencies. Even sympathetic historians have shown that England based his theory of so-called Holy Republicanism on selective evidence.[123]

To his credit, England paid more than lip service to the value of constitutional government. With the consultation of legal experts and leading members of his diocese, he drafted *The Constitution of the Roman Catholic Church of North Carolina, South Carolina and Geor-*

gia.[124] When he first arrived in his new see, Charleston was in the throes of a severe case of factious trusteeism. England studied the problem for almost two years. He familiarized himself with the American legal system, the constitutions of various Protestant churches, and Roman Catholic canon law. His *Constitution* is considered his "most lasting and most thoughtful response to the trustee problems and to the American environment which occasioned them."[125]

Similar to other non-Catholic American ecclesiastical constitutions, the *Constitution* outlined the principal features of church doctrine and discipline. It delineated the duties and rights of all in the church. It established a voluntary association among members of the diocese and created a legal corporation for handling and managing ecclesiastical funds, one of the bones of contention in trustee problems. Yet, as forward-looking as the *Constitution* was, it did not overcome the bias against women so typical of the Roman Catholic hierarchy. Membership in the diocesan corporation was restricted to baptized males, twenty-one or older, and in good ecclesiastical standing. This excluded the bishop's devoted sister Johanna, herself a loyal Catholic, as well as all the other women of the diocese.

In the area of church governance, separation of church and state was affirmed; infallibility of the pope without a general council, as a matter of doctrine, was denied. The Bishop of Charleston had been identified as a moderate conciliarist. He avoided the extremes of ultramontanism, which vested the pope with personal infallibility, and Gallicanism, which stressed the limits of papal power. For England, the highest tribunal of the church was a general council acting in union with the pope. He did believe, however, that in cases of dispute between the pope and the body of bishops, the decisions of the council overruled the pope. In his view, constitutional boundaries should be set for all powers within the church.

His diocesan *Constitution* provided for district churches, set up according to membership. Each was governed by a vestry composed of a clergyman appointed by the bishop and a number of laymen elected by members of the territory. It was the duty of the vestry to administer the local congregation's goods.

Each vestry had a degree of autonomy and could determine its own form of government and qualifications for membership within constitutional guidelines. England recognized that the laity had secular expertise to contribute and their majority vote alone in the vestry was required for financial agreements and contracts. If real property was to be alienated, however, episcopal consent was required, nor could the lay vestry withhold funds for support of the clergy. England's constitution made it clear that only the bishop had the power to appoint clergy or remove them in the event of irregularities. It provided for redress to a higher ecclesiastical tribunal should either priest or laity disagree with the bishop's decision.

One of the provisions of the constitution was that an annual convention of diocesan clergy and elected lay representatives from all districts meet annually with the bishop. After the celebration of an opening liturgy, the house of the clergy and of the laity would meet separately to discuss respectively the spiritual and temporal affairs of the diocese. Though not a specific part of the ecclesiastical government, the convention was a "body of sage, prudent, and religious counselors" to aid the bishop in the proper discharge of his duty.[126]

Another constitution that England framed was for the *Philosophical and Classical Seminary of Charleston*, which began operation early in 1822. The society was founded upon the principles of mutual aid and brotherly love. It was to promote sound literature and secure "meritorious candidates for Holy Orders."[127] Like John Carroll, England was concerned about a trained and worthy clergy. He confided to a friend that he was unwilling to receive "the refuse of the ministry to officiate in this country." He thought that this was about the only type of foreign cleric who would come to the South.[128] The *Constitution* reflected England's knowledge of South Carolina law and constitutional law. It carefully delimited the power vested in the office of the president who would be either the bishop or a vicar capitular. Outlining the rights and responsibilities of all, the constitution was adopted after "mature deliberation and frequent discussion."[129] Nevertheless, despite his best efforts and considerable expenditures, England complained that his seminary did not pay off in training priests for North Carolina.[130]

England extended his educational interests to include poor children. One of his first American ventures was to open a school for black children. It survived over a decade but was finally forced to close under pressure from slaveowners. England declared himself no friend of slavery; he was a spiritual egalitarian. He wrote that "when any man grows so fastidious as to imagine that God Almighty has revealed himself more or less for his negro than for himself, he ceases to be a Roman Catholic."[131] Eventually, however, he went on record in defense of slavery, partly because the abolitionists harbored a deep anti-Catholic animus.[132]

To the bishop of Charleston there was presented a splendid opportunity to answer several political objections against Catholicism in 1826. One month before he received his final citizenship papers, England was invited to address the Congress of the United States of America—the first Catholic clergyman to do so.[133] Described as a master orator gifted with a highly rhetorical style, England was able to present his arguments with brilliant effect. Essentially, he challenged the old accusations as he did in his exchange with Blanco White. He explained to the House of Representatives that he was spokesperson for a religion whose doctrines had been misunderstood. It was not his aim to try to prove that his position was the correct one. All he asked was a fair hearing and the equal rights guaranteed by the Constitution.[134]

That had not been mere rhetoric. In a private letter reflecting on his presentation, England commented that the members of Congress "must be instructed, not abused . . . they are not obstinate heretics— they are . . . thinking, reasoning, well disposed. I will add, a pious people." In the same letter, he confessed that he was "excited and flushed" as he began his oration, but felt "extraordinary gratification" at the attention he was accorded. "Every face seemed to say, 'go on'— but I thought two hours long enough for them and me."[135]

England never ceased advocating the American system of government even after Pope Gregory XVI published *Mirari Vos* in 1832.[136] Called "suave and power-conscious," Pope Gregory condemned the position of Félicité de Lamennais.[137] Lamennais urged the separation of church and state in his own country, and the *U.S. Catholic Miscellany* supported his position.[138] The pope upheld the union of the two and condemned liberty of conscience as an absurd and erroneous doctrine rooted in religious indifference. He also assigned to perdition all those who do not hold fast to the Catholic faith.[139]

For two years the *Miscellany* remained silent, but then it published *Mirari Vos* after it appeared in the non-Catholic press. England never offered a defense of the papal position. He counseled Catholics to remain steadfast in their faith but to condemn no one as heretical. God alone is the judge in religious matters.[140]

Death claimed Charleston's first bishop in 1842. After his American ministry of twenty-two years, there were only eight thousand Catholics in his diocese, most of whom were very poor. His successor, Bishop Ignatius Reynolds, tried to keep the *Miscellany* afloat. In order to generate funds, he edited and published the late bishop's works.[141] The books did not sell and the venture put the *Miscellany* more deeply into debt.[142] Subsequently, the *Miscellany* became one of the many Southern casualties of the Civil War. However, the journalistic work that England had begun in order to repel the Evangelical attack was extended to Catholic journals in New York, Philadelphia, Boston, Hartford, Washington, D.C., Bardstown, Cincinnati, and Saint Louis.[143]

As heirs to the Enlightenment, Carroll and England distinguished between religious toleration and religious indifference, an analysis that provided a basis for rational discourse with Protestants. However, by the time that the first Provincial Council of Baltimore had assembled, the heyday of interfaith amity was almost a thing of the past. A number of operative factors have been suggested.[144] The influx of Irish, French, and German Catholic immigrants was perceived as a threat to Protestant hegemony. This, in turn, provoked periodic outbreaks of nativism. In response to such hostility the Catholic church developed an institutional separatism. In the report sent to Pope Pius VIII in 1829, the prelates of Baltimore's First Provincial Council noted that six ecclesiastical seminaries had been established and three of the nine Catholic "colleges" had been granted state charters. There were thirty-three convents of religious women, and houses had been established for male Dominicans, Sulpicians, Vincentians, and Jesuits. In addition, there were many schools that provided free education for boys and girls. Hospitals, orphanages, and other charitable institutions ministered to Catholic needs.[145] The overall effect was that Catholic–Protestant interaction was severely restricted as both groups turned in upon themselves.

The new Catholic immigrants, future bishops among them, replaced the Anglo-Americans as the dominant factor in the church. As a result, the tradition of Enlightenment Catholicism was eclipsed. Most nineteenth-century American Catholic apologists tended toward the ultramontane wing of the European Romantic movement. Though ultramontanism was never a dominant factor in tradition, there was a desire to recapture the imagined glories of an age of an undivided Christendom; uniformity in church discipline was stressed by Catholic exponents of the faith. Any flirtation with the vernacular was proscribed by the successive councils of Baltimore, which insisted on strict adherence to the Roman ritual.[146]

The separation of church and state endorsed by John Carroll and John England was accepted by a vast majority of the Catholic community in the United States. Care of the civil realm was relegated to the state with some disastrous consequences. Catholics, in most instances, became uncritical supporters of American political institutions and decisions. Consequently, the Catholic bishops, representatives of a defensive minority, exercised no leadership in political issues with a decided moral component. Their silence in the face of the gross injustices of slavery and the genocidal wars against Native Americans have been singled out as graphic examples.[147]

CHAPTER
2
Romanticism: Orestes Brownson and the Young Isaac Hecker, 1830–1850

❧❧❧

*T*he First Provincial Council of Baltimore (1829) closed at the end of a decade already exhibiting America's transformation into an industrial nation. As the years moved on, more and more people joined the factory labor force, crowded into old cities, and forced the creation of new ones. The need for new roads, canals, railroads, and steamboats began a permanent transformation of the nation's economic and geographic contours. National expansionism moved at top speed as the westward trek began in earnest in the early 1840s. As the more venturesome moved out toward the prairies, equally daring immigrants began to flood the Eastern Coast. They precipitated an unprecedented population explosion.

The influx seriously affected some of the nation's churches, dramatically taxing their resources to the utmost. Large numbers of the German immigrants were Lutherans; many of the newly arrived Scots-Irish were Presbyterians. The Catholic church, however, had by far the largest numbers of immigrants and from the most widely varied nationalities.[1] Two hundred fifty thousand Catholics arrived in the 1830s; a decade later the number had nearly tripled. By the 1850s, Catholic immigrants nearly exceeded one million in number.[2] Coping with such burgeoning growth was one problem; dealing with the periodic waves of anti-Catholicism, spawned by the nativists' paranoid fear of a Catholic takeover, was another. The task of the

Catholic church was twofold: the immigrants and their ways had to be explained satisfactorily to the Yankees, and American political and social mores had to be transmitted to the immigrants. This was a major challenge by any standard. The challenge did not go unaccepted.

New leaders, cleric and lay, emerged within the Catholic community. Like John Carroll, some were native-born. Others were immigrants themselves, as was John England. A small but influential number were converts. The religious, educational, cultural, and political backgrounds of these future leaders were diverse. They frequently disagreed among themselves, even on substantive issues. Despite that, they shared a common love for, and loyalty to, the Catholic church, as well as a "romantic" intellectual orientation.

Attempting to define precisely what the term *romantic* means is, as one author has warned, a "hazardous occupation which has claimed many victims."[3] With that caution in mind, it seems safe to say at the least that romanticism was a reaction against the excessive objectivity and rationalism of the Enlightenment. The heart supplanted the head as ruler of human actions.

Johann Möhler was a significant figure in the Catholic Tübingen school that aimed to combat the rationalism of the Enlightenment with the intellectual tools of German idealism. The publication of his *Symbolik* in 1843 is considered a "theological event." Möhler realized that the zeitgeist pointed to a study of earlier church teachings, especially those of the pre-Reformation era. He was a pioneer in introducing the intuitive and historical approach to the development of doctrine.[4] His work was geared toward the theological elite. *Symbolik* was read and appreciated by some American Catholic thinkers.[5] Some readers were also influenced by Count Joseph de Maistre (1754–1821). Ruined and in exile as a result of the French Revolution, de Maistre was in search of a principle of unity that could bring order out of chaos. His *Du Pape*, published in 1819, is a defense of papal authority and infallibility. In general, it envisions an authoritarian system as the only one capable of saving a world falling into anarchy and unbelief. He distrusted anything new and wanted to destroy completely the spirit of the eighteenth century. He saw the Catholic synthesis of the Middle Ages valid for every period. He represented the extreme right wing of the romantic movement.[6]

Romanticism was neither uniquely European nor exclusively Catholic. Within American Protestantism there were various movements toward organic unity. One of the most striking of these was the "Mercersburg movement" spearheaded by Philip Schaff and John W. Nevin within the German Reformed Church. The New England Transcendentalists and those Episcopalians who took England's Oxford movement seriously were also operating out of a romantic context.[7] It has been argued that American Catholics were slower than both the Europeans and American Protestants to register the romantic impulse, owing to their excessive dependence on rationalism. This view has been challenged on the basis of the romantic orientation of such figures as Orestes Brownson, Isaac Hecker, and James A. McMaster, publishers of influential journals of the period. Among the hierarchy, Francis Patrick Kenrick, archbishop of Baltimore, and his successor, Martin John Spalding, were apologists who wrote from a romantic perspective. The latter's nephew, John Lancaster Spalding, was a prolific author who shared his uncle's views.[8]

This is not to suggest that the Enlightenment tradition was completely lost. Nor is it a claim that all, most, or even some serious Christians, Protestant or Catholic, favored an all-out retreat from rationalism. What it does suggest is that tensions did exist among church people as they sought to express their faith in the midst of a changing world. Some "liberal" heirs of the Enlightenment, for example, Father Isaac Hecker, wanted the church to affirm reason, modern progress, and liberty. They favored some ecclesial adaptations to the demands of the age. Other "conservative" romantics, such as Hecker's lay friend Orestes Brownson, in his later days took a jaundiced view of modernity and looked to the restoration of a single religion for the regeneration of social cohesion. As one author put it, most were attempting to balance multiple convictions in order to respond appropriately to complex experiences.[9]

The life and thought of Orestes Brownson provide useful insights into the political and ecclesial life of America covering a significant portion of the nineteenth century. Brownson made notable contributions to both the religious and intellectual history of his age. It has been claimed that no other American of his time observed society so profoundly as he did. Brownson was born in Stockbridge, Vermont, in 1802. His father died prematurely shortly after Orestes' birth. His mother, in straitened circumstances, was forced to send her six-year-old son to live with an elderly couple. They were kind but had no fixed religious affiliation. Brownson later recalled those years with them wistfully; he had acquired the manners "of an old man before ... [he] was a boy, and was brought up with no definite creed."[10]

Deprived of both a father and a religion, Brownson later developed a passion for both. True, his religious quest went through phases; at times his religious spirit was overcome, but it was never completely extinguished. Brownson's mature philosophical speculation on the problem of God expressed his longing to believe in a heavenly father, to quell the sense of loss he experienced because he never knew an earthly one.[11]

In his early teens, Brownson returned to live with his mother and had a brief formal education. At nineteen he became a Presbyterian. Brownson had made the decision to take the Presbyterian church as a guide and abnegate his own reason. Quickly he realized he had made a mistake. He said that he found the doctrine of unconditional election and reprobation "difficult to swallow and more difficult to digest." Brownson drifted to Universalism based upon a belief in the final salvation of all. In 1826 he became a Universalist minister. Three years later he became editor of the Universalist journal, *Gospel Advocate and Impartial Investigator.* He became the corresponding editor of *Free Inquirer,* which brought him into contact with the social reformers Robert Owens (commonly referred to as a utopian socialist) and Fanny Wright, a Scotswoman whom Brownson considered to be of "rare original powers."

With the zeal of a world reformer, Brownson promoted the platform of Wright and Owens—that the triple enemies to happiness were traditional religion, marriage or family, and private property. The three reformers agreed that American society needed radical transformation and emancipation from the clergy and from superstition. Part of the plan to bring about reform was the proposition that children, from the age of two on, would be maintained and educated at public expense.

Brownson joined the political Working Man's Party with the hope that it would come to power and adopt this educational system. He later admitted that, as a husband and father, he never really approved of Wright's and Owen's system of education or their view of marriage. After a year, Brownson left the Working Man's Party because he could not be a "party man," but he never deserted the cause of the "poorer and more numerous classes."

All the while, Brownson was struggling to find "the truth" so that he would know "with certitude what to do." In 1830 Brownson left Universalism. He declared himself an unbeliever and felt that he had "restored his manhood." Reflecting on this period of his life a quarter-century later, he admitted that he "rejected heaven for earth, God for man, eternity for time." Yet he was convinced that his honest avowal of unbelief was "a step that brought . . . [him] nearer the kingdom of God."

Brownson could not be without "religion" for long. By 1832 he had become a Unitarian preacher. He was drawn back to religion because he believed that only in religious ideas and principles, in the belief in God, in moral accountability, in duty, could one's passions and lust be restrained. Unitarianism attracted him because Dr. William Ellery Channing, the "patron saint" of New England Unitarians, and the other Unitarians whom Brownson had met were "educated, cultivated, and respectable." Brownson began a study of French and German rationalists, including the writings of Benjamin Constant.

Following Constant, Brownson understood religion as a natural sentiment of man embodied in institutions. As society progressed, new institutions developed. With the progress of civilization, older institutions were subject to criticism. Periods of destruction and transition of institutions did not signal the decline of civilization, but an advance.[12] Brownson found this theory of the progress of religion congenial with his notion of the progress of mankind, a belief widely held at the time. Indeed, the idea of the perfectibility of mankind and the importance of democracy and Christianity as mutually essential forces of society were part of the nineteenth-century American idea, with the notion of progress as its hallmark.[13]

Filled with his characteristic enthusiasm, Brownson hit upon the idea that what was needed was a new religious institution. It would embody the advanced intelligence of the age and would respond to its wants. This "Church of the Future" would contain within itself the principles of its own progress.[14] Thus he launched his "Society for Christian Union and Progress" in 1836, considered his most daring and challenging venture.[15] Brownson's "church" was of ecumenical intent. He did not aim at establishing a new sect, but wanted to effect unity and catholicity. With his mind still unsettled and with his characteristic frankness, he informed his congregation, mainly composed of disaffected workers and the unchurched, that he could not be sure that tomorrow his convictions would be what they were today.[16] During this period, Brownson published his *New Views of Christianity, Society, and the Church*.[17] Though Brownson would later admit that the work made no converts and contained "laughable blunders" in regard to Catholicism, this work was his rendition of the religious philosophy of the French utopian socialist, the Count de Saint-Simon.[18]

Influenced by French philosophers, Brownson stated that since religion is natural to humanity, when persons ceased to be religious, they ceased to be human. Religious institutions, as the forms in which religious sentiments are clothed, are mutable and transitory, regulated by the law of growth. Brownson sensed, however, that all was not well within the Christian empire; he believed that the sentiment of the holy had abandoned it.

Looking back to the birth of Christianity, Brownson began to view Jesus dialectically as the God-man mediating between the antitheses of spirit and matter. At the time of Christ, spirit was represented by the cultures of the Eastern world; matter by the cultures of Greece and Rome. The original sin of the Catholic church was that Christ came to be looked upon exclusively as the redeemer, rather than mediator. It failed to recognize Jesus' gospel of love, which bound together spirit and matter.

As a result, matter was seen as under a curse and the superiority of the spiritual over the material was idealized—church over civil society, celibacy over marriage. Catholicism represented the triumph of spirit over matter. Protestantism, for its part, was the triumph of the material over the spiritual. It had fostered the modern state, civil liberty, human reason, industry, and all temporal interests.

No church could quite satisfy Brownson during this period. He acknowledged the Bible as given by the inspiration of God, but insisted that the church had never sufficiently reflected what was in the "heart and life of Jesus." Brownson felt free to dissent from the Christianity of the church but said he would be content to "stand or fall for the Christianity of Christ."

Despite his indebtedness to other authors, Brownson felt that the ideas expressed in his *New Views* were "somewhat original," though he hastened to add that they were not the "only or even the most important views" that could be taken on the subject treated.[19]

Although Brownson would later, as a Catholic commenting upon his *New Views*, praise his insightful analysis—"remarkable," as he put it, "for its protest against Protestantism"—he pleaded ignorance in reference to his mishandling of Catholicism.[20]

Later authors would consider Brownson's *New Views* extraordinarily insightful in sensing at such an early period some of the failures of the Enlightenment. Brownson had opposed the atomistic and individualistic interpretation of both the American and French Revolutions. He had espoused a romantic philosophy of history as a basis for societal unity.[21] Out of this vision, Brownson launched another ambitious project, his own journal. The *Boston Quarterly Review* went to press in 1838; it was intended to enlist literature, religion, and philosophy on the side of democracy and reform. Impulses for reform were arising, and that same year the Chartist movement caused quite a stir in England. All segments of society joined protests against economic liberalism as labor agitated against government for improved working conditions. In America, humanitarian crusades were carried on to improve working conditions, and education was fostered to promote temperance and the rights of women. Campaigns to reform prisons, abolish slavery, and care for the poor and the orphans were widespread.

Between the years 1825 and 1837, literally hundreds of local trade societies, or Working Man's Parties, were established. The panic of 1837 and the subsequent depression led to massive unemployment and a loss of ground for labor unions.[22] It was in the aftermath of this crisis that Brownson published his essay "The Laboring Class," des-

tined to become a classic.[23] It began as a review of Thomas Carlyle's
study entitled *Chartism* (1839). As Brownson later recalled, he had
realized that the economic system was in dire need of change when
he wrote his essay. In it, he denounced industrialism, which had made
virtual slaves of the great masses of people. A democracy in which
one class of society owned the funds and another class was compelled
to labor under the harshest conditions was worse than the serfdom
of the Middle Ages.

In his view, Brownson declared that no two countries in all of
Christendom were so unfavorable to the poor as the United States
and Great Britain. Like corporations, they had no soul. Desperate situations called for radical solutions. Government must limit its own
powers, repeal all laws burdening the laborers, and abolish the banking system and credit. Monopolies must be destroyed. Following the
Saint-Simonians, Brownson called for an end to the inheritance of
property. A person's right to dispose of wealth ceased at death.[24]

The political campaign of 1840 was particularly ugly, and one in
which Catholic sensibilities were not spared. In the South the former
governor of Georgia, Secretary of State John Forsyth, suggested that
William Henry Harrison had been foisted upon Southerners by a cadre
of Catholic anti-Masons and Protestant abolitionists. Forsyth also
hinted that the British antislavery society had exerted some influence
upon Pope Gregory XVI and his letter of 1839 condemning the slave
trade. This drew the fire of John England, the bishop of Charleston,
South Carolina. England countered the accusation in his *Miscellany*
by rhetorically asking where the British influence had been when
popes from Pius II in 1462 to Pius VII in the early nineteenth century
had made similar pronouncements. Moreover, England continued,
what Pope Gregory had condemned was "what our laws condemn as
the 'slave trade' and not the sale and purchase which must frequently
occur in domestic slavery."[25]

John England's *Miscellany* declared itself unconcerned with party
politics and indifferent to the outcome of the election. What did concern it was a "large and powerful party" who, under the pretext of
protecting our liberties from foreign influence, had attempted to
"create a state of white slavery for all future Catholic immigrants,
and then to discover other modes of degradating those who cannot
be stripped of their citizenship."[26] Although Van Buren's defeat was,
to some degree, a nativist victory, Brownson made the dubious claim
that the beaten Democratic incumbent had blamed his loss on
Brownson's essay "The Laboring Class."[27]

In 1841, Orestes Brownson met Isaac Hecker, who like himself had
been involved in labor politics. In addition, they shared a general
world view steeped in a romantic notion of religion and culture.

Isaac Hecker was born in 1819 of immigrant German parents. Originally of Lutheran background, his mother had become a devout Methodist. Hecker was acquainted with the tenets of Protestantism, but he became dissatisfied with what the "sects" had to offer. When he met Brownson, he, too, was a religious seeker.[28]

Isaac's brothers, George and John, were successful bakers and later became prosperous as flour mill owners. The three Hecker brothers were committed to Jacksonian democracy. They accepted a fundamental natural and moral law as the basis of the Constitution; they exalted freedom and responsible individualism. They believed in the divine destiny and special mission of America.[29] They were sensitive to the great toll industrialization had taken on the working class. They were appalled at the widening gap between the rich and the poor. Politically, the Heckers allied themselves with the Loco-Foco party of New York City. The Loco-Focos were radical Democrats who were opposed to any form of monopoly. At the time of the economic panic of 1837, Hecker was not yet old enough to vote, but he made an early commitment to responsible reform and civic duty. It remained a lifetime interest.[30]

The brothers attended a lecture during which Brownson gave a talk entitled "The Democracy of Christ." As Hecker was later to recall, the thesis was that "Christ was the Big Democrat and the Gospel was the true Democratic platform."[31] Brownson befriended Hecker and influenced him to look from the "ballot to the book" for the key that would unlock man's destiny. They began to exchange letters that year and continued to do so for over thirty years. Despite the difference in their ages—Brownson was thirty-seven and Hecker only twenty-one—they shared in common a concern over the ills of society and a quest for religious truth. In the early years of their friendship, Brownson served as a kind of spiritual and intellectual mentor. Over the decades, Hecker came to know Brownson more intimately than any other of his friends.[32]

In 1842 Brownson sought intellectual stimulation at the Transcendentalist retreat Brook Farm, in West Roxbury, Massachusetts. Brook Farm, supported for a time by the leading intellectuals of the day, was one of the numerous utopian communities that flourished prior to the Civil War. The most eminent Transcendentalist, Ralph Waldo Emerson, said of the period that a draft for a utopia could be found in the waistcoat pocket of almost every reading man. The Transcendentalists, though no two thought alike, were generally on the liberal end of the romantic continuum. They believed in divine immanence, intuitive perception of truth, and complete self-reliance.[33]

At Brook Farm, Brownson wrote his essay "The Mediatorial Life

of Jesus," in which he tried to develop his own religio-philosophical
response to the ills of the age. Dedicated to William Ellery Channing,
the essay challenged Channing's thesis of the "divinity of humanity."
Brownson amassed evidence to the contrary from both tradition and
everyday experience. The doctrine of the depravity of humanity is a
universal tradition and, for Brownson, tradition was always a good
argument if the proposition was not intrinsically improbable. Drawing
upon his experience as the father of a brood of children, he pointed
out that even youngsters are not always innocent. Insightfully he
wrote, "The little rogues not infrequently show animation, spirit, intelligence only when doing some mischief."

Following Victor Cousin and Pierre Leroux, Brownson asserted that
"to live is to manifest ourselves, which cannot be done without communion with an object other than the self." Consequently, all life is
subjective and objective. Man's object, "by communion with which
he lives," is other men, God, and nature. Man communes with man
directly, with God and objects indirectly.

For Brownson, Jesus was a "providential man" in the strictest
sense. Since God is not reduced to the laws of nature, he must be
absolutely free, or he is not God; he can intervene in human affairs
in his providence. God did this in an extraordinary way in the person
of Jesus. Just as Jesus was not simply a special man, the Bible was
more than an edifying book. Both were supernatural. Modern philosophy, Brownson thought, has not begun to plumb the depths of
the New Testament, so it must have come from a "super human"
mind.[34]

Brownson also believed that he had discovered a rational explanation for the notion of the communication of supernatural grace.
Leroux, who was not wholly ignorant of Catholic theology, had given
Brownson a glimpse of the Catholic doctrine of grace. He concluded
that grace might be infused with no violence to nature or reason.[35]
Since Jesus lived in "unrestrained communion with God" and since
it is life that mediates, Jesus was able to communicate this life to his
disciples and thus virtually to the race. Brownson developed this idea
along the same lines he had used for his analysis of the transmission
of sin. Since the time of Jesus, however, sin could never get the upper
hand because man can always "refill at the divine well" through fel-
lowship. Actually, at the time, Brownson believed that the human
race was getting better.

Brownson drew several conclusions from his exposition of Jesus
as mediator. Brownson thought he and Channing should translate
this doctrine into "domestic and social institutions in obedience to
the strictest order and most unrestrained freedom compatible with
that order." It was the answer to the world's ills "sick with strife and

division." Brownson had found in the Gospel "Life and Reality which will unite all into the church [which] will become one in Christ." Brownson felt that now, as never before, he could really be a minister, not on his own authority, but because he had the "authority of God's Word."[36]

Brownson's disciple Isaac Hecker was driven by the desire for a more frugal life than that reputed to exist at Brook Farm, and accordingly he spent a little time at Fruitlands, a community of Transcendentalists in Boston. There the working principle was that man must regenerate himself before he can change his environment. Hecker sought transformation through strict mortification and self-denial. He lasted only fifteen days. Brownson was delighted. He told Hecker that he was glad his friend had quit that "humbug"—that he had never been keen on those communities.[37]

While Brownson had been working out his doctrine of life by communion, Hecker had been caught up in a series of ecstatic religious experiences. He was nervous and had bouts of depression. While he was physically ill in 1842, Brownson suggested that Hecker go to Brook Farm after all. Hecker took this advice and spent eight months associating with the leading intellectual and literary people of his day. He became exposed to the philosophy of Spinoza and Kant; he read the romantic writings of Schlegel and others;[38] and he was deeply affected by Johann Möhler's *Symbolik*.

In the early 1840s, Brownson and Hecker followed the English and American Oxford movements closely. Almost a decade earlier, the Anglican John Henry Newman had published a pamphlet on apostolic succession. This was the first of a long series called *Tracts for the Times*, which precipitated the Oxford movement, an intellectual revolution in England. In America, the movement developed as part of a larger religious desire for greater unity in the body of Christ.

Actually, the movement toward church union in America antedated the celebrated Oxford movement. The issues that the British Tractarians, as they came to be called, addressed—church authority, the sacraments, rituals, apostolic succession, and tradition as a source of revelation—had been discussed sympathetically in America as early as 1811. It was the Episcopalian bishop of New York, John Henry Hobart, who had reopened these questions and who had concluded that the Anglican high churchmen held the truly Catholic ground between the errors of Romanism and those of Protestantism. In Protestant America, the Oxford movement was protected by the High Church movement. In Anglican England, however, there was universal hostility toward the Tractarians. One author has suggested that the conversion of Anglicans to Catholicism in the two countries was in direct proportion to the amount of hostility the movement aroused in each. England, wherein the antagonism was high, produced a number of influential "defectors." In America, the High Church movement limited the number of converts.[39]

Francis Patrick Kenrick, coadjutor bishop of Philadelphia, was so encouraged by the development of the Oxford movement that (in 1838) he wrote a sixteen-page public letter inviting the Protestant Episcopal bishops of America to follow to a systematic conclusion the movement toward the Catholic church that had begun in England. He recommended that they read English Catholic Bishop John Milner's *The End of Religious Controversy*, which had already become a classic work of apologetics. Milner's essay, a good choice, discussed the principles underlying any religious quest, with a view to both convincing and converting.[40]

Kenrick was rebuffed by the offended Episcopalians. They reminded him that only when they were approached as already united in one faith, and not before that, would they be in a mood to consider any gesture of reconciliation.[41] Actually, this open letter was not Kenrick's first encounter with that group. He had addressed a "Letter on Christian Union" to the Episcopal bishop of Kentucky in 1836 and in the following year began a series of twenty-nine letters to John Henry Hopkins, the Episcopal bishop of Vermont.

Hopkins had published his argument that the Roman church had corrupted the primitive purity of the early church, particularly in its doctrines concerning the papacy and councils. In his response Kenrick defended the primacy, drawing support from scripture, the early church writings, conciliar positions, and other sources. Kenrick delicately sidestepped the question Hopkins had raised about the temporal rights of popes over sovereigns. Kenrick wrote that he would have nothing to do with this dispute, since times had changed and the pontiff was no longer recognized as the head of a Christian commonwealth, now that Europe was no longer Catholic.

The question Hopkins then asked was this: If thinking on the temporal power had changed, why cling to the "phantom of infallibility," a position which had not even been defined? Kenrick rejoined that the infallibility of the pope in general council was recognized by all and that no single dogma had ever been solemnly defined which was later abandoned or recalled. Kenrick registered shock at Hopkins's suggestion that the government should take a part in facilitating church unity. Kenrick said Hopkins left himself open to the accusation, so often leveled against Catholics, of "sighing after the union of Church and state."[42]

Kenrick was a scholar-bishop.[43] He wrote a four-volume work on dogmatic theology in 1839–1840, which was followed by a three-volume study on moral theology within the next three years. In his dogmatic theology, Kenrick minimized speculative questions; he treated the teachings of various Protestant sects. On undefined controverted issues, he stressed freedom of opinion.[44] It has been noted that one of Kenrick's remarkable contributions is his early and clear statement on the existence and function of episcopal collegiality. He defined the necessary collegial condition as existing not only when the bishops of the world gathered together, but whenever, even if dispersed over the globe, they spoke on one issue.[45] This was a clear exposition of a tradition that had been growing in the American Catholic church since the time of Bishop John England.[46]

Kenrick was a collegialist but no conciliarist. In treating the relationship between an ecumenical council and the pope, and the question whether the council would surpass him in authority, Kenrick responded that neither scripture nor tradition reported the existence of any acephalous council.[47] Kenrick's brother, Peter Richard, archbishop of Saint Louis, chided him for using only Latin in his books, an idiom in his judgment not suited to the times. Francis responded that his aim was to "teach what is right in language that is correct."[48]

In his moral theology, Kenrick followed Saint Thomas Aquinas and Saint Alphonsus. He made frequent use of non-Catholic, especially Anglican, authors. He was the first to translate the church's Roman law into the idiom of Anglo-American common law. A revised edition of his moral theology was later published in Belgium. Kenrick has been praised for his theological clarity and insight, if not for his originality. His works on moral theology were used in American seminaries into the twentieth century.[49]

As Isaac Hecker moved toward a religious decision between Rome and Canterbury, he had already determined, come what might, to dedicate his life to the church. After an interview with clergy of both Episcopal and Roman churches, Hecker chose the latter. He was conditionally baptized in August 1844. Several months later, his old mentor, Brownson, made the same move. The next year, so did John Henry Newman, one of the distinguished leaders of the British Oxford movement.

As a voracious reader of contemporary European thought, Brownson's interest in disputed questions took on a new urgency after his conversion. Like Newman, Brownson became involved with the struggle of his day between religious submissiveness and intellectual liberalism. He continued to grapple with the great political and social questions of the day. He would now reflect on them in the light of Catholic principles.[50]

After his conversion, Brownson admitted that he had a poor opinion of Catholics. Their apologetics were dry and lacked heart. He did not find Catholics at the head of any of the great intellectual, social, political, scientific, or literary movements of the day. It seemed to him that the great energetic nations were the non-Catholic ones: Great Britain, Russia, and, of course, America. In the so-called Catholic nations he felt that the leaders were "far from being attached to the Church." Since the problem could not lie within the nature of Catholicism itself, Brownson reasoned, it must lie in the policy of the clergy and "superannuated scholasticism." In light of Brownson's natural sentiments, it is easy to see why he considered his conversion a pure "work of grace."[51]

Brownson's one goal in editing the publication *Brownson's Quarterly Review* was to impart a freer and more elevated tone to Catholic discussion, not to convert Protestants. Before his conversion, the Yankee had been editor of the *Boston Quarterly Review* from 1838 to 1842. From 1844 to 1864 and again from 1873 to 1875, in his Catholic period, he was at the helm of the renamed *Brownson's Quarterly Review*. Brownson wanted to embolden Catholics to assert their rights. He intended to convince America that Catholicism and the political institutions of the United States were compatible. Moreover, he asserted that, as a bulwark against radicalism, the Catholic church was absolutely necessary to maintain American institutions.[52] "Infidelity, Protestantism, and heathenism," he wrote, "may institute a democracy, but only Catholicity may sustain it."[53] This was high new ground for American Catholic apologetics, usually on the defensive. History has credited Brownson with helping to convince non-Catholics that Catholics could be good Americans because of, not in spite of, the fact that they were good Catholics.[54]

Having been strongly influenced by Plato, Brownson disagreed with the Scholastics who held that the existence of God was not immediately self-evident or an innate truth, but known only by analogy and through effect to cause. For Brownson, God was the ideal, real, and necessary being who could be known by man intuitively but not explicitly. This emphasis on intuition was characteristic of the romantics. Brownson, however, went beyond them in his attempt to discover the ontological foundation for the knowledge of God.[55]

Like many nineteenth-century philosophers, Brownson employed unusual terminology. It has been suggested that Brownson's use of "intuition" was unfortunate. The term was commonly used to designate the immediate knowledge of self-evident things. For Brownson, "intuition" in the ontological order provided only the principles, the potentialities of reason.[56]

Brownson's understanding of the divine creative act, the dialectical principle of harmony, and his doctrine of life by communion were extremely important to him. By understanding the divine creative act, he felt he could explain natural revelation; through the doctrine of life by communion, supernatural revelation. The shared life of Jesus was an integrating principle; it was the foundation for the organic unity of tradition, history, and the church. The internal life of the church was clothed in external ecclesiastical structures. Authority and ecclesiastical unity were the visible manifestation of the inner authority and unity of the life of Jesus himself transmitted throughout the ages by communion with him.[57] This line of reasoning led Brownson to conclude that his own acceptance of the authority of the Catholic church was an intellectual one. He was most anxious to demonstrate this to his non-Catholic friends. They felt that he had restricted his mental freedom by embracing Catholicism and its dogmas.[58]

Some observers were of the opinion that, since he had changed his views so frequently, "Weathercock Brownson" could not be trusted to maintain them now.[59] Years later, Brownson's son came to his father's defense by explaining that as fast as he detected errors in his own or another's thoughts or glimpsed a new truth, he wrote about it. As a result, some who did not detect these changes as an abandonment of error judged Brownson "fickle and inconstant."[60]

Unfortunately, the elder Brownson had a natural talent for alienating people, prelates among them. One of his own prejudices, his anti-Irish bias, got him into trouble among ecclesiastical leaders. He confided in a personal letter to his trusted friend Hecker, "I do not like in general our Irish population." They did not clearly understand their religion. The Irish clergy were not much better, except for some unnamed "noble exceptions" to the rule.[61] Such confidences were safe enough, but what he printed for public consumption was quite another matter.

In the book *The Convert, or, Leaves from My Experience*, Brownson first confessed that he had found Catholics "superior to what I expected, more intellectual, more cultivated, more moral, more active, living and energetic," though not perfect. He then turned his attention to the large number of "nominally Catholic" Irish immigrants. He granted that they had suffered three hundred years of "bigotry, intolerance, persecution," which caused the "problem these immigrants create." Although "not as vicious as they appear," he found them guilty of a certain natural shiftlessness and recklessness.[62]

Brownson has been called too Yankee for the Catholics and too Catholic for the Yankees.[63] His solution to the Hibernization of the Catholic church was, as he wrote to Hecker, "American priests as fast as we can get them." Brownson honestly judged that a large portion of Catholic bishops and clergy had "a real dislike of the American people and character." He found the Irish laity "far less unamerican than their clergy."[64]

Brownson envisioned two Americas at war: the old constitutional and British order was in conflict with the new Jacksonian one, heir of the anti-Federalists and inspired by the French Revolution and foreign anarchists. It was the old constitutional republicanism that Brownson believed was compatible with Catholicism. Brownson feared that true Americanism was losing out to a false Americanism that grew out of "universal red republicanism."

What disturbed Brownson so much about "democracy"—and this had been evident earlier in his opposition to nativism—was the growing numbers of unpropertied workers whom industrialism had spawned. It was inconceivable to Brownson that government could survive if it were entrusted to the instincts of the illiterate and impoverished mob. They could be no more trusted than the greedy oligarchy.[65]

Brownson believed that only one strong and conservative institution could save the nation—the Catholic church. His staunch espousal of and high praise for things Catholic were repugnant to some of his readers. His offensive "excess in lauding things our own," Francis Kenrick wrote to his brother Peter, "we must be ready to pardon" since it comes from "a spirit which errs by fervor of affection."[66]

That loving but sometimes imprudent spirit led Brownson to examine the nature of the relationship between the spiritual and temporal orders in five successive issues of his *Review*. Both orders, Brownson argued, were established by God, with the spiritual superior to the temporal. God in Christ established the Catholic church. Since the temporal is ordered to the spiritual, "the pope, then even by virtue of his spiritual authority, has the power to judge all temporal questions, if not precisely as temporal, yet as spiritual." In the same vein he argued that non-Catholics, if they examined the matter fairly, would agree that it would make "good sense to see that, if the Pope be the vicar of Christ on earth . . . he must be independent and supreme before the secular authority."[67]

Brownson almost reached a point of obsession when he pointed out that the pope had the power of deposing secular rulers. Brownson admitted that this could not happen in any but a thoroughly Catholic state—an ideal that, of course, excluded America. That fact did not mean that the principle was not still in force.[68] By comparison with Brownson, de Maistre almost paled.

As a result, Brownson was denounced by Catholics and non-Catholics alike. Francis Kenrick told his brother that the newly Catholic editor was "piling up trouble for us, defending that temporal power of the pope which is generally not accepted" as essential to the pope's

office. Kenrick characterized Brownson's style as "not temperate"—
an understatement, to say the least. What really hurt Kenrick was
Brownson's insinuation that the issue of temporal power was "the
one genuinely Catholic teaching we fear to handle." Kenrick may have
seen this comment as a personal reproach, since he had prudently
avoided the issue in his own writings. What disturbed Kenrick further
was the nagging fear that non-Catholics would later take up Brownson's accusation and make just "such charges against us," especially
the charge that fear had dictated Kenrick's position.[69] It was not fear.
Kenrick wrote to a lay friend that he had gone "quite as far as my
convictions lead me."[70]

Several bishops reacted vocally. Archbishop John B. Purcell of
Cincinnati thought Brownson should be excommunicated. Bishop
Michael O'Connor of Pittsburgh made a public response in the *Met-
ropolitan*.[71] Archbishop John Hughes of New York City loudly criticized Brownson and was instrumental in having the Roman Office
of Propaganda examine Brownson's articles on papal temporal power.[72]

The upshot of the entire fracas was that members of the hierarchy
pressured Francis Kenrick to request that Brownson cease publishing
in his journal the letter of support that the bishops had given him in
1849.[73] Kenrick complied, but never abandoned Brownson even
though he did not always agree with him.

For his part, Brownson, who had moved from Boston to escape
episcopal control, discovered that New York was not large enough
for both Hughes and himself, two independent men. He moved once
again, this time to Elizabeth, New Jersey, where the convert Bishop
James Roosevelt Bayley would be his episcopal superior. For Hughes
it was good riddance. He had trouble with convert editors like
Brownson and James A. McMaster of the *Freeman's Journal*. He found
they sometimes unhappily betrayed the absence of "original Catholic
discipline." Hughes's famous retort to Brownson's expression of independence was, "I will suffer no man in my diocese that I cannot
control."[74]

In retrospect, Brownson's son, Henry, asserted that his father's
views on the pope's temporal power were opposed, not because they
were unorthodox, but because they were "inopportune, imprudent,
and likely to expose the Church to unnecessary odium."[75]

Henry was probably correct on all scores. The Office of Propaganda
found nothing doctrinally suspect in Brownson's articles.[76] Brownson
himself claimed that a number of bishops agreed with him in private.
What galled Brownson was that the same men turned their backs on
him in public. Understandably, this led Brownson to hold some bishops' integrity in suspicion.[77]

It should be pointed out that, in Brownson's opinion, his extreme ultramontane interpretation was the only form of Catholicism to which Americans would ever be converted. He believed it was the "only form congenial to their stern republican character."[78] It formed an essential principle of his politico-religious philosophy; he expounded it without reserve.[79]

CHAPTER
3
Isaac Hecker, an American Saint Paul, 1850–1880

While Brownson's excessive attachment to Rome was getting him into trouble at home, his friend Hecker was in Rome trying to have domestic problems resolved—problems that had developed because of his attachment to America. Hecker had become an ordained Redemptorist priest in 1849. During the years that followed, he decided to write a book addressed to non-Catholics. This resolve had grown out of the long years of his own painful religious quest. Like his mentor, Hecker wanted to show that only the Catholic church could adequately answer the ultimate questions every one raised. *Questions of the Soul*, a quasi-autobiographical work, was published in 1855. In it, Hecker undertook a demonstration to show that "the destiny of the soul . . . is to be one with God . . . and without God [man] is incomplete and his actions [are] ineffectual." Since one is "weak, frail, sinful," one cannot fulfill one's own destiny. However, God did not abandon everyone. He showed them a way. The influence of Möhler and the deep, powerful incarnational bent of Hecker's theology are evident in his assurance that one's destiny has already been accomplished in the God-man, Jesus Christ, "the model man and the way." When Jesus died, he left us his church, his bodily extension.

Hecker blamed the unbridled individuality of Protestantism for the confusion and apostasy of the age. Humanity and science had marched into the nineteenth century leaving God and traditional values behind. Hecker agreed with Brownson on this point. They both viewed history through romantic and Catholic eyes in spite of their widely diverse views on other issues regarding Catholicism. Thus, theirs is a good case in point to illustrate just how broad the appellation "romantic" really is.

Hecker believed that the Catholic church's reaction to the unrestrained individualism engendered by the Protestant revolt of the sixteenth century necessarily caused the church to emphasize its divine authority. In turn the church became externalized and extremely hierarchical. Hecker thought that this phase of the church would pass. The church should become a more dynamic and appealing spiritual body. Since Protestantism was dying—so Hecker thought—it would no longer be a threat.

To the modern reader, Hecker's treatment of Protestantism may appear polemical. Its general approach, however, did mark a new departure in Catholic apologetical literature. He offered no dogmatic defense of Catholicism drawn from Scripture or history. He did not set out to refute the errors of Protestantism or answer charges against Catholicism. Hecker simply delineated in a positive, appealing, and noncontroversial manner the instincts and cravings of human nature.[1] Such writing is all the more remarkable given that, during the period in which it was written, nativism was running amok.

The "Know-Nothings," formally known as the Secret Order of the Star-Spangled Banner, had begun to harass Catholics and other foreign-born citizens during the decade prior to the Civil War. Not every non-Catholic joined in the hysteria of the period. Abraham Lincoln, for example, saw the Know-Nothings for what they really were. If they should gain control, he worried that the national degeneracy, already in progress by the denial of equality to blacks, would continue at such a rate that the phrase "all men are created equal" would read "all men are created equal, except Negroes, *and foreigners and Catholics*." If it should come to that, Lincoln said, he would prefer to emigrate to a country where despotism was open, and not concealed by hypocrisy.[2]

Brownson welcomed Hecker's *Questions of the Soul* as a breath of sanity in a country gone slightly mad. He called it one of the few original, true American books.[3] The work was inclined to be mystical and ascetic. It was intended to show that only the Catholic church could satisfy the cravings of the human heart. Shortly after the book was published, the author confided to Brownson that there was still a need to demonstrate that the Catholic church answered the wants of the intellect as well; the head was left to be converted.[4]

Aspirations of Nature was intended to remedy this need. It was released in 1858 when Hecker was in Rome. Although it was more ambitious and more fundamental in nature than *Questions of the Soul*, the approach was the same. Hecker proceeded from the condition of humanity's needs to their fulfillment in the church. As with *Questions*, the essential goodness of human nature was Hecker's point of departure. Since there is a limit to the power of the intellect, the author argued, it cannot know the divine plan of life in all its fullness—this demands a revelation from God. From these correlatives, reason and revelation, Hecker demonstrated that neither philosophy nor Protestantism could answer humanity's intellectual quest adequately. Only the Catholic church could, for "in her bosom, the whole man— reason, heart, senses, all is turned to the worship of its creator."[5] This principle, enunciated in both *Questions* and *Aspirations*, grounded his later theological elaborations.

Hecker had gone to Rome to try to explain the situation in which he and several of his priest companions found themselves. They had run into difficulty with the predominantly German culture of the Redemptorist American houses. Many of the American-born Redemptorist priests wanted to extend their apostolate beyond ministering to German Catholic immigrants, and they hoped to reach out to Protestants as well. They also thought that an "American" house should be established by the community. This would work to the good of the immigrants and could hasten their Americanization. These Redemptorists were anxious to counter one of the nativist accusations against the Catholic church—that it was "foreign" in character. In Rome, Hecker petitioned the Redemptorist general, Father Nicholas Mauron, for the foundation of an American house. A series of misunderstandings, plus a latent suspicion of rebelliousness in the character of the petitioning American priests, led the general to expel Hecker from the order in August 1857. Hecker appealed his case to Pope Pius IX.[6] During the months that Hecker spent anxiously waiting for a final decision, Brownson published a devastating review of *Aspirations of Nature*. Brownson disagreed with Hecker's estimate of the spiritual and moral qualities of the American national character, with his desire to recast the church in an American mold, and with his desire for what Brownson called "too hasty" acculturation of immigrants. The reviewer disagreed sharply as well with the author's general estimate of human nature. Hecker believed that original sin deprived the soul of grace but did not intrinsically disable nature. Brownson, now holding a position closely akin with the Protestant Reformers, accused Hecker of overestimating the human capacity to do good after the fall.[7] Brownson secretly thought that Hecker was a semi-Pelagian without knowing it; Brownson himself was perhaps a Lutheran without knowing it.

Hecker was dismayed by Brownson's review. He told his old mentor that he had read the review "again and again." Hecker found it a "source of great regret that men who have the same noble and let me say, divine work at heart, should find so many differences between them." Hecker chided Brownson for the unfortunate and inopportune release of the review. He felt it would increase suspicion against him in Rome and have a "terrible effect" on the American fathers.[8] Brownson replied that he thought the "animus of the review" was not unkind. He explained that he had disagreed with Hecker on several points that were "more matter of opinion." He admitted that he was less sanguine than Hecker about the immediate success of converting America. Brownson thought that the prevalent disposition of non-Catholics and the lack of missionary spirit among Catholics were serious obstacles. Brownson confessed that what he was most anxious to do was disabuse the public of the notion that there is "formed amongst us an American party or an American clique. . . . You know," Brownson continued, "we none of us want a native party, or entertain any other than true fraternal feelings towards our Catholic brothers of European birth." Brownson feared that talk of America's conversion could be construed to mean putting the government of the church here in the hands of native-born Americans and refusing to have any but native-born clergy and prelates.[9]

With genuine fraternal affection, Hecker understood that some of the negative comments Brownson had printed about his work were the very points on which Archbishop John Hughes of New York City had challenged Brownson himself. Hecker forgave his old friend, who was in ecclesiastical trouble himself and wanted to distance himself from Hecker's problems.[10]

While in Rome, Hecker wrote a lengthy article for the Jesuit periodical *Civiltà Cattolica*. In it he attempted to explain to Europeans the situation of the Catholic church in the United States. He wrote that in the providence of God, every nation, just as every individual, is at some moment offered the grace of conversion. Hecker believed the moment for America was at hand and had to be seized. Drawing upon his Brook Farm and Fruitlands experiences, he described the spiritual tendencies among Americans. He contrasted what he called native species of socialism and communism with the European varieties. The latter repudiated the church with hostility; the former led upward and toward the church.

Hecker's love for and optimism about America are quite apparent when he discusses the special character of America's political institutions. To fend off any attack against the separation of church and state as they exist in America, he alluded to the trend in Europe "to tyrannize over the Church" at the very time when the United States Constitution was being framed. For Hecker it was the finger of divine providence directing the framers of that Constitution in the path that would lead to the triumph of the Christian faith.

Hecker reasoned along the following lines. It is axiomatic in America that people are capable of self-government. This is worked out in principle through universal suffrage. The democratic system assumes the basic integrity of human nature, the existence of natural rights, law, and justice—precisely what Catholicity teaches. It is Calvinism and Protestantism that teach the natural depravity of humankind. Therefore, the principles upon which the American republic is founded are not only congenial to Christianity but are Catholic in their source. Any political institution upholding these principles disposes its people to the Catholic faith.

To counter the European accusation that Americans are materialistic, Hecker used an interesting ploy. He claimed that America's wealth worked to the advantage of its conversion. No potential candidate for Catholic baptism could be deterred from entering the church, even if his employer should attempt to tyrannize him. The neophyte did not have to fear his boss, "since lucrative employment is easily found."[11] This may have been true in Hecker's circle; his own brothers had become quite prosperous. In general, his romanticized view of the labor opportunities had little factual foundation. His attempt to give a "religious" interpretation to "materialism" is too contrived. He apparently found his thesis somewhat difficult to defend. In his subsequent interviews with Pius IX, the pope brought up Americans' preoccupation with material pursuits. Hecker replied, "True, Holy Father, but the holy Faith is there."[12]

Hecker's *Civiltà* article was translated and carried in the chief periodicals of France, Germany, Belgium, and the United States.[13] The early seeds of Hecker's "Americanism" were being sown. Fortunately for American Catholic history, the pope dispensed Hecker and four other American Redemptorists from their vows. He encouraged them to operate as a community to work for the conversion of America. All five men had themselves been converts. Several had been members of the Oxford movement at the General Theological Seminary in New York. In 1858, Hecker and three of the group became known as the Missionary Society of Saint Paul the Apostle.[14]

Isaac Hecker developed a unique Catholic apologetic, one influenced by his romanticism and his experiences as a Protestant. The convert took the objections of Protestants seriously and was willing and anxious to debate with them. He traveled widely and lectured extensively, and he was completely at ease among non-Catholics. A former seeker himself, Hecker was confident that he would be heard because he believed that the religious arguments he presented were true and answered the natural cravings of heart and head, intellect and will. Like other nineteenth-century theorists, Hecker believed that religion was important in all spheres of life, including the political. Hecker's respect for American political institutions was rooted in his belief that the American theory of natural rights was linked with the Catholic theory of natural law, a position unique to Hecker. He believed that the weakness of the English liberal tradition was its lack of an institutionalized authority to protect individuals' rights and liberties. In Hecker's vision, the Catholic church, once America had been converted, would be the institution for political virtue.

Hecker was optimistic about the possibility of reconciling liberalism and Catholicism. Brownson, however, was not. Although Hecker and Brownson had cut their teeth on Jacksonian democracy and shared a common view of the relationship between religion and politics, Brownson grew disillusioned. He bitterly questioned whether a democratic society could ever support Catholicism. By contrast, Hecker never gave up on the American experiment. He is credited with having formulated the first optimistic Catholic political theory of liberal democracy.[15]

Spiritually, Hecker had lifelong mystical tendencies. Early in Hecker's religious journey, Brownson, who completely failed to grasp this dimension of his friend, warned Hecker against his mysticism and "undue subjectivism." "Here is the rock," Brownson admonished, "on which many a great soul has been wrecked."[16] Nonetheless, Hecker's mysticism has been suggested as an important element in shaping his attitude toward women.[17]

Hecker's early diary reveals his high valuation of the feminine. In one entry, which has a very contemporary ring about it, the youthful Isaac wrote, "Man requires a new birth, the birth of the feminine in him." A month later his reflections continued along this line as he noted his inclination "to think . . . that the same individual should unite in his own being both sexes." This union in one individual mirrored Christ "who has united in him the perfect lovefulness [sic] and tenderness of woman with the wisdom and strength of man."[18] After Hecker had established the Paulists, he tried to establish a parallel group of laywomen, who also would not profess vows. He recruited potential candidates from among the women whom he directed spiritually, but the plan never materialized. One of Hecker's spiritual daughters, Mrs. E. M. Cullen, was an ardent suffragist. Hecker had adopted the position that women would not even be demanding the vote if they still occupied the place society once gave them. He based his view on the Catholic stock-in-trade antisuffrage argument. Hecker advanced the position that cloistered women of the Middle Ages had the advantages of education that many males did not. In some instances, abbesses held monastic power over men. It was Luther and the Reformation that eroded women's position when convents were closed. Despite that alteration of circumstances, Hecker contended that the contemporary church still gave "full scope to women's capacities and powers."[19]

The argument did not convince Mrs. Cullen. The lot in life of the married medieval woman was rarely, if ever, expounded in the Catholic defense of the status quo. Cullen chided Hecker for his retrograde views. She attributed them to the fact that he was a member of the "bachelor order." Most men who supported the suffrage movement, she noted, were married.[20]

Hecker's *Catholic World* carried articles more favorable than *Brownson's Quarterly Review* on the woman question. But it has been argued that after the 1860s, as Hecker became a more active participant in male-dominated ecclesiastical affairs, he showed little concern for women and failed to move beyond the conventional Catholic wisdom on the question. As his most recent biographer has noted, this was unfortunate in light of Hecker's promising beginning. Judged against Brownson's standards, however, Hecker emerges as a champion of women. The difference between their perspectives became acute during the late 1860s. Hecker remained constant in his moderately liberal outlook; Brownson set to battle in earnest "the spirit of the age."[21]

During this period, Hecker emerged as spokesman for a group of well-educated and monied Catholic laypeople. They were Yankee Catholics; many among them were converts. Anxious to advance the cause of the church and play a role in the shaping of American society, they nevertheless often found themselves on the fringe of both society and church. The particular message that Hecker preached, called a kind of "American Messianism," was critical of both American nationalism and European Catholicism. Neither seemed able to accommodate Hecker and his like-minded associates. As a result, he elaborated a vision of church and society that would allow Yankee Catholics full stature.[22]

Hecker was on the periphery of another group of American Catholics composed of "radical" New York priests.[23] As a result of facing the political issues precipitated by the Civil War, some clerics applied the principle of "democracy in action," which they had recently witnessed, to ideas about reform in American Catholicism. One of the things that had galled many of these clerics was the arbitrary transfer of priests, or even their dismissal, at the whim of autocratic bishops.

In 1865 this small group of liberal clerics formed a theological society, which they named the Accademia. Although it was disbanded the next year, five or six of the former members continued to meet regularly. The views that they held have been judged radical for their day. About issues concerning the papacy, their views were rather predictable: they opposed the temporal power of the pope; thought of infallibility as ecclesial, not papal or personal; and were uncomfortable with the doctrine of the Immaculate Conception, which rested on papal authority alone. In scriptural matters they even held open views on the questions of inerrancy and inspiration. In disciplinary matters they opposed extreme legalism and favored the vernacular for devotion and eventually for the liturgy. There is a contemporary note in their advocacy of general absolution for large congregations and in their opposition to mandatory celibacy. They were irenic in their outlook. They favored public schools over a rival and costly Catholic school system. At least one member of this society, Edward McGlynn, joined with non-Catholics in order to pursue shared values, usually in a liturgical context.

These so-called radicals were held in suspicion by their superiors and some fellow priests. The issues raised by the Accademia were not resolved, but this is not to say that they went away. Some would resurface during the Americanist crisis, others during the modernist conflict. A number would be resurrected during Vatican II.[24]

The desire to define the basis of ecclesiastical authority in an age of revolution motivated Pius IX to convoke the First Vatican Council in 1870.[25] The dogmatic commission appointed to assist in the work of conciliar preparation made an early decision to use Pope Pius IX's *Syllabus of Errors* as its base. The *Syllabus* was at odds with most of the liberal thought of the nineteenth century. The Roman preparatory commission followed the pope's lead and was also bent on condemning deviations, old and new.[26]

On the other side of the ocean, Isaac Hecker typically viewed the upcoming council as providential. It would work as an agent of reconciliation between church and society. He believed the outcome of the council would usher a new and glorious era into church history, one in which the American Catholic Church was destined to play a major role.

Hecker arrived in Rome in November of 1869 as procurator for a nonattending bishop of Columbus, Ohio, Sylvester Rosecrans. During the council, Hecker was named personal theologian to Archbishop Spalding of Baltimore, an appointment that gave him access to all the documents of the council and made him privy to all conciliar discussions.[27]

It quickly became evident that there was a strong ultramontane faction afoot advocating the definition of papal infallibility. Eighty percent of American bishops opposed the move on the ground that it was at the very least inopportune. They feared a proclamation of infallibility would rekindle nativist hostilities.[28]

Martin John Spalding wrote to Cardinal Alessandro Barnabò, secretary of the Sacred Congregation, *Propaganda Fide,* to the effect that the American bishops believe in papal infallibility ex cathedra, but were inclined to think its "formal definition unnecessary and perhaps inexpedient." Spalding was also privately concerned about the possibility that the council would stretch and generalize the principles of the Syllabus.

As the determination of the ultramontanes became clearer, Spalding attempted to promote a compromise. He had drawn up a formula for an implicit definition of papal infallibility. Rather than use the word "infallibility" and promulgate a new definition, earlier condemnations of opponents to the papacy, particularly the Gallicans and the Jansenists, would be reiterated.[29]

Hecker had associated himself with the anti-infallibilist faction led by Bishop Félix Dupanloup of Orleans. For some months the Paulist founder acted as an intermediary between North American opponents of a definition, notable among them Archbishop Thomas L. Connolly of Halifax and Archbishop Peter Richard Kenrick of Saint Louis, and the majority who favored a definition. Much of Hecker's effort was directed toward preventing the question from ever coming before the council for discussion.[30]

Peter Kenrick became the most outspoken American to question papal infallibility on theological grounds. He argued that neither Scripture nor tradition made the doctrine clear. He was provoked that Archbishop Spalding had presumed to speak in the name of the American bishops when he presented his compromise proposal.[31] Several years prior to the council, Kenrick had expressed his belief that bishops were vested with the Holy Spirit. It was they who had the right to determine how to rule their own sees. They were not simply to follow instructions from Rome. Rome made too many decisions based on scanty or faulty information.[32]

Frustrated by the insufficient time he was given on the council floor to present his views in the debate over papal prerogatives, Kenrick published his *Concio in Concilio Vaticano habenda at non habita.*[33] It surprised even the members of the minority. Peter Kenrick was particularly angry with Irish Cardinal Paul Cullen's mishandling of a quotation from the work of his brother, Francis Kenrick, presented in support of the infallibilists' position. Peter agreed that his brother had devotion to the Holy See, but insisted that he taught that the consent of the episcopacy was necessary if a decree were to be declared infallible.[34]

Peter denied that the letter the American bishops sent to Pope Pius

IX at the close of the Second Plenary Council implicitly recognized papal infallibility. He deftly pointed out that Spalding, author of the letter, was also author of *Lectures on the Evidence of Catholicity*.[35] In that book Spalding held the position that infallibility ex cathedra was a more or less certain theological opinion. He added that the power was exercised rarely and only in conjunction with bishops in council or dispersed over the world. This was the same position Francis Kenrick had presented in his book *The Papacy*.

Peter argued that a definition of papal infallibility would augment the current trend to overcentralization already crippling ecclesiastical administration. Infallibility denigrated the individual position and collegial status of bishops. A definition would be psychologically detrimental to the church. If a bishop voted in favor of definition without giving serious thought and thorough study to the question, he would be guilty of grave sin.[36] Generally conservative, Bishop Bernard McQuaid of Rochester shared some of Kenrick's concerns. He worried that episcopal collegiality reaffirmed in 1866 at the Second Plenary Council of Baltimore Council could not be safeguarded against the position being championed by the majority.[37]

The question of papal prerogatives was not the only item on the conciliar agenda that held American interest. The last five of twenty-one canons appended to the schema on the church dealt with the issues of church-state relations. Hecker avidly participated in the discussion initiated by the schema. It gave him an opportunity to demonstrate that the experience of the American church could be paradigmatic for resolving European church-state problems. It was during the council, one author has argued, that Hecker began to see more clearly what he considered to be the providential mission of the United States—to solve in advance the problems of Europe where the separation of church and state was becoming inevitable.[38] Concomitant with that view was his growing conviction that the Paulists should expand their mission to Europe and even beyond. They would be the bearers of "the light derived from American civilization" and agents of Europe's "political regeneration" and religious renewal.

Hecker's optimism about the outcome of the council declined sharply in the midst of the controversy that raged when the unavoidable question of papal infallibility was finally introduced in March of 1870. At the same time, Hecker's health began to fail. By April he complained that he was habitually exhausted. By the end of the month Hecker had left Rome, three months before infallibility was brought to a vote.

Hecker was bothered by the fact that the proposed definition was a step away from the primary Catholic truths of the Trinity with the attendant notion of the indwelling of the Holy Spirit and of the Incarnation reflected in Hecker's understanding of a providential theory of history. The definition and the machinations of the ultramontanists were victories for absolutism and monarchy. The movement was completely out of step with the time. Hecker could accept that the bishops were "by divine right, judges of what is of faith."[39] His problem was reconciling this definition with his understanding of providential events in history and his penchant for reading and interpreting these as signs of the times.

On July 18, 1870, a formal vote was taken on the constitution *Pastor Aeternus;* papal infallibility and jurisdictional primacy were defined.[40] Of the American bishops who had remained in Rome, twenty-five voted yes, one no. Peter Kenrick and two other American prelates were among the fifty-five bishops who left on the eve of the definition. They wanted to spare Pius IX the embarrassment that their negative votes would have caused him. The other eighteen American bishops had already gone home.[41] The day after the issuance of the decree, France declared war against Prussia. This set off a chain of events necessitating that the council be prorogued.[42] In assessing the overall contribution of the American bishops, James Hennesey has remarked that they neither took the council by storm, nor failed to contribute "something of the ideas and peculiar genius of their own country."[43]

Eventually, all the American prelates accepted the definition. For a few like Purcell and Peter Kenrick it was not easy.[44] Kenrick refused to retract what he had published in his *Concio.* He would not write a pastoral letter on the council or send a personal letter of submission to the pope. When the Italian army occupied Rome in late September of 1870, he refused to sign a letter of sympathy to the pope.[45]

Reactions to the definition among the general American public were mixed. The ultramontanes, James A. McMaster, editor of the *Freeman's Journal,* and Brownson, were ebullient.[46] Brownson interpreted papal primacy to include the right to depose rulers and absolve subjects from their allegiance. He thought that it mandated the recognition of the legitimacy of the temporal power of the pope. It was precisely these political implications that caused some serious misgivings among members of the secular and religious press. In this context it has been argued that nineteenth-century anti-Catholicism was more political than theological. Protestants perceived the Catholic church as the defender of the old order, reactionary and intransigent. It was seen as a threat to the American ideas of freedom and democracy.[47]

With hindsight, one fact emerges clearly. *Pastor Aeternus* moved the Catholic church, American branch included, a giant step along the path of Romanization, the peculiar social form that the church assumed during the century-and-a-half prior to Vatican II.[48] One his-

torian has indicated that the definition of infallibility and concomitant
political events contributed to the unique nineteenth-century phenomenon that produced the image of the pope as a father figure. At
the same time, the papacy acquired the aura of martyrdom. The image
was fed by Napoleon's persecution of Pius VI and Pius VII. It was
enhanced by the treatment of Pius IX at the hands of Garibaldi and
Cavour. It reached its apogee in Pio Nono's self-imposed incarceration
as the "prisoner of the Vatican."[49]

By the time papal infallibility had been defined, Brownson had
already viewed himself as an "old fogey" in his views and sympathies.[50] In an essay entitled "Church and State," he acknowledged he
had come to realize that the zeitgeist was against any form of union
between church and state.[51] He felt that the movement was a complete
sundering of the two, with the state as supreme authority. He believed
that what the pope had condemned in the Syllabus was political atheism, the independence of the temporal from the law of God.[52] He
thought that this, in fact, had happened in America. Brownson wrote:
"The American democracy is not what it was in 1776. It was then
christian after a protestant fashion; it is now infected with European
liberalism . . . If we had to induce the American system now, we should
not be able to do so."[53]
    The entire world, in Brownson's extreme view, was in need of re-
conversion, but there were only "wooden bishops and priests to do
it with." He no longer believed that the churches fared well in the
United States. On the contrary, the church had never faced such a
hostile order as it had in America. He thought that Hecker's notion
that democracy was favorable to the promotion of the Catholic church
was just plain foolishness.[54]
    The aging Brownson resumed publication of Brownson's Quarterly
Review in 1873, the year that the nation suffered an economic collapse
and panic, which left 3 million workers unemployed. The Review was
terminated two years later. The days of the publication's greatest
popularity were long gone.[55] Brownson died the following year.
    The events of the Vatican Council permanently directed Hecker's
view toward Europe. The aftermath of the definition had left the European church weak. Johann Ignaz Döllinger and the "old Catholics"
had refused to accept papal infallibility and the latter went into open
schism. Politically, Hecker was appalled because he feared that Catholics in Italy, France, and Spain were under the rule of a small group
of atheists. As he pondered the question of the proper means for church
renewal, he concluded that only a faithful discipleship to the immediate and interior promptings of the Holy Spirit would be adequate
to meet the needs of the age.[56]

Suffering from a protracted illness, Hecker was advised by his physician to take the nineteenth-century cure-all—to travel for his health. For two years he toured Europe, Egypt, and the Holy Land. His European travels brought him into contact with influential intellectuals and old friends who shared his progressive views. They discussed the renewal of church and society, which could only be effected by a heightened attention to the action of the Holy Spirit within the soul, the church, and society. He published his program for renewal in 1874. Entitled "Exposition on the Needs of the Church and the Age," it was received positively.[57] It encouraged him to continue to air his views. Essays written during this period were printed in book form as *The Church and the Ages*.[58] In this work Hecker's passion for the American church was subordinated to his consciousness of the universal mission of the church. Hecker had grappled privately with the question of his own role in the global scheme of things. In a memorandum written in Europe he mused:

> What else has been my exile from home for unless to make my life-experience applicable to the general condition of the Church and the world in its present crisis? The past was for the United States, the future is for the world . . . I now see why I called myself an "International Catholic."[59]

The Church and the Ages is permeated with variations of a double thesis: America is most congenial to Christianity; the task of the church in the United States is to show its citizens, and ultimately European societies, that only Catholicity can effect the synthesis between Christianity and republicanism.[60] Hecker was well aware that neither national nor racial lines could contain the church, since it was independent in its origin, essence, and institution of every race and nation. It was destined to embrace all humanity in unity. In writing to a friend about spiritual renovation based on "certain general ideas" formulated according to "uncontested principles of grace," Hecker insisted that the "application should be regulated by different ecclesiastical authorities according to different countries and circumstances." His correspondent understood that Hecker did not wish to impose "on each individual the Anglo-Saxon character."[61]

Hecker's experience of democracy strongly colored his emphasis on the role of intelligence, and especially of liberty, in the development of the full human personality. Humanity was better prepared than ever to respond to an even greater outpouring of the Holy Spirit, which would "elevate the human personality to an intensity of force and grandeur productive of a new era to the Church and to society . . . difficult for the imagination to grasp."

When Hecker described the role of the Holy Spirit in the church, he generally spoke of it as twofold: exterior and interior. The external aspects through which the Spirit operates are sacraments, worship, the practice of virtue, and the exercise of church authority. The interior function of the Spirit—the "final aim of the Church"— is the deepening of the interior life of the individual and the immediate union of the soul with Christ. The external aspect of the church, Hecker insisted, must be subordinated to, and can never be substituted for, the final end of the church.[62]

Hecker read the works of Cardinal Henry Edward Manning, which expounded devotion to the Holy Spirit. Manning was the major European promoter of this devotion; however, the emphasis of the American and Englishman differed. Manning recommended outward devotion and prescribed prayers within a structured relationship. The hallmark of such devotion was loyalty to the institutional church. Hecker's emphasis was mystical, intuitive, and interior.[63]

The importance Hecker attached to the function of the laity in the church is in direct proportion with the importance he attributed to individual initiative. "Let there be individual initiative," he said. "Laymen need not wait for priest, nor priest for bishop, nor bishop for pope while the Holy Ghost sends down the reproof that he is prompting each one and no one moves for him."[64] Hecker never separated the idea of individuality from that of sanctification; otherwise, the balance between natural and supernatural would be disturbed and end in pride and egotism.[65] He saw the need for the formation of confessors who would be prepared to deal with a spirituality of personal initiative applied to contemporary souls.[66] No other American or European Catholic of the time has been judged so respectful of the role of the laity as Hecker was. He saw the layperson's work in society and family as morally significant and central to the church's mission. Only the laity could exert Catholic influence in the midst of contemporary society.[67]

Some of Hecker's interpretations were at least novel, if not radical. He considered the church "the most democratic institution." His highly controversial interpretation of papal infallibility has been called, without exaggeration, one of the most unusual in the nineteenth century.[68] Hecker wrote:

> For the definition of the Vatican Council, having rendered the supreme authority of the Church, which is the unerring interpreter and criterion of divinely revealed truth, more explicit and more complete, has prepared the way for the faithful to follow with greater safety and liberty, the inspirations of the Holy Spirit. The dogmatic papal definition of the Vatican Council is therefore the axis on which turn the new course of the Church, the renewal of religion, and the entire restoration of society.[69]

His proposition that the origin and destiny of the Catholic church and the American nation were the same has been called "outrageous."[70]

When speaking of members of the hierarchy Hecker avoided the traditional designation "prince of the church," which suggested monarchy. Rather, he speculated on the consequences of widespread democracy among Catholic nations:

> It would result in the College of Cardinals being made a representative body of all mankind. It would be the religious senate of the world. Its decisions would be the religious decisions of all humanity.

He opposed the monarchical form of government on theological grounds. To Count Joseph de Maistre's dire prediction that the United States would not last, Hecker retorted that "Catholicity in religion sanctions republicanism in politics, and republicanism in politics favors Catholicity in religion."[71]

The last manuscript Hecker prepared, a brief tract, was concerned with the renewal of Christian life. No longer as hopeful as in his earlier works, he admitted that times were not improving but getting worse. But his old optimism reappeared as he recalled that, at the beginning of every new age or critical period, the Holy Spirit called forth new religious institutes that understood and responded to the needs of the times. Ignatius Loyola aided the church in its struggle against the Protestant Reformation. He symbolized the era of the church when it necessarily emphasized "divine external authority." That age came to a close with the definition of infallibility, which secured "the sphere of divine external authority." Philip Neri, on the other hand, typified the new age of the church by his emphasis on the interior action of the Holy Spirit. Such a shift in emphasis implied "nothing else than a more perfect evolution of the essential nature of the Church." Members of new religious orders must be penetrated with a sense of God's immanence and transcendence, since the age had lost a sense of God's existence. The new religious will foster an appreciation of the natural sciences which the impious had snatched from the hands of the church.[72] Hecker concluded by noting that various aspects of education—literature, science, teaching, formerly the exclusive province of religious orders and clergy—had rightfully passed into the hands of the laity. This freed the clergy for the study of theology, the "noblest employment of our best faculties." This does not imply a disjunction between the sacred and the secular in Hecker's thought. He never accepted a separation of religion and culture, as had his European contemporaries. This would make the church simply one agency of goodness among many. Hecker believed that the church was necessary for the security of faith and the full realization of shared humanity. According to Hecker there was no instrument more efficacious for effecting social reconciliation than the priesthood.[73]

Shortly before Hecker's death he revived his desire to establish a

Paulist-like movement throughout Europe. He envisioned the community as an agent of renewal and regeneration. He worked on this plan in conjunction with his old friend, Bishop John J. Keane. Death left Hecker's dreams unfulfilled.[74]

Contemporary religious historians have begun to uncover the richness of thought and breadth of apostolic vision of the man who has justifiably been called "the Yankee Paul."[75]

CHAPTER
4
The Catholic University and Americanism, 1880–1900

~~~~~~~~

$\mathcal{T}$he idea of establishing a Catholic university in the United States was first mentioned by Archbishop Martin John Spalding in preparation for the Second Plenary Council of Baltimore. The project was greeted with little enthusiasm on the part of the bishops. With so many pressing needs facing the post–Civil War church, university education, while on the conciliar agenda, was not high on it. The seed, however, was sown. The task of nurturing the idea and bringing it to fruition fell to the archbishop's nephew, John Lancaster Spalding.[1]

The young Spalding received his clerical training at Louvain, Belgium, enrolling in 1859 at the age of nineteen. The professors there had developed a synthesis of modified traditionalism and Augustinian ontologism. They accepted the principal thesis of ontologism, that ideas are "seen" immediately in God in the sense expressed by Saint Augustine. In his *Confessions*, Augustine wrote that God is the immutable truth above changeable, created minds. When the finite mind turns to the principles by which it is governed, in reality, it turns to God.[2] From modified traditionalism, the Louvain professors accepted the thesis that God had made a primitive revelation of divine ideas. These ideas were not the actual cause of the first principles of knowledge, but an indispensable condition for knowledge. This primitive revelation was transmitted to successive generations through language. Education acquired through society was the necessary condition to bring innate ideas from their virtual condition into actuality.

Speculative thinking apparently excited the young and talented Spalding. After two and a half years abroad, he wrote to his uncle enthusiastically, "I am German, I am so mysteriously and deeply philosophical. . . ."

By the time Spalding left Europe, he had been exposed to "Louvain ontologism" with its appreciation for the development of thought through changing historical and cultural circumstances. He was committed to education as the key to religious and cultural advancement. He had also developed a proficiency in German, which gave him access to the romantic writers of the period. Spalding later developed a passion for the works of the great Johann Wolfgang von Goethe (1749–1832).

Not too long after Spalding's return home, James McMaster, editor of the *Freeman's Journal*, published a disturbing article in 1867. He claimed that the works of one of Louvain's professors, Canon Gerard Casimir Ubaghs, had been condemned by the Holy Office. Spalding challenged McMaster and published a defense of Ubaghs and the faculty of his alma mater. The matter ended rather ingloriously for Spalding.[3] Ubagh's *Theodicea* and *Logica* had actually been banned from use as textbooks in Catholic schools in 1866. Prior to the Roman proscription, Ubaghs and his confreres had been accused of traditionalism. They successfully cleared themselves of that charge, but their opponents, still suspicious of their orthodoxy, made a direct appeal to the pope. Ubaghs and his crew were shipwrecked on the Rock of Peter. The Louvain philosophers were not the only casualties. By the end of the 1860s, Rome had condemned virtually every major philosophical force in Catholic theology except scholasticism. The solution that the scholastics proposed as the antidote to rationalism was to try to persuade modern philosophy to revert to the position it held prior to Descartes. Only then could it rebuild itself on sound Christian principles. This school argued that the philosophy of Saint Thomas Aquinas alone held the key to determining the proper relationships between faith and reason, grace and nature, and, by extension, altar and throne.[4]

During the reign of Leo XIII, neo-Thomism triumphed. In the 1879 encyclical, *Aeterni Patris*, scholasticism—which became almost completely identified with the supposed system of Saint Thomas Aquinas, was decreed the philosophy to be taught in all Catholic colleges and universities.[5] Thus, neo-Thomism became the orthodoxy against which to judge Catholic philosophers operating out of different philosophical frameworks. Because neo-Thomists could not think historically, they could not accept the concept that ideas necessarily developed through the force of the changing conditions of history. They were neither prepared for, nor kindly disposed to, Catholics who tried to deal creatively with the pressing questions of the modern age. As a result, within a quarter-century after the publication of *Aeterni Patris*, painful crises wracked the Catholic intellectual community in Europe and in America.

John Lancaster Spalding's own career was tainted by the suspicion that he was an ontologist. Before he was appointed first bishop of Peoria in 1877, he had to be cleared of that accusation as well as for his reservations about the definition of papal infallibility.[6] Spalding had an inquiring mind and, though he is generally described as essentially conservative on some issues, he was by no means rigid in his intellectual outlook.[7] One constant in Spalding's life, however, was his dedication to higher education and a concomitant disdain for mediocrity, wherever it was found.

About the time Spalding had begun to agitate for a Catholic university, the National Teachers' Association passed a harsh judgment on all existing American institutions of higher learning. They argued that no native school, despite what it might be called, came anywhere near the ideal of a true university in the European sense. The convert Bishop Thomas A. Becker of Wilmington concurred with that opinion.[8] So did Spalding, and he wanted to do something about it.

In an article commemorating the centennial of the Declaration of Independence, Spalding painted a rather bleak picture of America's intellectual landscape. He readily acknowledged the accomplishments wrought over the past hundred years. What was notably lacking was the independent thinker. "We are," Spalding lamented, "a commonplace and mediocre people; practical, without high ideas, lofty aspirations or excellent standards of worth and character." In his judgment, Americans were inferior to Europeans "in philosophy, in science, in literature, in art, in culture." Ever the national heroes, Washington and Lincoln were referred to as "common men." Orestes Brownson was singled out as the "ablest man" who discussed "religion and philosophy, or probably any other subject, in the United States during the last hundred years." Yet Brownson himself did not pass muster. Something was "wanting" to make him a "great" philosopher, theologian, or even a "perfect master of style." What really troubled Spalding was that there seemed to be no replacement on the horizon to fill the shoes of the recently deceased Yankee convert. The solution to the problem was a university where an elite could be trained to "further Catholic ends."

To quell the fears of Protestants over the expansion of Catholicism in America, Spalding assured his readers that, even if America should become 90 percent Catholic, the principles of religious liberty would stand intact. Actually, Spalding continued, Protestants should rejoice that the Catholic population was growing. Catholics were the surest antidote to the threat of anarchy, which America's "unbridled liberty" could surely provoke. Only the Catholic church with its "great and sacred authority" was the safeguard of sanity.[9] Even as Spalding wrote, the *Kulturkampf* was being waged in Prussia and other German states. It supported universal education, on the one hand, and suppressed Catholic seminaries, on the other.

True civilization, Spalding argued, could not be fostered through the pragmatic, but only through the aesthetic sense. It is the power of art when "made beautiful and sublime in poetry, in song, in eloquence . . . that moulds the national character." Spalding insisted that religion could exist without culture, but that true culture could not exist without religion. He returned to this theme frequently in subsequent writings.[10]

During this period, Spalding publicly worried about the fate of his beloved, aesthetic Germany in the wake of Bismarck's "cultural war." In this context, Spalding had some harsh things to say about Goethe, suggesting that the blame for Bismarck's attempt to control clerical education could be laid at the poet's feet. That "idol of German literature, to whom the very sign of the cross was so hateful," Spalding lamented, had referred to himself as a non-Christian. In the American's opinion, the root of Goethe's anti-Christian attitude was his disgust at the thought of sacrifice, odious to his "lustful and all-indulgent nature." The god of Goethe's heart was "sensualism and sexualism."[11]

In 1878 Spalding was asked by several bishops to take the lead in promoting clerical education, since no one else was doing so. Several years later, Spalding wrote to Archbishop James Gibbons of Baltimore that he would be happy to go to work in a university that would educate priests and would be willing to dedicate his life to the work.[12]

Spalding was given the opportunity to make a plea for the establishment of a Catholic university before the assembled prelates at the Third Plenary Council of Baltimore in 1884. He had already tweaked a few conciliar noses by his opposition to any exercise of democracy within the church. One of the reasons the bishops had assembled in Baltimore was to discuss more representative ecclesial government. There had long been agitation among the American clergy to give them greater voice in nominating their bishops.[13] Spalding contended that if priests were given a say, the laity would then demand a voice. Spalding never trusted the masses. "Where they are King," he said, "fools inevitably rule." His biographer has wryly noted that John Lancaster Spalding never forgot that he could trace his family back to another Lancaster, King Edward III of England.[14]

In his address before the council, Spalding again displayed his elitist strain. He noted that it was "fashionable" to affect contempt for people of "superior culture"; education was seen only as utilitarian. In calling for a university, Spalding made it clear that he was not asking for more technical training for the clergy. That was the work of the seminaries. What he envisioned was an institution that would help priests develop a philosophical habit of mind. It is possible, he argued, for a priest to be a skilled and erudite theologian and still lack mental culture. Specialization tended to make a person one-sided. Priests, "the first teachers of the race," should have unbiased minds. They should be open to the comparison of ideas and truths with one another. The very defense of religion demanded priests of excellent intellectual qualities. They would be honest in their appraisal of modern science and its limits. Only when there were a sufficient number of "cultivated intellects to treat religious subjects" could Catholic theology come out of "its isolation in the modern world." In Spalding's opinion, "the best cultivation of mind" ranked a close second to the priest's need for virtue.

Spalding concluded his conciliar address by arguing that no "enlightened bishop" could oppose a university as he described it. The only question was its feasibility. Spalding thought that such an institution was possible if one were content with modest beginnings.[15]

Spalding had brought more than rhetoric to the Plenary Council. He had put some teeth into his plan with the promised help of a young New York heiress. Miss Mary Gwendolyn Caldwell had agreed to donate $300,000, a sizable portion of her wealth, toward the construction of the proposed institution; however, she had attached some strings, which Spalding had approved. According to the stipulations, the location had to be in the capital city of the nation and the twenty-one-year-old Miss Caldwell had to be considered founder.

Despite his careful plans and passionate pleas, Spalding proved to be not much more convincing than his uncle had been at the previous Plenary Council. The university project would have died if Archbishop Gibbons had not rescued it. He appointed a committee of prelates and laymen, with Spalding as chairman, to study the matter. This decision has been called one of the most memorable actions taken by the council.

Some of the bishops were not pleased with the proposed site; others wished that funds could be found other than those offered by the bossy Miss Caldwell. When the smoke cleared, and despite some episcopal reservation, Spalding was nominated as rector for the Catholic University. For some curious reason, he declined. He did, however, deliver the address at the ceremonial laying of the cornerstone in 1888. The event was attended by President Grover Cleveland, several cabinet members, and some thirty bishops. Spalding's address is widely recognized as a turning point in his career.[16]

There was enough in Spalding's talk to offend more than a few pious ears. Anyone who harbored suspicions about the spirit of the age, the American experience, or Miss Caldwell was sure to be wounded. Spalding opened and closed his address with references to the young benefactress. The first was in the context of the opposition Columbus had experienced in his attempt to discover a new world. His folly was in reality the "conviction of God" which found backing in "a woman's heart." No great stretch of the imagination is needed to see the veiled allusion to the Spalding-Caldwell duo.

Spalding had high praise for the accomplishment of the United States with its democratic principles of fraternity and equality, the very message preached by Christ. He lauded the successful separation of church from state in government, "a form rarely tried, even on a small scale."[17] Any tentativeness Spalding may have earlier expressed about the character of contemporary times was clearly resolved.[18] He extolled the accomplishments of his own age as superior to all others, including those of ancient Greece and Rome and the church during the Middle Ages. Rather than look to past glories, Spalding argued that the church had to look to the future. This was precisely why the establishment of the university was so important. The contemporary age was intellectual, not devotional. The new scientific views of the universe carried with them new problems in religion and morality, politics and science. Science and morality, Spalding continued, need religion as much as thought and action require emotion. The knowledge of the age determines what is demanded of scholars. Those who "uphold religion must confess that faith which ignorance alone can keep alive is little better than superstititon." Stupidity, Spalding argued, was to be dreaded more than "malignity; for ignorance, and not malice, is the most fruitful cause of human misery." Spalding concluded his address with "the name of her whose generous heart and enlightened mind" gave the impetus to the incipient university— "Mary Gwendolyn Caldwell."[19] Most of the leading Catholic newspapers and the dailies in the East carried the address. Spalding had come to be recognized by most as an authority on Catholic education and perhaps the most scholarly and cultivated member of the American hierarchy.[20]

In 1888 John Keane was appointed the first rector of the Catholic University of America, which was due to open the following year. As noted, he had been influenced by Isaac Hecker, whom he had met in 1866. Keane was so impressed with him that in 1872 Keane asked his archbishop, James Roosevelt Bayley, for permission to join the

Paulists. He and Hecker both felt that his attraction to the community was a call from the Holy Spirit. However, Bayley felt conscience-bound to retain Keane because he was an excellent priest and was sorely needed.[21] Keane continued to maintain a close bond with Hecker and remained his spiritual disciple.[22] Devotion to the Holy Spirit became the foundation of Keane's spirituality. In 1879 he established the Confraternity of the Holy Ghost. It emphasized interiority and individual initiative. In the guidelines Keane drew up for the membership, he tried to reconcile a strong, republican, lay voice with the hierarchical constitution of the church.

Like his mentor, Keane had a strong sense of the providential destiny of America. He worked toward a convergence between Catholicism and American civilization. His republican political orientation led him to emphasize the universal aspiration for enlightenment, the capabilities of reason, and the rights of conscience.[23]

Shortly after Hecker's death, Keane eulogized his old friend. He wrote that some thought Hecker a visionary dreamer or a dangerous theorizer; these were petty minds who looked with suspicion on whatever transcended their narrow conservatism. There are always "little embodiments of precautionary prudence . . . ever eager to whisper or to squeak their wee note of alarm and to cry, 'Down brakes.' " Keane continued that Hecker neither despised their words of caution nor let them scare him into inactivity. While Hecker's "course was ever onward, it was ever careful."[24] Within a decade after he wrote those words, Keane would find himself embroiled in the Americanist controversy and chosen as the special object of Père Charles Maignen's wrath; this avowed monarchist saw Keane as the embodiment of all that Hecker stood for and all that Maignen condemned.[25]

It would take time and dispassion to put Isaac Hecker's influences into proper perspective. Interest in his life and thought have grown over the past few decades. One historian evaluated Hecker's contribution admirably when he wrote, "Probably no nineteenth-century Roman Catholic in America so clearly foreshadowed the *aggiornamento* which Pope John XXIII would begin to call for when he became pope—on the centenary of the Paulists' founding."[26]

Keane had become identified with several other "liberal" prelates because of his sympathies with the Knights of Labor. Keane had met twice with the "Grand Master Workman," Catholic Terrence V. Powderly, during October of 1886 to discuss the relationship between the Knights and the Catholic church.

At the end of that month, Keane departed for Rome with Archbishop John Ireland of Saint Paul to secure permission for the establishment of the Catholic University of America.[27] After Ireland and Keane left America, Archbishop Michael Corrigan, Ireland's counterpart among the conservative American prelates, withdrew from the board of trustees of the proposed university. The Jesuits of Georgetown also opposed the plan.[28]

While Keane and Ireland were in Rome, other issues concerning the American church arose, among them the condemnation of the Canadian branch of the Knights of Labor. The American hierarchy, with the exceptions of Corrigan, Silas Chatard of Vincennes, Indiana, and Bishop James Healy of Portland, Maine, were reluctant to interpret this condemnation as applicable to the United States. James Gibbons, now a cardinal, presented a memorial—actually prepared by Ireland and Keane—to Pope Leo XIII. It pointed out the harm that would be done to the Catholic church in America if the Knights were condemned. Gibbons urged rather that an encyclical be published that would set guidelines for social issues.[29]

The Oxford convert, Cardinal Henry Manning, a friend of labor, sent a letter of praise to Gibbons after an unauthorized version of the memorial was leaked to the press. Keane was instrumental in having Manning's letter published. A condemnation of the Knights was averted; Keane and Ireland were introduced to the power of the press, which would give them instant access to the international flow of Catholic and secular news for the next thirteen years.[30]

Another factor that had complicated the labor question was the closely related issue of the orthodoxy of Henry George's "single-tax" theory. In his book *Progress and Poverty*, George had argued that private right to land had no more foundation than the private right to air; the land of every country belonged to all. Private occupancy and use of the land, however, were right and good. The rent derived from the land should be used for the benefit of all, which would be more than sufficient to meet government expenses. The government would levy just one tax, that on rent.[31] Some interpreted the Protestant George's idea as a denial of the right to private property.

Edward McGlynn, New York priest, prominent member of the defunct "Accademia," powerful orator, and avid advocate of social reform, publicly supported George.[32] He infuriated Corrigan because he refused to cancel a speech on behalf of George despite the archbishop's order. McGlynn challenged the hierarchy to prevent him from exercising his civil rights as an American citizen. The upshot of the affair resulted in McGlynn's excommunication.[33]

Neither Gibbons, Keane, nor Ireland espoused George's theories, but Gibbons argued against a condemnation of *Progress and Poverty*, the "work of a humble artisan," because it would be "neither appropriate nor useful."[34] The book was finally put on the Index, but publication of the condemnation was prohibited, to the chagrin of the conservatives. McGlynn was eventually reinstated through the intercession of John Ireland. *The New York Tribune* interpreted McGlynn's restoration as a sign that Catholics were adjusting to free institutions and as a mortal blow to ultramontanism.[35]

Hecker had been frankly shocked by McGlynn's actions in support of George. He felt the radical priest had divorced religion from politics. The episode left Hecker troubled.[36] James McMaster, editor of the *Freeman's Journal*, suffered no such scruples over McGlynn. He excoriated him on a number of issues,[37] and only death at the close of 1886 stilled the pen of that feisty opponent of any form of liberal Catholicism.

One final problem that faced Keane and Ireland during their Roman trip was the petition presented by Father Peter Abbelen of Milwaukee to Propaganda, in which he had demanded equal status for German-speaking Catholics. Keane and Ireland strongly opposed the move as an attempt to "germanize" the church. The Abbelen petition was defeated, which earned the antipathy of the German party and all whom they could influence. Each victory won by the Americanizing bishops deepened the rift between them and their fellow prelates of a more conservative mindset.[38]

When Keane and Ireland returned from Rome, they brought with them what has been called a cluster of convictions about the Catholic church in America, which they began to preach with missionary zeal. The vision they propagated was called Americanism, and the Catholic University of America played a central role in the Americanist drama.[39]

In the closing decade of the century, the university was drawn into a highly charged controversy over the school issue. Some Catholics had resented the state's constantly growing role in education as a violation of parents' rights as individuals. They opposed what they viewed as a kind of paternalism on the part of the government. In a pamphlet entitled "Education: To Whom Does It Belong?" the erudite Thomas Bouquillon, professor of Moral Theology at Catholic University, responded.[40] The Belgian-born Bouquillon had a well-established reputation as a moral theologian even before his appointment to the Catholic University. He was also one of the four professors at the university who had examined the orthodoxy of McGlynn. They concluded that he was not espousing anything contrary to Catholic faith. Their decision, which contributed to McGlynn's reinstatement, also deeply angered the archbishop of New York.

In his pamphlet, Bouquillon presented a theoretical analysis that gave the state rights on which the church had never pronounced. He refused to admit that the American state was too un-Christian to exercise more than police powers, and he argued that it had the right to use all the legitimate temporal means it judged necessary for the attainment of the temporal common welfare. Since an educated citizenry was essential, the state had a clear right to provide a public school system.[41]

A quick rejoinder was made by the conservative Jesuit René Holaind of Woodstock College.[42] His and Bouquillon's pamphlets were commented upon in the *American Ecclesiastical Review*.[43] The *AER* favored the conservative side of the issue. Holaind congratulated its editor, Herman Heuser, for starting the reaction that was "going to swamp the whole conspiracy." He advised Heuser to "keep Bouquillon lively but smiling, and kill mercilessly any plan which would surrender 'our boys', i.e. the future of the Catholic Church in this country to a pack of evolutionists and freemasons." Holaind believed that the whole controversy was a consequence of a "leaning towards paternalism in sociology."[44] Keane, of course, defended Bouquillon against his adversaries. John Hogan, the Sulpician rector of the Divinity College at the University, asked Heuser to give Bouquillon a fair hearing. He wrote, "All my life I have been witnessing men wronged . . . by inaccurate reports of their teachings. And don't raise the cry of liberalism which has wrought so much evil for half a century."

Hogan concluded by remarking that he would like to see "all shades of Catholic thought and Catholic opinion feel equally at home" in Heuser's journal.[45] Subsequently, the Jesuit *La Civiltà Cattolica* of Rome launched an attack—on both the theory as presented by Bouquillon and the practice promoted by John Ireland—that was much more bitter than anything envisioned by Heuser.

John Ireland had made an arrangement with the school boards of Faribault and Stillwater, Minnesota, to lease their parochial school buildings. For a one-dollar annual rent, they would be state schools during school hours. Before and after, however, they would be parochial schools, at which time religion would be taught.[46] Ireland had modeled his plan on a program inaugurated by Father James Nelson, an alumnus of the Accademia group (described in Chapter 3), at his parish in Poughkeepsie, New York, some years earlier.[47] Both schemes were opposed by Corrigan and his suffragan bishop Bernard McQuaid of Rochester, N.Y. Spalding expressed the opinion that a majority of the hierarchy opposed "Faribaultism." A large number of American and Roman Jesuits were also hostile to the idea.

Bouquillon had prepared his treatise on the issue in response to the requests of Cardinal Gibbons and Archbishop Patrick Ryan of Philadelphia. Ryan had accurately foreseen that a "war of pamphlets" would follow. Bouquillon was hurt that *Civiltà* had accused him of liberalism and state idolatry,[48] and Gibbons worried about the damage the controversy could cause the fledgling university. The setback appeared only temporary, for Ireland went to Rome and successfully defended himself and Bouquillon. Nevertheless, it was a pyrrhic victory for Faribaultism; after a trial run, the plan failed.

The German immigrants, who had opposed Bouquillon, also resented Ireland and Keane's opposition to their countryman, Catholic Herr Peter Cahensly, secretary of the Saint Raphael Society, founded in 1871 to aid immigrants. In 1891, he had proposed to the Holy See that greater recognition be given foreign groups in America to prevent their loss of faith. The Americanizing faction quickly attacked the Germans. Spalding came to their defense.

The Germans were the second largest Catholic immigrant block after the Irish. They were a well-established group with deep cultural roots and a self-conscious, vigorous German Catholicism. Spalding respected the Germans' character. They had proven themselves industrious, law abiding, and supportive of religious and social liberty. Spalding claimed that it was ludicrous to see any kind of treason in Cahensly's desire to care for the spiritual needs of his people. To cast any suspicion upon their loyalty to America was patently unfair.[49] Once again, Cardinal Gibbons intervened. He prevented the hierarchy from being divided along nationalistic lines. Keane, however, censured his German professors, Joseph Schroeder and Joseph Pohle, for publicly aligning themselves with the German faction.

Another issue irritating to the Germans was Keane's activity in the Temperance crusade, which tended to identify the university with that cause. As far as the Germans were concerned, intemperance was an Irish vice, not theirs. Keane's position as rector of Catholic University became even more precarious when he decided to attend the World Parliament of Religions scheduled for 1893. Keane knew that his participation would be looked at askance by all the ultraconservatives, but he took the risk.[50]

The Parliament of World Religions was held in conjunction with the World's Fair or Columbian Exposition in Chicago. It was a celebration of the four-hundredth anniversary of Columbus's discovery of America. Immediately prior to the parliament, the Second American Catholic Congress met. According to the agreement reached in 1889 at the close of the first—all lay—Catholic congresses, both clergy and laity were represented on the program. The job of organizing the educational materials used in the Catholic school system for display during the Columbian Exposition fell to John Lancaster Spalding. He worked hard to prove to his countrymen, Protestant and Catholic, that the parochial schools could provide quality secular education as well as religious instruction. In the field of higher education, Spalding had already begun to extend his campaign for intellectual cultivation to include women.

During the 1890s Spalding advocated the advancement of feminine education in general, and teacher training for religious women in particular.[51] He wanted teachers' colleges to be established in conjunction with universities. In his view, professional knowledge alone for teachers was not enough. The key to successful pedagogy was possession of a philosophic mind. The function of a true teacher was not to impart learning so much as to engender in the student a habit of inquiry and a desire for self-cultivation.[52] "Is it not plain," Spalding wrote, "that the impulse the teacher gives us is more important than the knowledge."[53]

Spalding considered Catholic colleges for women the logical outgrowth of the secondary schools. When he suggested that a women's college be established near the all-male environs of the Catholic University, the mere rumor made some Roman officials very nervous.[54] Once again Cardinal Gibbons came to the rescue and defended the project. This allowed Spalding the freedom to argue that, since the Civil War, women had been brought up to trust their own intelligence. One of the chief glories of the nineteenth century, he said, was the opportunity given to women, particularly in the United States. Spalding chalked up to "inveterate prejudice" the opinion that women were inferior to men. Anyone opposed to education for women either did not understand what education really is, or did not believe in its "divine efficacy."[55]

Women, Spalding contended, were not only equal to men in their scholastic ability, but they surpassed men in their eagerness for self-improvement. It was to the female sex that Spalding paid his highest compliment: women, not men, were "the great readers of books, especially poetry." Poetry, given that it was "genuine poetry," Spalding valued as the "finest educational influence" available.[56]

Things were not going well for Spalding's favorite project in 1894. The enrollment at the Catholic University had dropped. The board of trustees requested that the rector, Keane, go to Rome to outline the cause of the difficulties. In an audience with Leo XIII, Keane blamed the dearth of students on opposition from the Germans, the Jesuits, Archbishop Corrigan in alliance with Bishop McQuaid of Rochester, and all who opposed the policy of the recently appointed apostolic delegate, Archbishop Francesco Satolli, who was living at the Catholic University and whom the conservatives had identified with it. Keane returned home satisfied that he had been successful. Both the pope and Mariano Rampolla, cardinal secretary of state, assured him that they had not been impressed by the insinuations made against the university. Leo promised that he would speak favorably of the Catholic University in his forthcoming encyclical.[57]

When *Longinqua Oceani*, the first encyclical ever addressed to the American church, appeared in 1895, Leo's reference to the university was rather restrained. The pope spoke of the benefits America would accrue "if the professors and students (as We doubt not they will) be mindful of Our injunction, and, shunning party spirit and strife, conciliate the good opinion of the people and the clergy." There was more, but it was worse in the eyes of the Americanizers. While paying high praise to the American nation and the young, vigorous church there, Leo cautioned that it would be erroneous to conclude that the situation in the United States presented "the most desirable status of the Church, or that it would be universally lawful or expedient for State and Church to be, as in America, dissevered and divorced."[58] Ireland was dismayed. He complained to Gibbons, "That unfortunate allusion to the Church and State cannot be explained to Americans."[59] John R. Slattery, founder of the Society of Saint Joseph or the Josephite Fathers in 1891 and a warm supporter of the Americanists, was left disillusioned by Leo's letter. It appeared that the pope had reversed his position on republicanism. Leo's apostolic delegate to America had already taken a conservative turn. Satolli blamed Slattery for omitting two of his conservative speeches in a collection of his addresses, *Loyalty to Church and State*, which the Josephite had edited. When replaced as apostolic delegate, Satolli returned to Rome as a curial cardinal and made life difficult for the Americanists.[60]

The tide was turning against the liberal party. The first to feel its force was Monsignor Denis J. O'Connell, recognized by all parties as the Americanists' Vatican agent. In June of 1895, he was asked to resign the rectorship of the American College in Rome. Cardinal Gibbons did not save him from this fate, but made it possible for O'Connell to remain in Rome with some dignity;[61] Slattery, however, was scandilized by what he interpreted as the Cardinal's self-serving refusal to defend his friend.[62]

In September of 1896, Keane was removed from the rectorship of the Catholic University by Leo XIII himself.[63] The blow shocked Keane and his supporters. It cheered the hearts of his opponents who thought that Rome had at last recognized the failure of the university. Spalding worried that rebuking Keane would be the blow that would also kill the fledgling Catholic University.[64] However, though the liberals had suffered a setback, they were not discouraged. The end of 1897 found O'Connell rejuvenated. His Roman apartment, dubbed "Liberty Hall," became the meeting place for the "Club" or the "Lodge." The members, cleric and lay, shared a common desire to modernize the church. The group included Keane, now living in Rome; an American, John

Zahm, C.S.C., of Notre Dame; the Italian brothers, Cardinals Serafino and Vincenzo Vannutelli, "conciliationists" (that is, advocates of rapprochement between the Vatican and the kingdom of Italy); and other leading figures. On the fringe were the Frenchmen Félix Klein, Alfred Loisy (described by O'Connell as the "leading biblical scholar in the Church"), and others.[65]

O'Connell was consciously forming a party of international dimension that would implement the Americanists' platform. It was at this point that he urged Ireland to try to gain support for the movement from German liberals. Ireland complied by delivering an address in 1897 in which he made it clear that it was not Germans per se whom he opposed, but "refractaires." Leo XIII had used this term to identify those who refused to follow his *ralliément* policy in France.[66] This won the support of German liberals, but there would be a price to pay. O'Connell, meanwhile, arranged for Ireland's speeches to be translated into Italian.[67]

At the same time, a French edition of Walter Elliott's biography of Hecker appeared.[68] Elliott's original work, which had received little notice, contained a number of unfortunate inaccuracies that obscured Hecker's thought on several controversial topics. Elliott, a close associate of Hecker, had prepared his manuscript in the midst of pressing responsibilities and recognized that his work was "of home-made quality."[69] The translator and Félix Klein, the editor, added their own interpretation to Elliott's original. Nonetheless, Elliott apparently found no serious fault with the rendition.[70] The French *Vie* was greeted enthusiastically by O'Connell; he believed that it gave the "movement" its "supernatural" philosophy.[71]

In a general mood of euphoria, O'Connell, Keane, and Zahm attended the International Catholic Scientific Congress in Fribourg, Switzerland, in August of 1897. Because of the ferment Klein's *Vie* had caused in France, O'Connell used the congress to clarify any misrepresentations of Americanism and to promote the "movement" at the same time. In his presentation, "A New Idea in the Life of Father Hecker," O'Connell distinguished between "political" and "ecclesiastical" Americanism. This was part of his plan to shift the focus from theological questions, which the *Vie* had raised, to the political plane.

Political Americanism, O'Connell instructed his audience, was, in principle, in close conformity with the human rights tradition rooted in natural law. He noted that "some germs of these same principles were found in the Magna Charta of Runnymede and thence they passed into the common law of all English-speaking nations." O'Connell then explained the "due process" this law provided:

> No free man shall be molested in his life, his liberty, his property or his honor except by speedy and public trial before an impartial jury, after

having been made fully acquainted with the nature of the accusation, confronted with witnesses, and furnished with means of defense; and this not as a privilege, but as a natural right—and the government was there to see that it was respected."

To point out the deep significance of political Americanism, O'Connell contrasted this system with that of the Roman Empire, chosen for "brevity's sake"—and chosen, no doubt, to conceal his attack on contemporary European monarchical and nonrepublican forms of government as well as to mask his criticism of church canon law. In Roman public law, O'Connell continued, persons as persons had no rights; any they later received were a free gift of the state in their quality as citizen. The arbitrary will of the emperor was law. The whole system of political Roman law was deficient to the core. American political law recognized the dominion of God and natural law; Roman law did not.

He followed this with a veiled attack on canon law. It deserves to be quoted at length:

And even as regards the Civil Code or Private [Roman] law, if the Church sometimes makes use of it and most wisely, she is nevertheless not dependent upon it, nor blind to its defects. For hundreds of years she lived without it at Jerusalem, at Alexandria, at Rome, under her own laws, the spontaneous outgrowth of her own divine constitution. She can take up these laws again when she will, and her trend is to create eventually an entirely complete code of Christian law, bearing throughout and in every part the imprint of the Incarnation.

O'Connell said that Hecker accepted political Americanism because he believed Protestants could be converted to "Catholic truth" quite easily, but never to "Roman political or public law."

In his exposition of "ecclesiastical" Americanism, O'Connell described the advantages accrued by the church when it does not "enjoy government patronage." O'Connell showed his own political skill when he referred to the favorable comments of Leo XIII and Archbishop Satolli about the Constitution of the United States.[72] O'Connell's interest in the renovation of canon law based on the common law tradition, a view judged more radical than that of the most advanced thinkers among the clerical members of the Accademia group, was shared by other Americanists, but it did not preoccupy them.[73]

Bishop Charles Turinaz of Nancy raised some objections against O'Connell's presentation in Fribourg, but the majority of the audience praised his delineation.[74] However, O'Connell's speech added fuel to the fire already smoldering in the conservative camp. They had interpreted it as a direct criticism of the church in western Europe, which, of course, it was.

A presentation made by the Americanist Zahm was equally well received by the liberal element of the Fribourg audience. This well-respected scientist, elected international vice-president of the Congress and president of the Anthropology section, delivered a paper called "Evolution and Teleology." American Catholic intellectuals had shown some interest in the theory of evolution since Charles Darwin's *Origin of Species* appeared in 1859; Orestes Brownson at first took a mediating position against both those theologians who repudiated science when it appeared to be in conflict with Catholic faith and those scientists who made exaggerated claims deduced from hypotheses and experiments.[75] The Civil War distracted most Americans from further speculation about the topic. However, when Darwin threw caution to the wind in his *Descent of Man* in 1871, Brownson became a violent foe of materialistic science and claimed that Darwin and his kind were enemies of both religion and science. Brownson argued that the hypothesis of progress or development was "unquestionably repugnant to the whole Christian doctrine and order of thought. If it is true, Christianity is false." The first man was "not a monkey or a tadpole . . . but full grown in the integrity of his nature, instructed by his Maker." According to Brownson, an extranscendentalist, the history of the human race was not one of progress but of decay. He believed that evolution contradicted the whole teleological order; it denied that creation had a purpose and was ordained to an end. The problem was that science not only ignored theology but pretended to be capable of existing without it.[76]

Many among the Catholic clergy accepted the mediating position of the British zoologist St. George Mivart, a convert to Catholicism. In his *Genesis of Species*, published shortly prior to Darwin's *Descent*, Mivart accepted the evolution of lower animal life but insisted that the soul was directly created by God.[77] Liberal Catholics agreed that revelation had spoken too unequivocally on this position to permit acceptance of any speculational hypothesis about the evolution of the soul.[78]

Keane and Ireland had tried to have Mivart appointed to a chair of natural science at the Catholic University, but failed. Their efforts were blocked by Archbishop Corrigan and Archbishop Patrick Ryan. Until his death in 1900, Mivart's theory continued to be the major alternative to Darwinism.[79]

Conservatives continued to defend the belief that God created human beings directly as an immutable and distinct species. The *American Catholic Quarterly Review*, which began in 1876, took a strongly conservative position on the issue. During the same period, the *Catholic World* showed little sympathy for Darwinism, but the evolutionary climate was changing. Discoveries of fossils, publications of biological treatises, and lecturers and popularizers of Darwin's views drew an ever-widening audience. The *Catholic World* frequently carried articles on evolution during the 1880s, cautiously carrying the banners of scientific criticism and thought.[80] The first American Catholic book on the subject, *Modern Scientific Views and Christian Doctrines Compared*, was published by Father John Gmeiner in 1884. At the time, he was a professor at Archbishop Ireland's theological seminary in Saint Paul. In the work, Gmeiner presented a theistic interpretation of Darwinism and claimed that evolution actually supported Christianity. God's design and providence were even more wonderful when executed gradually.[81] John Slattery's first attempt to reconcile contemporary science and the church was precipitated by reading Darwin's works. Like Gmeiner, he argued in the mid-1880s that theistic evolution and divine creation were compatible.[82]

Catholic journals of the 1890s reflected the variety of opinions about evolutionary theory. The *American Ecclesiastical Review* published a lengthy review of Salvatore di Bartolo's *Criterions of Catholic Truths*. The Italian priest denied that popes in the past often spoke infallibly, and he believed that researchers could continue to hold scientific opinions that disagreed with revealed truths until such opinions were given further examination and reflection. Without agreeing with all of di Bartolo's conclusions, the *Catholic World* noted that the book would help remove suspicions that the church was intolerant. Cardinal Gibbons concurred with that assessment. Not so the *American Catholic Quarterly Review* or the *American Ecclesiastical Review*. Both were openly hostile to the book. In a series of four articles entitled "Theological Minimizing and Its Latest Defender," Joseph Schroeder, professor of Dogmatic Theology at Catholic University, lashed out against di Bartolo. What angered Schroeder most was the author's assertion that the infallibility of the church did not extend to "dogmatic facts." Schroeder contended that infallibility could be extended to include not only revelation but also truths not revealed yet connected with revelation.[83]

As the liberals were preparing to reply, *Criterions of Catholic Truth* was put on the Index. At that point, the editor, Herman Heuser, stopped the discussion in the *American Ecclesiastical Review*, even though Schroeder had prepared several additional articles. However, the climate of opinion was to change. A few months later the same journal published a series of articles by John B. Hogan, a Sulpician of Americanist leanings, pleading for the natural sciences to be taught in seminaries; Hogan believed they had a legitimate place in the curriculum of any liberal education.[84] Increased openness to new currents of scientific thought had been given support by Pope Leo XIII's *Aeterni Patris.* He recommended that all students familiarize themselves with the findings of contemporary science.[85]

In 1892 the *American Ecclesiastical Review* carried an article by another professor of the Catholic University, Joseph Pohle.[86] Pohle held that anything but Godless evolution was amenable to a theistic interpretation. John Lancaster Spalding argued eloquently that there could be no incompatibility between science and religion. In his poetic prose, Spalding admitted that there appeared to be "oppugnancy between the belief of an all-wise, all-good . . . God, and belief in the divine origin of nature, whose face is smeared with filth and blood"; but this was a phantom contradiction due to a failure of imagination. Science, Spalding argued, was the "widening thought of man working on the hypothesis of universal intelligibility . . . religion is the soul, escaping the labyrinths of matter . . . on the heights they meet and are at peace."[87]

By the mid-1890s members of the Catholic Reading Circle affiliated with the Catholic Summer School were hearing lectures by Mivart and Zahm and were reading "Man's Place in Nature." The work implicitly accepted the assumption that the human race had material origins.[88]

In the debate precipitated by di Bartolo's position on the limited extent of revelation, Leo XIII issued "Providentissimus Deus" in 1893. The pope encouraged the study of Oriental languages and the art of biblical criticism, which were held in high contemporary esteem. He warned, however, against an "inept method, dignified by the name of 'higher criticism.' " In Leo's opinion, the non-Catholic "higher critics" were trained with a false philosophy. For Catholics to accept their method in trying to determine the integrity and authority of each book of the Bible from internal evidence alone would be perilous. The conclusion of the patristics would be ignored, the teachings of the church would be overlooked, and the supernatural would be forgotten.[89]

Predictably, liberals and conservatives interpreted Leo's words differently. Some rejoiced that the pope had dealt a blow to theological minimizers. Others, like Charles Grannan, a professor at Catholic University, held that "true higher criticism" and intelligent study of the Bible had not been censured. Zahm agreed with that opinion. In his *Bible, Science, and Faith,* he quoted Leo's statement that the purpose of the Bible was to teach religious truth, not science.[90]

Zahm, professor of Physics at the University of Notre Dame, had originally viewed Darwinism with suspicion. However, his contacts with Catholic clerical and lay scholars at the International Scientific Congress, held in Paris in 1889 and 1891, left Zahm convinced that

Catholic faith could not be damaged by studying evolution, if understood correctly. Since Catholics were being drawn into the topic of evolution, according to Zahm, they should be prepared. To that end, he published *Evolution and Dogma* in 1896.[91] He argued that evolution was in perfect accord with science, with scripture, and with patristic and scholastic theology. The world was indebted to scientists like Lamarck, Darwin, and Mivart. He predicted that these pioneers had "ushered in a new era and are the kings and prophets of the most active and prolific period of research that the world has yet witnessed."[92] Zahm was convinced that the evolutionary theory would soon be the accepted one in both Christian philosophy and apologetics. It has been argued that it was more Zahm's vigorous style than what he actually wrote that caused a storm of controversy.[93] *Civiltà Cattolica* gave the book an adverse review.[94] An article entitled "Is Zahm a Heretic?" appeared in the New York *Herald*. Apparently, Zahm had what one historian has called a penchant for sensationalism; it seems that Zahm himself edited the newspaper story. The priest-scientist and his theory were assailed by Bishop Sebastian Messmer of Green Bay and other clerics; he was defended by Edward Pace, professor of Philosophy at the Catholic University and by reviewers in virtually every major American Catholic journal.

The controversy, despite Zahm's thinking to the contrary, did not interest Americans generally. Most Protestant and secular evolutionists viewed the quarrel within Catholicism as rather parochial and antiquarian.[95] However, Zahm's book did win praise outside Catholic circles. Zahm released to the press William Gladstone's laudatory letter, and a New England Protestant paper asserted that *Evolution and Dogma* put "the case of Christianity against agnosticism and atheism as clearly, ably, liberally and convincingly as it has yet been done."[96]

Before Zahm had reached Fribourg, rumors of an impending Roman condemnation of *Evolution and Dogma* were in the air. As it turned out, his Fribourg address, "Evolution and Teleology," was Zahm's last presentation on a scientific subject. Despite the efforts of his Roman friend, Cardinal Serafino Vannutelli, to prevent the publication of the decree, *Evolution and Dogma* was proscribed by the Sacred Congregation of the Index. Bishop Keane urged Zahm to "stoop to conquer."[97] Zahm told his Italian translator to withdraw the book in all languages. Despite that, he had not changed his opinion on evolution. He privately wrote,

> My views may not be looked upon with favor by all in Rome. I do not expect so much and I do not care for the approval of everyone. But I know that every eminent man of science throughout Europe is in perfect sympathy with my views. I venture to say that the twentieth century

will not be very old before nine out of ten thinkers will be evolutionists as opposed to believers in special creation.[98]

Zahm, who had earlier written that if Saints Augustine and Thomas Aquinas were living today, they would not be pathetically defending past solutions to modern questions but would be the boldest and most liberal minds the world had ever known, now found himself on the defensive.[99] In some Vatican quarters, Zahm was seen as a vulnerable symbol of the highly suspect liberal movement in American Catholicism. O'Connell interpreted Zahm's fate in that light; he wrote to his scientific friend, "Naturally one must consider the maneuver as a recognition of the part you played in Americanism." Rome's disapproval of Zahm's work marked the end of his labors in the field of science and on the question of the relation between science and religion. Under pressure, his defenders fell silent. His loss to scholarship, unfortunately not an isolated instance, contributed to the gulf growing between American Catholic thought and American scientific thought.[100]

Despite the setback, O'Connell and his friends remained hopeful. At Félix Klein's suggestion, O'Connell sent copies of his Fribourg address to every bishop and Catholic newspaper in the United States. It was also widely circulated throughout Europe and beyond.[101]

Keane tried his own hand at dispelling conservative European Catholics' "complete misunderstanding" of conditions in America. In his "America as Seen from Abroad," Keane claimed that differences in traditions and institutions caused minds, molded by ancient custom and prejudice, to judge as heterodox things actually in complete harmony with the teachings of the church. Keane noted, however, that Americans had little chance for a reputation of orthodoxy since they had been tagged with "the label of liberalism"—an epithet more awful than heresy.[102]

Slattery rallied enough enthusiasm to congratulate Keane for his literary salvo. After years of separation, Slattery declared, Hecker and Keane were "invading Europe and knocking at the Vatican. Hecker in his Americanism: Keane, its embodiment."[103]

The America that Keane's intended European audience was viewing with increasing suspicion was the young, Protestant, republican nation. The acknowledged industrial leader of the world was reportedly preparing for war against old, Catholic, monarchical Spain. Many Americans were sympathetic with the Cubans' attempt to gain their independence from Spain. Initially, John Ireland favored the Spanish side of the issue, and at the request of Leo XIII he interceded with President McKinley to prevent any outbreak of hostilities. But Ireland proved unsuccessful. He blamed it on Leo's eleventh-hour decision to intervene. The sinking of the *U.S.S. Maine* in Havana's harbor did not help matters. Once war was declared, Ireland was heartily for the cause of the United States.[104]

The climate in Rome became increasingly hostile. A slanderous work by the avowed French monarchist, Père Charles Maignen, appeared. It was not bad enough that his *Etudes sur l'américanisme: le Père Hecker, est-il un saint?* answered the rhetorical question with a resounding "no!"[105] The book villainized Klein and the Americanists at the same time. To make matters worse, it had been published in Rome and carried the *imprimatur* of the Dominican Alberto Lepidi, master of the Sacred Palace.

Maignen was a French integrist who had opposed Leo XIII's *ralliément* as liberalism and any rapprochement with non-Catholics as doctrinal minimalism. He considered the church and modern society divided in principle, and he held in contempt the Anglo-Saxon mystique common to the Americanists. Klein's *Vie*, according to Maignen, was "no mere book . . . it was a flag, a party badge, an engine of war— a sort of Trojan horse carrying within its sides the whole phalanx of the chiefs of Americanism."[106] Keane, attacked by Maignen unmercifully, was furious that an *imprimatur* had been given. Together with Cardinal Gibbons and John Ireland he protested the matter to Cardinal Mariano Rampolla, Leo's secretary of state. Their response came not from Rampolla but from Lepidi himself. Lepidi, one of Europe's leading neo-Thomists and theologians at the Papal Court, said that he had granted the *imprimatur* because it was his duty to safeguard faith and tradition. In his opinion, Maignen's work would lead to a thorough discussion "of Americanism to which were attached doctrines which lent themselves to false and dangerous interpretations."[107]

Rampolla himself also responded, somewhat evasively, to Gibbons's protest. He told the cardinal that the pope intended to send him a pontifical letter concerning the Hecker case. The Sulpician Alphonse Magnien, the superior of Saint Mary's Seminary and a confidant of Gibbons, wrote to Félix Klein to apprise him of the situation.[108]

Years earlier, Magnien had been Gibbons's personal secretary and confidant, and, through Gibbons, Magnien met the leading Americanists. He had backed Keane's liberal leadership at the Catholic University and Ireland's school plan, and he was instrumental in prodding Gibbons to request that Rome make Ireland a cardinal. The Vatican's refusal and the apparent ascendancy of the Corrigan forces disconcerted Magnien. He worried about the contents of the projected letter hinted at by Rampolla.[109] If things went badly, Magnien thought he knew where to fix the blame. He complained to Klein that the Americanists' "three implacable enemies [in Rome were] Mazzella, Satolli and Brandi, and they have the old Pope in their power."[110] The extent of this influence over Leo XIII cannot presently be determined; however, Magnien was not wrong in assessing their power.[111] In 1879 Leo had resorted, as one historian put it, "to Draconian measures" in his determination to make the Gregorian University in Rome a center of Thomism. Camillo Mazzella was appointed to the faculty to replace a professor not enthusiastic about implementing *Aeterni Patris*.[112] The neo-Thomists Satolli and Brandi were considered "experts" on American affairs: Satolli in his former capacity as apostolic delegate to the United States and Brandi as a former professor at the Jesuit scholasticate in Woodstock, Maryland. As editor of *Civiltà*, the Jesuit organ devoted to implementing neo-Thomism, Brandi showed no sympathy for the Americanizers.

For their part, Ireland and his friends thought that an American military victory in the Spanish-American War would be in their favor and might even prevent a condemnation of Klein's *Vie*. They knew that Leo XIII understood political power. O'Connell was convinced that Spain's defeat would force Rome to come to terms with America. He wrote to Ireland that "the nonsense of trying to govern the universal Church, from a purely European standpoint . . . will be glaringly evident."[113]

Near the conclusion of the brief war, O'Connell confronted Lepidi, a suspected Spanish sympathizer. He demanded to know why the Italian priest had granted an *imprimatur* to Maignen's book. Lepidi, in turn, requested that the American scribble down a few lines embodying what he had said at Fribourg. Much to O'Connell's chagrin, Maignen later published eclectic selections from the notes O'Connell had given to Lepidi. Later, O'Connell complained to Walter Elliott that he never realized he was being fooled into furnishing ammunition to the man against whom he was protesting. "These men are not honest," O'Connell concluded, "and it is an illusion to treat them so."[114] Despite this setback, and for a variety of complex reasons, O'Connell continued to be optimistic. At the end of 1898, he was "certain that there [would] be no encyclical at all."[115] The following month, to his and his friends' dismay, Leo XIII published *Testem Benevolentiae*, the promised letter on Americanism.[116]

Six months earlier, Spain had signed an armistice with the United States; Cuba, Puerto Rico, and the Philippines came under American control. It is tempting to speculate what would have happened to the Americanists had war been averted. It is even more tantalizing to imagine their fate had Spain been victorious. Several historians have demonstrated that all papal condemnations of the second half of the nineteenth century had political links.[117] *Testem* itself has been interpreted as a reproach to victorious America.[118] The United States may have won in the political order, but *Testem* made it clear who controlled the power in the ecclesiastical sphere. The letter makes clear that no heresy was involved. For their part, the Americanizers had no unified theological "platform."[119] They did hold some common views, however, not least of which was their enthusiasm for the American political system. In addition, they had all, in varying degrees, adopted aspects of the new approach to apologetics with its historical consciousness and respect for subjectivity.

The roots of the Americanists' conflict were deep. It is not an exaggeration to claim, as one historian has done, that from the time of the papal definition of the Immaculate Conception in 1854, conservative Europeans and Americanizers, such as Isaac Hecker and others, were set on a collision course. Europeans interpreted the dogma declaring that Mary alone was sinless as a condemnation of self-government.[120] They reasoned that the effects of original sin, a weakened intellect and disordered will, make democracy a dangerous illusion. What was needed was an authoritarian, repressive, and preventive government.[121] Hecker and the Americanists not only praised their free and democratic political system, but saw it as universally valid.

Leo XIII's attempt to universalize neo-Thomism was inaugurated precisely to maintain a correct relationship between faith and reason, grace and nature, altar and throne. It is true that Leo supported the French republic, but he believed that the country, called the eldest daughter of the church, was "naturally Christian."[122] His *Longingua Oceani* to Protestant America made it clear that the American political system was tolerable, but certainly not a model to be exported. *Testem Benevolentiae* shows that Leo had not changed his mind on this issue.

Charles Maignen boasted that every error that he had identified in his *Père Hecker* was censured in *Testem Benevolentiae*,[123] but that certainly was an exaggeration: his venom and name-calling were deleted, and the gravity of the "errors" Maignen attacked was toned down. The basic orientation, however, was his. Seven years earlier, Maignen had published a book, entitled *La souveraineté du peuple est une hérésie*, in which he claimed that the doctrine of popular rule derived from Luther and Calvin.[124] In his *Père Hecker*, he called his subject and the Americanizers a "liberal and innovating party" who preached that "things fundamentally American [are] God's will for all civilized peoples of our times." The American ideal was, in the French priest's mind, one in which "authority is reduced within the limits of the least possible, that is, democracy."[125]

Much of *Testem Benevolentiae* reflects Maignen's hostility toward the spirit of the contemporary age. The text of *Testem* had been drafted by the neo-Thomists, Mazzella, Satolli and Lepidi. Mazzella has been judged lacking in any real understanding of modern science and culture, and Lepidi as blind to subjectivity and history.[126]

To reinforce Leo's thinking on the issue of civil liberty, *Testem* refers to his *Immortale Dei*, "The Christian Constitution of States."[127] When he composed this document fourteen years earlier, Leo was not enfeebled by advanced age.[128] In both encyclicals, "civil liberty" bears a pejorative connotation. The historical perspective from which Leo had judged the democratic state focused exclusively on the situation of secular antinomial Europe. There the "sovereignty of the people" was defined with no reference to God—authority had as its origin and end the people alone. Law made no provision for matters of a religious nature; such were consigned to the domain of individual conscience. The theory of separation of church and state as worked out in practice on the Continent was one generally hostile to the interests of the church. Its sphere of freedom, influence, and property was either diminished or destroyed. Consequently, the "civil liberty" advocated in society could be understood by Leo only as synonymous with "unbridled license." The separation of church and state was judged an irreligious aberration, one ultimately leading to atheism.

"The Christian Constitution of States," therefore, had been addressed to a reality which held little in common with the situation in the United States. Hecker and the Americanists, however, had consistently interpreted Leo's words and actions in light of their own concept and experience of democracy. They seized upon *Immortale Dei*'s conclusion that "forms of government are contingent," and the support given in *Au milieu des sollicitudes* to the French Third Republic, as a papal endorsement of democracy. They failed to recognize that Leo was in no way ready to admit that the ideal form of government could be anything other than one in which the Catholic church enjoyed a privileged position, protected and fostered by the state; indeed, one in which they were united.[129]

Central to the diverse opinions about liberty held by Leo XIII and the Americanists is their estimate of the maturity of contemporary individuals. References to the dignity of the human person are not absent from the pope's writings, but these are not the most luminous aspect of the Leonine corpus.[130] Historically, it was the "unformed and illiterate masses" that Leo had in mind. Hecker and the Americanists, who understood democracy as the natural and ultimate expression of the authentic Catholic teaching about the worth of the individual, considered their peers possessed of ever-expanding intellect with a concomitantly fuller exercise of liberty. They were prepared to share in the powers of a government whose role was to facilitate and make more possible the exercise of rights and duties. By contrast, the attention of *Immortale Dei* is directed to the "prince" or ruler who acts as a "father" toward his "infant-subjects," who are characterized by obedience.

Given Leo's understanding of the liberty advocated in the political order, one can understand the near-hysterical tone *Testem* assumes in rebuking suggestions that liberty be exercised in the religious domain.[131] To Hecker and the Americanists, however, there was nothing un-Christian about their advocacy of individual initiative in the church with a consequent deemphasis on its authoritative aspects. They did not reason from the liberty granted in a democracy to a greater liberty that should be allowed in the church. Rather, it was the reverse that they held—democracy was so congenial to Christianity because "the principles of Catholic teaching are at the core of civil liberty."[132]

Testem Benevolentiae's emphasis on the virtue of obedience in the religious order flows logically from Leo's theory of the subject in the political order. If one is ill-fitted to judge in the civil realm, one is even less competent to do so in matters that pertain to a superior and supernatural order. Hecker's encouragement of initiative in religious matters, understood as a function of the Holy Spirit given freer reign in man's developed nature, was bound to be suspect.

The very suggestion made by the Americanizers, that they had legitimate ideas to offer about ways the church could engage the contemporary age, was less than appreciated. If anything, *Testem* underlined the role of papal authority, needed more than ever "in order to safe guard the minds of the Church's children from the dangers of these present times." *Testem* stands squarely against change of any kind. True, Leo conceded that church discipline had changed in the past and that, theoretically, it is mutable. *Testem*, however, gives no hint that contemporary change is necessary or desirable. Rather, *Testem* assumes an offended air at the suggestion that "the Church could frame a code of laws useless or heavier than human liberty can bear."

Testem called for unity, not only in doctrine, but "unity of government" centralized in the "chair of Blessed Peter" in the "rightly called Roman Church."[133] *Testem*'s designation of the universal church as "Roman" is worthy of several historical notes. It has been recorded that many of the American bishops attending the Vatican Council in 1870 had taken a dim view of the insistence that the adjective "Roman" be included in the official name of the church. They made the point that it was Christ, not Peter, who was the principle of unity in the church.[134] On the other side of the ocean, an Italian-American newspaper, *The True American Catholic*, claimed in its first issue on February 4, 1899, that in Rome "Christ himself is Roman."[135] *Testem*, of course, never went that far. In the text, *Testem* distinguished between "theological" Americanism and "political" Americanism. If the notions described as theological were being propagated, *Testem* states, they should be stopped. If all that was meant by "Americanism" was the "political condition and the laws and customs by which you are governed," *Testem* conceded that "there is not reason to take exception to the name."[136]

There are some curiosities about *Testem* that have intrigued historians for years. Hecker is the only name mentioned in the encyclical, and it is in connection with the stir created by the French translations of Elliott's biography. As a result, some have argued that *Testem* was really sent to the wrong country, though this hardly seems likely.[137] Whether *Testem* censured any of Hecker's authentic thought and whether the Americanizers adequately understood Hecker are still being debated.[138]

All those directly involved in the controversy disclaimed any adhesion to the points questioned in *Testem*. Several of the conservative prelates thanked Leo XIII for his timely intervention. Corrigan congratulated Leo for embodying in one document the manifest errors that had been put forward as sound doctrine.[139] The German bishops of Milwaukee agreed and expressed disapproval of the subterfuge resorted to by some unnamed parties in order to evade condemnation. Some of the French claimed that the errors indeed existed in America but not in France, and so it went.[140]

One of the things *Testem* did not do was resolve the tensions that existed between the conservatives and liberals in America. There developed, as one historian of Americanism expressed it, a kind of armed truce on the issue because of its volatile nature.[141] The shadow cast upon the liberal proponents of Americanism followed them for the rest of their lives.

Testem Benevolentiae flowed logically from Leo XIII's identity with neo-Thomist philosophy. The Americanists were operating out of a different context. Their efforts have been characterized as the "inchoate groping of Catholics formed in a tradition both indigenous and derivative."[142] Their epistomological and philosophical starting point was at variance with Leo's. If that was judged wrongheaded, any attempt, rudimentary as it might be, at theological elaboration would necessarily be perceived as deficient. The age of legitimate philosophical pluralism within the Catholic church simply had not yet arrived.[143]

The Americanizers tended to be as monolithic in their views about what was good for the church as were the authors of *Testem Benevolentiae*. Those who praised the progress of the United States were blind to the dangers of American materialism. They were not critical enough when identifying human advancement with their own nation.

It may be noted, however, that although they accepted the doctrine of "manifest destiny" along with the majority of the population, the Americanizers expressed some reservations about America's expansionism.[144] Keane expressed the fear, early during the Spanish-American War, that the United States was going into the colonizing business.[145] Ireland later criticized America's crassness in attempting to acquire the Panama Canal.[146] Yet the Americanizers were not sufficiently self-critical. Unlike John Lancaster Spalding, other Americanizing prelates had no sympathy for some immigrants' desire for cultural pluralism within the church. Ireland was so narrow in his view that he actually precipitated an ecclesiastical schism. He refused to accept under his jurisdiction Ukrainian Catholics of the Greek Rite. The issue was their married clergy, a legitimate option for priests outside the Latin Rite. Ireland created such hard feelings that the Ukrainians severed their centuries-old ties with the See of Rome and joined the Russian Orthodox church.[147] Only in recent decades has the desirability of cultural pluralism been universally recognized within the Catholic church.

Some of the legitimate aspirations of the Americanists found expression in the documents of Vatican II. Foremost among them is the declaration on religious freedom, *Dignitatis Humanae.*[148] *Lumen Gentium*, with its emphasis on the role of the laity and its movement away from hierarchical centrality through episcopal collegiality, are features akin to Hecker's fondest hopes.[149] The use of the vernacular, one of the results of the liturgical renewal outlined in the Constitution on the Sacred Liturgy, *Sacrosanctum Concilium*, had been recognized as a need for the American church from the time of its first bishop, John Carroll.[150] The questions precipitated by the conciliar decree on the Appropriate Renewal of the Religious Life, *Perfectae Caritatis*, how best to give evangelical witness to contemporary society, were the same kinds that led Hecker to the foundation of the Paulist Fathers.[151]

It was perhaps the Paulists themselves who suffered the most after *Testem.* In 1900, Walter Elliott admitted that the Paulist staff of the *Catholic World* were "under a scare" and afraid of their own shadows near to "a veritable panic . . . [yet required to] keep up appearances of indifference."[152] The passage of time did not ease Elliott's mind. The long-range effect of *Testem* is reflected in a letter he wrote to Heuser in 1909. The Paulist had congratulated the editor of the *American Ecclesiastical Review* on an article he had written urging the use of the vernacular in the liturgy. Heuser requested permission to publish Elliott's letter in the *Review.* Elliott responded negatively. He believed it would damage Heuser's standing as a "solid conservative man" to have his name linked with the Paulist's. Elliott wrote, "I am quite differently regarded, though my intimate friends are better acquainted with my shrinking from all that is 'novel' in the doctrinal meaning of the term." He continued by referring to Archbishop Corrigan's reaction years earlier to an article Elliott had published on the same subject in the *Catholic World*. "He simply foamed at the bare mention of vernacularity," Elliott told Heuser. He added that although Corrigan was dead, his kind were not: "The Latin mentality is dead set on Latin universality—unless, indeed, one of those quick and radical changes of spirit in our rulers, noted in the history of the Holy Church, has been vouchsafed us." Several days later, Elliott wrote to Heuser to inform him of the outcome of his meeting with Cardinal Gibbons. When Elliott asked the prelate if he thought it would be prudent to request the archbishops of America to petition the Holy See for use of the vernacular in *"extra-missam* services," Gibbons responded that it would not be. That the divisions among the American prelates had not been healed is clear. Gibbons feared that a request of that nature, coming from him, "would lead to hot protests from the super-orthodox."[153] The unfortunate effect of *Testem* was that it left the major problem of the controversy—the proper relationship, if any, between Catholic faith and contemporary American culture—unresolved.

The consequences of *Testem* extended into the realm of spirituality. Devotion to the Holy Spirit, so central to Hecker's thought, came to be interpreted in a restricted manner by the Paulists after 1899. As one author has observed, the role of the Spirit had to be confined to the interior realm, thus limiting its social, political, and ecclesiological consequences. The type of devotion that came to flourish outside the Paulist community was one in which the role of the Spirit fostered dedication to hierarchical authority and to unity in Catholic dogma, discipline, and devotion.[154]

Nine months after *Testem Benevolentiae* had been published, the fiercely independent John Lancaster Spalding gave what has been called "his most notable pulpit performance."[155] In the Church of Gesu in Rome, and in the presence of Sebastiano Martinelli, apostolic delegate to the United States, Spalding delivered a sermon entitled "Education and the Future of Religion." Reiterating one of his favorite themes, Spalding insisted that there was no contradiction between God and the universe, nature and supernature, faith and knowledge. Spalding boldly asserted that "all truth is orthodox, whether it come to us through revelation" or whether it come in the form of certain and scientific knowledge. He assured the congregation that a true Catholic held fast to the principles of authority, but insisted that the mind is free and "has the right to inquire into and learn whatever may be investigated and known." He made a spirited defense of Catholic freedom, not only to learn but also to teach. He repeated his plea that the church, priests and laypeople alike, not ignore philosophic, scientific, or historical problems if Catholics were to be effective in contemporary civilization. His historical timing is clear. He challenged the climate of Roman opposition to free inquiry. "What is there to fear?" Spalding asked, since human error could not prevail against truth. That Spalding was not impressed with Roman apologetics is evident when he insisted that true religion does not need the "defense of concealment, or of sophistical apology, or of lies." Spalding urged research into the history of the church where "good has been mingled with evil." What Spalding said of church history, he applied to higher criticism of the Bible. "No facts connected with its composition can obscure the light of God's word." From that point on, Spalding became even more daring. He excoriated the church for its treatment of those "who labor with honest purpose and untiring zeal for deeper and truer knowledge." The church censured those in the vanguard, allowing the great body of Catholics "to fall into the sleep of a self-contented ignorance" while the "great world moves on," leaving them in the grave. If mistrust of the church's able minds were permitted to exist, the inevitable result would be "a lowering of the whole intellectual life of Catholics."

To make his point about free inquiry in the church, Spalding used the history of biblical interpretation as an object lesson. If the inspired writers of the sacred books have been misunderstood by honest minds and enlightened theologians, should the noninspired minds of talented and dedicated scholars who attempt to bring new knowledge to "clothe the old truths" be treated with less than good will and kindness?

Spalding was highly critical of philosophical and theological scholasticism without naming it. He satirized a system of "crystallized formulas" that took no account of the general culture of the age. Theology must not rest content with presenting "the old truths in the old way, as merely a larger catechism."

Throughout his address, Spalding spoke of the need for a thoroughly cultivated priest. He should not confine himself to the monastery, but he must go forth into the world as a guide and leader. Only then will the laity resume any active interest in the welfare and progress of the church. Spalding let fly his best salvos toward the end of his address. He said that he spoke as an American. He made it clear that the history of the church in the English-speaking world of the nineteenth century was one of "real and great progress." This progress was made possible by the freedom afforded to the church separated from the state. In countries like America, people "live with the old truths, while they walk unafraid in the midst of the vast development of science, culture, and material wealth." Spalding obviously did not share Leo XIII's interpretation of the contemporary age. He claimed for English-speaking Catholics "triumphs and conquests which have not been achieved by Catholics elsewhere in the wonderful century that is now closing."[156]

Historians have recognized that Spalding's address contains doctrines very compatible with the Americanists' ideals.[157] O'Connell was delighted with Spalding's Gesu sermon. Félix Klein, who translated the address into French, claimed to have "discovered" Spalding.[158]

This address certainly puts Spalding in the Americanist camp, despite his earlier opposition to them on various issues. Only Spalding and O'Connell refused to send letters of submission to Leo XIII after *Testem* was published. A French contemporary considered the Gesu address Spalding's answer to the papal censure of Americanism.[159]

By the time *Testem Benevolentiae* was written, Spalding had developed a keen appreciation for the spirit of the age, perhaps under the influence of his growing appreciation of Goethe.[160] When Spalding first wrote about Goethe in the 1870s, he portrayed him as a sex-crazed enemy of Christ and religion. A quarter-century later, with accumulated life experiences and insight, Spalding had an entirely different conception of Goethe. He now called him the "German apostle of culture" who possessed a religious spirit.

The key to Spalding's admiration was Goethe's own passion for self-culture. The bishop said that the problem Goethe had to solve for himself was the question of his own vocation—to follow it seriously and with perseverance. He had to educate himself, for only then would he be worthy of service to God and man. This made Goethe special to Spalding because, in his view, most did not understand their vocations as being valuable chiefly as their means of mental and moral improvement. It certainly seems that this is the way Spalding understood his own priesthood and that of his confreres. He believed that priests should be the first teachers of the race in all the aesthetic arts, poetry, music, painting, sculpture, and the rest. True religion, as Spalding never tired of saying, appealed to humanity's highest faculties and necessarily promoted true culture.[161]

Spalding, the bishop of Peoria, was not in the forefront of the Americanist struggles, but he was a talented intellectual leader. He articulated the ideals of the Catholic University and the Americanist vision of the church in the United States.

CHAPTER
5
Modernist Scholarship and Progressive Social Thought, 1900–1920

෴

*D*efinitive historical judgment has yet to be passed on the significance of Leo XIII's signature on *Testem Benevolentiae* or the felicity of the neo-Thomistic renewal. In America, the years between 1899 and 1907 have been described as the threshold to a potential "golden age" of American Catholic clerical intellectual development.[1] Among the factors responsible were the contributions made by faculty members at the Catholic University, the growing number and improved quality of clerical publications, and the trend toward questioning and searching that priests had inherited from the previous decade. The Catholic University counted among its faculty a core of scholars of high caliber.[2] Henri Hyvernat, one of the country's foremost Orientalists, taught Old Testament and cognate literature. Another professor of Scripture, Charles P. Grannan, was a member of the Pontifical Biblical Commission and an advocate of higher criticism. Philosophy professor Edward Pace, a pioneer in experimental psychology, established the second psychological laboratory in the United States at the Catholic University in 1891.[3] Thomas Bouquillon did more than teach moral theology. He is considered a "precursor" of the incipient social sciences developing at the University in 1897.

The Catholic University was not the only institution of higher learning with a faculty interested in contemporary questions. Saint Paul Seminary, located in John Ireland's archdiocese, had one of

Bouquillon's protégés, John A. Ryan, who went on to distinguish himself as a theoretician of social justice.[4] Saint Charles Seminary in Philadelphia was the home of the *American Ecclesiastical Review*. Under the editorship of Herman Heuser, professor of Scripture, *AER* carried articles on recent biblical studies, higher criticism, and the advantages and limits of the neoscholastic method.[5] Edward J. Hanna, professor of Dogma at Saint Bernard's Seminary in Rochester, had a broad acquaintance with contemporary trends.

The Sulpicians, considered the most liberal clerics of the period along with the Paulists, staffed seminaries in Boston, Baltimore, San Francisco, and New York. Some among the Sulpician ranks were in the forefront of progressive scholarship.[6] John Hogan's *Clerical Studies*, published in 1898, was a comprehensive call for faith and fearless scholarship as the order of the day for seminarians.[7] The French translation, which appeared three years later, was used widely by progressive French bishops in reorganizing their own seminaries.[8]

Unquestionably, the most progressive of the Sulpician seminaries in America was at Dunwoodie in Yonkers, New York. The historian of the Sulpicians has pointed to the ironic fact that they came to Saint Joseph Seminary at the 1894 invitation of the conservative Archbishop Corrigan. He had passed over members of his own diocesan clergy in favor of the Sulpician leadership in order to avoid liberalism. However, two of the most notable Sulpicians in the United States, Hogan and Alphonse Magnien, were closely, though covertly, associated with Corrigan's nemesis, the Americanizers. Both Sulpicians worked to give their society in the United States a distinctively American character.[9]

Although officially under Sulpician direction, eight of the fourteen faculty at Dunwoodie were members of the diocesan clergy. The entire seminary faculty has been judged probably the best in the United States.[10] The Sulpician Superior, Edward Dyer, set the tone for Saint Joseph's. His pedagogy was progressive, and he tried to work out a relationship with Columbia University and New York University that would allow him to send Dunwoodie's best seminarians there for classes. In 1902, Dyer became vicar-general of the Sulpicians in the United States and was replaced by James Driscoll, who had been a student of Hyvernat when the latter taught in Rome. Driscoll was far more au courant regarding intellectual trends than Dyer.[11] He shared with his fellow Sulpician and colleague Francis E. Gigot, progressive biblical insights. Gigot was the most advanced Catholic scripture scholar in the United States and its most knowledgeable authority on European Catholic studies in biblical higher criticism.[12] When Gabriel Oussani became professor of Oriental History and Biblical Archeology in 1904, Dunwoodie was in the forefront of Catholic biblical scholarship in the United States with Driscoll, Gigot, and the Baghdad-born Oussani.[13] Francis P. Duffy, a New York archdiocesan priest, was professor of philosophy, but his scholarly interests included theology, history, and science. It was Duffy, together with fellow faculty member John F. Brady of the same department, who conceived the idea for a scholarly English-language journal that would address the major theological problems that had emerged in light of the scientific and historical research of the previous half-century.[14] These men were concerned that some of the solutions being proposed were irreconcilable with any rational interpretation of historic Christianity. Driscoll warmly supported the idea and he and Duffy agreed to become the editors. John F. Farley, who had succeeded Corrigan as archbishop of New York, welcomed enthusiastically the idea that the proposed review would be published out of his seminary, under his official sponsorship and with his *imprimatur.*

According to the editorial policy, the review intended to treat contemporary theological, scriptural, and philosophical questions "in a scholarly fashion," intelligible to the ordinary cultivated mind. The editors recruited the most eminent scholars, European and American clerics and laypeople. The first issue of the *New York Review* appeared in June of 1905.[15]

The *Review* showed a respect for tradition but an awareness that the religious and scientific conditions demanded, according to the *Review*'s historian, a "reconstruction" of time-honored truths. The divinity of Christ, the inspiration of the Bible, and the very possibility of belief were being challenged outside the pale of traditional Catholic scholarship. The journal fundamentally supported the approach of the new apologetics, which incorporated the subjective element of religious experience. In the spirit of fairness and free inquiry, the *Review* also published articles that pointed out weaknesses in this approach and defended systematic scholastic objectivity. Scriptural articles were written from a perspective of higher criticism. Other signs of the *Review*'s caliber were the articles on the cognate sciences, including Egyptology, Assyreology, archeology, and philology.[16] Essays on dogma followed the developmentalist approach of John Henry Newman and promoted the cardinal's suggestion that the faithful be consulted on doctrinal questions.[17] Clearly, the journal represented scholars in the advanced wing of Catholic thought. At the same time, Rome had set its face firmly in the opposite direction.

In 1902 Alfred Loisy, a French biblical exegete, published *L'Evangile et l'église.*[18] In the work, Loisy attempted to present a modern apologia of Catholicism against scholars whom he judged heterodox. In the process, he proposed a complete reinterpretation of Christianity.[19] Loisy's work sparked a controversy that reached proportions of enormous magnitude. *L'Evangile et l'église* was put on the Index in

1903. The relationship between Loisy and Rome grew stormy. In England, the Jesuit George Tyrrell was developing a new religious synthesis, drawing on Newman's ideas, in order to formulate a more inclusive and more democratic ecclesiology. Tyrrell's immanentist philosophical approach, among other things, got him into trouble with his superiors and he was dismissed from the Society of Jesus in 1906.[20]

The Italian version of modernism was of a more sociopolitical nature, but it touched on areas of religion and theology. Ernesto Buonaiuti, the most prominent figure, became intrigued with immanentism and moved in the direction of a social messianism.[21] He and others, such as Romalo Murri, were part of a new generation of Italian clerics who supported Christian democracy with its demand for political independence from the hierarchy. The old guard continued the papal obsession with the occupation of the former Papal States by the Italian government.[22]

Because the currents of Catholic liberal thought touched so close to home, Leo XIII's successor, Pius X, viewed them as poisoned at their very sources by godless rationalism and Protestant subjectivism.[23] On July 3, 1907, the Vatican Holy Office published the decree *Lamentabili*. It listed sixty-five propositions that were considered in opposition to orthodoxy. Two months later, Pius X issued *Pascendi Dominici Gregis*, a condemnation of modernism, considered a "synthesis of all heresies."[24] The letter was aimed principally at the works of Loisy and Tyrrell, generally considered the leading modernist figures. There were others in various European countries who were also placed under suspicion. To define precisely what the label "modernist" meant is a difficult task. Modernism was a spontaneous intellectual phenomenon rather than an organized movement. Positions among those designated as heretical varied; however, they all shared some general characteristics. Most were priests who rejected traditional scholastic metaphysics in favor of nineteenth-century historical methodology. They attempted to develop a synthesis between Catholicism and modern scientific, political, and social ideas. Many of the questions raised by the modernists were legitimate; some of their answers were at variance with the articulation of dogma.

With the publication of *Pascendi*, a siege mentality deepened in the church. The heavy-handed global war on modern thought was lamented immediately by one of Pius X's loyal subjects. Father Louis Birot wrote that he submitted to the encyclical "with a sad heart, for its sharp doctrinal severity is constructed on the most artificial of misunderstanding. . . . The Pope is like an artillery colonel high on the crest of a hill who bombards armies of both parties [friends and foes] . . . and in the melee wipes out the best of his own troops."[25]

This was certainly the case on the American scene. Not that any individual was singled out for censure; it was the *New York Review* that was cut down in its infancy. The issues surrounding the demise of the *Review* are somewhat complex. The *Review* was openly sympathetic to modernist views, and it published articles by Tyrrell, Loisy, and others who were later condemned. Driscoll had a warm and ideologically compatible relationship with Loisy.[26] The Paulist Richard McSorley, staff member of the *Catholic World* and contributor to the *Review*, was Tyrrell's "plenipotentiary" for the publication of his work in America.[27] Rumors came back to Farley that New York seminarians studying in Rome were in contact with condemned Italian modernists. The proximate reason for the suppression of the *Review* was an article by Edward J. Hanna of Saint Bernard's Seminary. His essay was called "The Human Knowledge of Christ."[28] At the outset, Hanna made it clear that his position was purely speculative and tentative. He cited several scriptural texts—Luke 2:52 and Mark 13:32—that suggested limits to Christ's human knowledge. He also examined the position of the early Christian writers on the question. In his conclusion, Hanna indicated that, in Jesus' humanity, he shared to some degree the restrictions common to human consciousness. This ran contrary to the teaching from the time of Pope Saint Gregory the Great in the seventh century. Gregory held that Jesus had unlimited knowledge. Hanna's article appeared prior to *Pascendi* and caused scarcely a stir in America, though it did precipitate a bit of a squall in Rome.[29]

The timing of the article was unfortunate. Immediately prior to the condemnation of modernism, Hanna's name was presented to Rome as the leading choice for coadjutor to the archbishop of San Francisco, with the right to succession. Subsequently, suspicions were raised about Hanna's orthodoxy in Rome.[30] With post-*Pascendi* zeal, all of Hanna's writings were collected for investigation. This brought the *New York Review* under suspicion. Although Hanna's work was not condemned, he was asked to write a follow-up article on the question of Christ's knowledge according to the lines dictated by the Propaganda. It was to be published in English, French, and German.

Hanna was a protégé of Bishop McQuaid. He resented the suspicion cast on his seminary professor and, indirectly, on his own seminary. There is a touch of irony in McQuaid's defense of Hanna. The bishop of Rochester had been a fierce opponent of the liberal Americanizers. He, with a few others, had held that the "errors" censured in *Testem Benevolentiae* did indeed exist in America. When Roman suspicion hit home, however, the bishop of Rochester supported the respected scholar whose liberal ideas, incidentally, touched much more closely on doctrinal questions than those of his old foes.

Farley and Cardinal Gibbons journeyed to the Eternal City in the summer of 1908 to present a defense of Hanna. Among other things, they complained about the confusion in Rome which identified Americanism with modernism.[31] Understandably, the nervous American prelates insisted that the condemned modernism was theological and nonexistent in their country; Americanism, they claimed, was merely functional. From the Roman vantage point, both "isms" were infected with the same pernicious virus, liberalism. From a totally different perspective, some post–Vatican II reinterpreters of Americanism and modernism have been willing to connect the legitimate aspirations of each as distinct species of the same genus.[32]

Hanna complied with Rome's request and wrote a sequel to "The Human Knowledge of Christ." The toll *Pascendi* was exacting on scholarship is clear in the cautious and conservative tone that Hanna adopted as he presented the case for Christ's unrestricted human knowledge.[33] Despite Hanna's show of good faith, he was not vindicated until 1911 when he finally became auxiliary bishop of San Francisco.[34]

Events moved much more swiftly in the opposite direction. The *New York Review* ceased publication in 1908. It was suppressed by Farley under pressure from Rome.[35] The next year the archbishop ousted Driscoll as Rector in an effort to free his seminary from the suspicion of heterodoxy. In what can only be interpreted as a humiliating demotion, Driscoll, with no practical pastoral experience, exchanged places with Father John R. Chidwick, who had no academic credentials.[36] Rather symbolically, Chidwick had been chaplain to the New York Police, and at Saint Joseph's, he patrolled his forces well. One of the new rector's first moves was to sever the relationship with Columbia University. He went on to inaugurate a first at Dunwoodie: all classes were to be conducted in Latin. Driscoll obediently became pastor of Saint Ambrose in Manhattan; his scholarly career was finished.[37]

Francis P. Duffy was another tragic loss to scholarship. In 1912, Duffy told Farley that he was closing his books forever and wanted a nonintellectual assignment. Actually, his scholarly career had ended in 1908. If Duffy is remembered at all, it is as America's most famous Army Chaplain with the "Fightin' Sixty-Ninth" in the First World War, and not as a foremost priest-scholar for fifteen years. Oussani continued teaching at Dunwoodie, but he did no more scholarly writing, and his students were denied any advanced biblical insights. Oussani later hinted at the wholesale climate of fear that followed in the wake of *Pascendi*. When a seminarian asked him if a particular French author had ever been suspected of modernism, Oussani assured him that anyone alive at the time was under suspicion.[38] Gigot also remained on Saint Joseph's faculty, and he, too, stagnated.

For complex reasons not directly linked with the *New York Review*,

Saint Joseph's Seminary had passed from the control of the Sulpicians to that of Archbishop Farley in 1906. Christopher J. Kauffman has suggested that, had that transfer not taken place, Dunwoodie would have been better able to resist the total romanization of seminary life that ensued. This did not happen in the other seminaries which the Sulpicians conducted in the United States.[39]

The inquisitorial spirit unleashed by *Pascendi* took a bizarre twist in the case of a professor at the Catholic University. In what could be described as a comedy of errors if the consequences had not been so tragic, Dutch-born Professor of Scripture Henry A. Poels was dismissed from the faculty.[40] Part of the problem had been caused by a decree issued by the Pontifical Biblical Commission of 1906. It required scholars to hold the position that Moses was the "substantial" author of the first five books of the Bible. This opinion ran contrary to the theories proposed by higher critics for decades. Poels spoke with Pius X about his scholarly difficulty with the decree. The pope agreed to allow Poels to continue teaching scripture as long as he showed respect for authority and did not dispute the Biblical Commission's decision. Poels agreed with the stipulation.

A year later, Denis O'Connell, the rector bishop of the Catholic University, complained to the pope about an unnamed professor on his faculty. The priest in question reportedly presented his students with the questions raised by modern scholarship, but not their solutions. O'Connell had Charles Grannan in mind; the pope thought he was talking about Poels. In the massive confusion that followed, Poels was requested to sign an oath reportedly drawn up by the pope himself. Cardinal Merry del Val, papal secretary of State, interpreted the oath to mean that Poels had to profess belief in the Biblical Commission's decree concerning Mosaic authorship. Poels understood this to be a violation of his conscience and refused. Although the board of trustees at the university realized that Poels was an innocent victim, only bishops Camillus Maes of Covington, Kentucky, and Matthew Harkins of Providence, Rhode Island, came to his defense. O'Connell, earlier the champion of canonical due process, and Cardinal Gibbons, defender of the Knights of Labor against Roman suppression in the 1880s, did precious little to protect Poels. In the aftermath of *Testem Benevolentiae*, both men were anxious to prove their loyalty to Rome at the expense of another man's honor. Poels's contract with the Catholic University was not renewed in 1910; he returned to Holland.

One historian has pointed out the theological implications. Beyond the personal pain suffered by Poels, the hierarchy's insistence that he sign the oath virtually wiped out scripture scholarship in the United States for several decades. More seriously, the American bishops allowed their strong collegial tradition to be eroded by yielding their legitimate episcopal authority to the Roman Curia, a body with no scriptural foundation. This move toward Roman centralization and ultramontanism was not reversed until the American hierarchy rediscovered collegiality during the Vatican II era. Finally, one issue raised by Poels when he was arguing his own defense has yet to be resolved. The Dutch scholar made an important distinction between the adhesion owed to statements made by the Pontifical Commission, composed of a group of cardinals, and that owed to infallible declarations made by the pope himself. The subtlety of the position was not appreciated in his and similar cases. Consequently, there developed, as the same historian put it, "a blurring of the distinction between infallible and noninfallible statements of the magisterium, between statements of the magisterium and statements of the curial congregations, and between magisterial statements and theological interpretation."[41] As a result, the question of legitimate scholarly academic freedom vis-à-vis noninfallible magisterial teachings perennially haunts the halls of Catholic academe.

There were few priests in America who left the Catholic church over modernism.[42] The most celebrated case occurred before *Pascendi* was issued. John Slattery, first superior general of the Josephites and friend of the Americanizers, had grown disillusioned with the church's efforts on behalf of black Catholics and with what he perceived as ecclesiastical politics. One historian has determined that by the early 1900s, Slattery had abandoned all hope that the church could be reformed.[43] He announced his withdrawal from the Roman Catholic communion in 1906.[44] Another hearty Americanizer, the Paulist William Sullivan, declared himself a modernist and left the church several years after *Pascendi* was released.[45] The decision for both men was painful.[46] Neither Slattery nor Sullivan, however, was a major figure on the modernist landscape. The greatest single loss to American Catholic scholarship was, beyond doubt, the *New York Review*. No other journal of the *Review*'s caliber would fill the void until *Theological Studies* began publication in 1940.

Saint Joseph Seminary, home of the *New York Review*, was not the only institution of higher learning touched by *Romanità*. The situation was duplicated across the country. Unlike the German bishops, not one of the American hierarchy protested the "Oath against Modernism" which required adhesion to *Pascendi* and was mandatory for seminary faculties, theology professors, pastors, and church officials.[47] Intellectual sterility set in. One historian of the post-Modernist church has written:

> We shall never know how many valuable shoots, which might have
> brought forth good fruit, were killed, alongside the dangerous errors,

when the bomb *[Pascendi]* dropped, nor how many men were prevented, thereafter, from ever thinking at all because some had fallen into error in their thinking.[48]

In less bellicose but equally poignant words, the modernist William Sullivan lamented:

Never again in our generation will scholarship weary the Church with importunities nor democracy disturb the echoes with its robust and ringing call. The entire procession of modern ideas and modern men has gone another way, and over the schools and sanctuaries of Catholicism broods in Buddhistic calm the new Pax Romana.[49]

History has proven that Sullivan's pessimistic prognostication was essentially accurate. One noteworthy exception was the production of the *Catholic Encyclopedia*, considered "the greatest single monument to scholarship to have appeared under American Catholic auspices" in the early twentieth century.[50] The *Encyclopedia* grew out of a concern expressed by the Jesuit John Wynne in 1902. In an article entitled "Poisoning the Wells," he expressed his consternation over the fact that new editions of general encyclopedias either misrepresented or ignored Catholic contributions to culture.[51]

This deficiency Wynne attributed either to ill will or ignorance. He decided that an English-language encyclopedia written from a Catholic perspective was sorely needed. With what a contemporary described as "indomitable energy" and "fertility of resources in leadership," Wynne began to recruit help for the project.[52] By 1905 a board of editors had been formed who agreed to undertake the herculean task. Doctor Charles Herbermann, lay professor of Latin and librarian of the New York City College, was editor-in-chief. Condé Pallen, former editor of *Church Progress and Catholic World*, was the managing editor. He later became president of the Encyclopedia Press, Incorporated, and served in that capacity until 1920.[53] Pallen invested more than his time in the project. He financially backed the venture with a loan of $84,500 and bonds worth $50,000.[54] Two priest-professors of the Catholic University, Thomas J. Shahan and Edward A. Pace, joined Wynne to complete membership of the board.[55] Shahan, professor of church history and patrology, was well-abreast of the currents of recent scholarship. The *Catholic University Bulletin* under his editorial guidance maintained high scholarly standards from 1895 until 1909, when he became rector of the university. His concern for the institution's intellectual advancement won for him the designation "rector scholar."[56] Shahan contributed some two hundred articles to the *Encyclopedia* and translated another hundred, far more than any of the other editors.[57]

In all truth, however, the *Catholic Encyclopedia* can rightly be called the "great Wynne Encyclopedia"; Wynne was the force behind the project.[58] Like Shahan and Pallen, Wynne had prior editorial experience. He guided the Jesuit literary publication, the *Messenger*, from its inception in 1902 until 1909, when its name was changed to *America*. Jesuits from across the country contributed to the new weekly journal of opinion whose editor Wynne remained for another year.[59] He drafted the layman Thomas F. Meehan from the staff of the *Catholic Encyclopedia* and placed him in charge of editorial production of *America* early in 1909; Meehan served as editorial assistant for over three decades.[60]

There are several points of similarity between the scholarly *New York Review* and the *Catholic Encyclopedia*. Their editorial policies were remarkably alike, though the *Encyclopedia*'s scope was far more ambitious; it intended to present its readers "with the full body of Catholic teaching." The work was to be entirely new, not a mere compilation or translation of other encyclopedias. Like the *Review*, the *Encyclopedia* aimed at intellectual honesty. In disputed questions, "different views of acknowledged authorities" were to be presented with no special pleading for the conservative or the progressive cause. The most recent scientific methods were to be employed and the "results of the latest research in theology, philosophy, history, apologetics, archeology, and the other sciences" would be given.

The editors of the *Encyclopedia* did not limit their scope exclusively to church matters. They recognized that there was no specifically "Catholic science," but they felt that it was important to register Catholic contributions to every department of learning at a time when it was commonly asserted that Catholic principles were an obstacle to research.[61]

The international character of the *Encyclopedia* is evidenced by the list of close to 1,500 contributors from forty-three different countries. The writers were members of the clergy and laity, represented at a ratio of about three to one. Of the 145 women authors, 40 percent belonged to various religious communities. Over one-third of the total number of contributors were Americans among whom clergy and laity were represented at about the same general ratio.[62] The latter represented a variety of backgrounds; they were teachers, doctors, lawyers, journalists, bankers, contractors, artists, and so on.[63] The women among them contributed an impressive number of articles, primarily biographical sketches and histories of religious communities.[64] Blanche Kelly, an associate editor of the *Encyclopedia*, compiled the index volume. The *Encyclopedia* was published in New York by the Robert Appleton Company, founded exclusively for that purpose.[65]

Archbishop Farley gave the editors a vote of confidence by constituting them the ecclesiastical censors.[66]

Two cataclysms that the board of editors had not foreseen in the early stages of planning and production almost shut down the operation. The modernist scare threatened the life of the *Encyclopedia* in its first year of publication. Later, World War I brought the venture to the brink of financial ruin. Reportedly, a strong protest from the American hierarchy averted the first disaster.[67] The second was forestalled primarily through the dogged perseverance of Wynne, coupled with an aggressive fund-raising and marketing campaign engineered by the board of editors.[68]

However cautious the contributors to the *Catholic Encyclopedia* had to be, many were not closed to the findings of recent scholarship. A good example of the attempt to present a balanced approach is found in the article "Biblical Criticism," a very sensitive issue. It was written by the American priest-professor of Hebrew and Sacred Scripture, George J. Reid of Saint Paul Seminary.[69] In a careful way, he presented a summary of the history of higher criticism in general and of its adoption by Catholic exegetes. In accordance with editorial policy, Reid presented the positions of the Catholic "progressive school" and the objections raised by their conservative opponents. He refrained from promoting either camp's platform. It is only in the concluding paragraph that a clear sense of the growing power of the Roman curia is found. There, Reid gave the prevailing conservative view. In the area of disputed questions, it was not the biblical scholars who were the ones competent to judge the merits of a case, but the Pontifical Biblical Commission. In what can be considered an official policy statement, Reid wrote:

> The Church warmly recommends the exercise of criticism according to sound principles unbiased by rationalistic presuppositions, but it must condemn undue deference to heterodox writers.... When doubt arises about the permissibility of hypotheses, it is for ecclesiastical authority to decide.[70]

Not every author reflected Reid's attempt at scholarly objectivity. Arthur Vermeersch assumed a thoroughly polemical tone in the article "Modernism."[71] The Belgian-born Jesuit had earlier collaborated in the 1904 compilation of the Code of Canon Law under Pius X.[72] Understandably, Vermeersch's treatment of modernism was extremely sympathetic to the papal position on the subject. It also displays that peculiarly Roman penchant for viewing the church almost exclusively in terms of its relationship with the state. As one historian has observed, Rome was more at home with a tract on political science than

it was with a treatise on ecclesiology.[73] In one sentence that identified
modernism's "essential error," the Roman-trained Vermeersch joined
immutable doctrines with political contingencies. He wrote:

> The definition of an unchangeable dogma imposes itself on every Catholic
> . . . and it necessarily supposes a Church legislating for all the faithful,
> passing judgment on State action—from its own point of view of course—
> and that ever seeks alliance with the civil power to carry on the work of
> the Apostolate.

In the author's view, the center of theological modernism was Italy,
even more so than France. Vermeersch stoutly defended the action
of the Italian hierarchy who had "imposed social and political di-
rections which call[ed] for the sacrifice of humanitarian and patriotic
ideas and dreams." From their perspective, restoring the lost Papal
States was integral to a defense of the faith.

In a complete departure from the *Encyclopedia*'s editorial guidelines, Vermeersch offered his own opinion on an open question. He
represents the extreme right wing, which tended to judge as infallible
every statement issued by the pope. The Jesuit admitted that scholars
differed about the degree of authoritativeness *Lamentabili* and *Pascendi* carried. To his way of thinking, however, they were infallible,
at least in their doctrinal conclusions.[74]

Interesting contrasts can be drawn between two other articles that
dealt with ecclesio-political relationships. The authors basically represent the quasi-official Roman view of the issue in contrast with the
liberal and American perspective. Charles Macksey, Jesuit professor
of ethics at the Gregorian University in Rome, wrote the entry "State
and Church." He looked to Pius IX's Syllabus of Errors as his guide
and presented the union of church and State as the ideal. Despite his
American birth, the best that the former Woodstock faculty member
had to say about separation of the two authorities in pluralistic countries was that it was a "practical" modus vivendi necessitated by "evil
times."[75] Macksey evidently had imbibed some of the Woodstock animus against the Americanizers.

In sharp contrast to Macksey's article stands the English Jesuit
George Haywood Joyce's essay, "Church." Citing the authority of Leo
XIII, this convert from Anglicanism gave a very positive assessment
of the separation of church and State. Nowhere is union of the two
even hinted at as an ideal. Quite the contrary, Joyce pointed to historical eras when "ecclesiastical authorities have grasped at power
which by right belonged to the state" and vice versa.[76]

It is not surprising that, in an encyclopedia treating over 30,000
subjects in some 350,000 articles, a variety of perspectives would find
their way into print.[77] It was, however, the conservative element that

had the final say in the Americanist affair. Condé Pallen, old foe of Ireland and his friends, wrote the entry on *Testem Benevolentiae*. After giving a concise summary of the errors outlined in the encyclical, Pallen ignored the liberal prelates' insistence on American Catholic theological innocence. Rather, he presented a modified version of the New York-Milwaukee oppositions' interpretation. Pallen agreed that the censured deviations had existed in the United States, though they were not so "widespread or systematic" as Klein's *Vie* made them appear.[78]

All in all, the contemporary religious and secular press roundly praised the *Catholic Encyclopedia*. It was called the "greatest triumph of Christian science in the English tongue." High grades were awarded for "exactitude and precision."[79] What particularly pleased the staff of the Encyclopedia Press was the fact that non-Catholics were "astonished" by the *Encyclopedia*'s "fairness and scholarship" as much as by its "universal scope."[80] The *New York Evening Post* offered the suggestion that the *Encyclopedia*, if used by non-Catholics, would go a long way toward "correcting" erroneous opinions and "breaking down existing prejudices."[81] To the extent that this outcome actually happened, Wynne accomplished his original objective. Despite some initial reservations, the pope himself honored the diligent and circumspect board of editors. When publication of the *Encyclopedia* was completed, Pius X conferred the papal decoration "Pro Ecclesia et Pontifice" upon Wynne and his colleagues.[82]

While the editors were being feted by Rome, a hue and cry were raised against them in England. Members of the Catholic Women's Suffrage Society there were furious about the *Encyclopedia*'s article "Women," which appeared in 1912. It had been written by an Austrian antifeminist cleric, Augustine Rössler. In the eyes of the CWSS, he represented the "crude arrogance" of those Christians who shudder at the very thought of women in power.[83] The entire tone of Rössler's essay was baldly chauvinistic, but one particular sentence bothered the women especially.[84] The Austrian had made the doctrinally unsound claim that "the female sex is in some respects inferior to the male sex, both as regards body and soul."[85]

The pressures for orthodoxy from England were apparently not taken as seriously by the *Encyclopedia*'s editors as had been those from Rome. For five years, members of the CWSS tried to get the offensive sentence corrected. Finally, the editors suggested that they omit it in future editions.[86]

The *Encyclopedia* did carry a much more nuanced article on women that immediately followed Rössler's: the American William Fanning's "Woman in English-speaking Countries." While he basically agreed with Rössler's judgment that a majority of Catholics were opposed to women in politics, Fanning was much more open to the possibility. He pointed out that some distinguished prelates, among them Cardinal Vaughn of England and Cardinal Moran of Australia, favored women's suffrage. The majority of American and Irish bishops, however, were of the opinion that women and politics should not mix.[87]

In 1919, Pope Benedict XV privately expressed his desire to see woman's suffrage granted universally. Coincidentally, the following year, the Nineteenth Amendment to the Constitution of the United States was ratified. For some women, Catholics among them, this was not an end but the beginning of a long and bitter struggle to have the federal government pass an equal rights amendment that would free women from all legal disabilities.[88]

Once the Nineteenth Amendment was a fait accompli, Cardinal Gibbons, dean of the Catholic hierarchy, urged women to take the franchise seriously. The social reformer John A. Ryan, who had earlier been ambivalent on the issue, expressed the hope that women would not fall prey to machine politics as some of their masculine counterparts had. It was up to the fairer sex to set an example and use the ballot box with integrity.[89] Ryan was no feminist by contemporary standards. Like most Catholics, he believed that women belonged in the home. He was realistic enough, however, to recognize the stark fact that many poor women had no alternative but to enter the work force. To his credit, Ryan championed the cause of equal pay for equal work, a plea that has a very contemporary ring about it.[90]

Ryan, a farm boy whose Irish immigrant parents had settled in Minnesota, cut his teeth on the philosophy of populism. The People's Party had been formed in the Midwest after the election of 1890.[91] Farmers and some city workers organized in an attempt to return political power to the ordinary citizenry. Not unjustifiably, they believed that state governments were manipulated by big business, and business was booming.

The United States led the world in industrial output well into the twentieth century. The titans of industry controlled the market through monopolies. Railroads, steel, and oil dominated large segments of the economy. The victims of progress were the exploited factory workers and farmers, who organized in self-defense. Unfortunately, they met with little success. Government, then as now, largely supported the business side of the coin.[92]

The Catholic church was keenly aware of the plight of poor workers. A large proportion of unskilled laborers were recent immigrants; many of these were Catholic. Italians, Poles, Slovaks, and others from Eastern Europe, along with the Mexican-Americans of the Southwest, were among the church's poorest members.[93] Resources were strained as attempts were made to respond to pressing needs. Most efforts tended to be geared toward alleviating the effects of poverty. Unlike Orestes Brownson, who understood the systemic cause of indigence, most American Catholics continued to interpret poverty as a personal rather than as a social problem. Consequently, Catholics were generally slow to respond to the problems inherent in industrialization. They were suspicious of the progressive movement, largely a middle-class Protestant effort tinged with nativism. For their part, the progressives opposed ruthless laissez-faire capitalism and condemned both the immigrants' attachment to labor unions as inimical to a classless society and party machine politics as detrimental to the common good. From the Catholic perspective, there was a deep fear of the progressives' socialistic tendencies.

There were a few lay Catholic reform editors—John Boyle O'Reilly, George Deering Wolff, and Patrick Ford—who had begun a critique of America's economic system in the 1870s.[94] There was, however, no unified approach to the problems of industrialization. The church lacked any national organizational structure. No Plenary Council had been held since 1884, and the annual meetings of archbishops were of an unofficial character. Even Leo XIII's celebrated labor encyclical, *Rerum Novarum*, was interpreted largely as a condemnation of socialism rather than as a critique of capitalism.

John Ryan proved himself a remarkable exception and his influence reached far beyond the Catholic community. Ryan was part of the clergy formed under the influence of Archbishop John Ireland in Saint Paul. He later acknowledged his indebtedness to Ireland and his friend, Cardinal Gibbons, though he admitted that Ireland, the millionaire, sided with the "pillars of the contemporary economic order" and not with their critics.

More profound impressions were made by the American Protestant reformer Henry George and the English Catholic publicist William S. Lilly, who saw industrial reorganization as a moral imperative. Another American-English duo, Richard T. Ely and John A. Hobson, also exerted a great influence on Ryan's thinking. Ely, political economist at Johns Hopkins University and founder of the American Economic Association, held the position that laissez-faire is "unsafe in politics and unsound in morals."[95] He advocated government ownership and operation of natural monopolies like railroads, a graduated tax on land speculation, an eight-hour workday, and the abolition of child labor; and attempted to indicate issues on which socialists and reformers could agree.[96] From Hobson, Ryan borrowed the thesis that "underconsumption and oversaving are the main cause of industrial slumps and depressions." It became the cornerstone of his own theory.

As a student at the Catholic University, Ryan greatly admired William Kerby, professor of sociology, social reformer, and founder of the National Conference of Catholic Charities in 1910. Ryan, the "Populist boy from Minnesota," who was not prone to flattery, called his professor of moral theology, Thomas Bouquillon, the "most erudite man" he had ever known.[97]

Like the Americanists before him, Ryan was looking for a way to reconcile the Catholic church with American society. It was specifically the reformers whom Ryan wished to engage. He found the springboard in Leo XIII's *Rerum Novarum*. Ryan's popularism disposed him to read the encyclical selectively: he has been called a double revisionist. As a progressive, he recognized the flaws in the Lockian natural rights theory that undergirded the Declaration of Independence and the American Constitution. Locke had stressed self-interest and negative government. The reformers wanted rights to be balanced with responsibilities and expected the government to play a positive role in effecting the common good. With progressive eyes, Ryan read *Rerum Novarum* from a distinctly American perspective. Consciously or not, he toned down the differences between the progressives and the pope. Consequently, Ryan was as selective in his interpretation as were his contemporary critics who reached diametrically opposed conclusions.[98] Ryan thought that Leo's position on state intervention for the amelioration of social ills had radically altered the traditional Catholic view that private charity was the panacea.[99] However, many Catholics feared any form of state intervention as creeping socialism.

It was primarily in the field of ethics that Ryan saw neo-Scholasticism's utility. It presented objective and universal principles of natural law and yet was flexible enough to allow them to be applied to modern social conditions.[100] This was the foundation upon which Ryan built a theory that gained him public recognition. His doctoral dissertation, *A Living Wage*, was published in 1906.[101] The work was dedicated to Richard Ely. Ely returned the compliment and wrote that, as far as he was aware, *A Living Wage* was "the first attempt in English to set forth a Roman Catholic system of political economy" that went beyond "vague and glittering generalities to get to precise doctrine, from sentiment to reasoned arguments."[102]

The keystone of Ryan's ethics was his insistence that human nature is created by God and destined for a reasonable life. Consequently, the universally equal dignity of humans had to be protected and nourished. Ryan's thesis that the dignity of the individual is sacrosanct has been pinpointed as the fundamental common ground between Catholicism and the reform movement.[103]

Ryan argued from the priority and independence of natural rights to the state's will in the ontological order. Consequently, it was the duty of government to promote, and not merely to protect, human rights. Ryan recognized that the ideal of fair and adequate compensation for most workers was a distant reality. As an interim measure, he advocated an eight-hour workday, called for subsidized housing, and argued that an old-age pension was needed to support laborers too poor to save for their later years. He wanted legislation enacted that would exact a hefty inheritance tax and a graduated income tax.

One of the merits Ely saw in Ryan's work was his concreteness. Based on a careful analysis of living expenses, Ryan estimated that an annual income of $600 was the minimum salary necessary for an urban dweller to live with decency. At the time, the average yearly pay was $571, and an overwhelming 60 percent of the industrial labor force was earning far below that.[104]

Ryan ended *A Living Wage* with a recognition that recourse to religion alone would not solve the labor problem, but he did not believe that a permanent solution could be found without it.[105] Throughout his work, Ryan assumed what has been called a pragmatic and gradualistic approach. To Leo XIII's natural law emphasis on balance and harmony, Ryan added the note of expediency. He recognized the limitations of treating ethical issues exclusively within a philosophical and theological framework. If public well-being is the determining criterion, Ryan concluded that moral values and genuine expediency are identical.[106]

A Living Wage was widely noted and the reviews were mixed. In some quarters it was highly praised; others roundly condemned Ryan, not for opposing socialism as he claimed, but for preaching it in its entirety.[107] Ryan's book, however, proved to be an important impetus in the movement for minimum wage legislation. He was one of the drafters of a model law passed in Minnesota.[108]

Ryan believed that he had found in *Rerum Novarum* the leverage necessary to push Catholics out of their indifference to contemporary social problems. Instead of simply denouncing Marxism, he urged that they try to understand the amount of truth in socialism. He especially wanted Catholic laymen to lead a reform movement. He said that their womenfolk could put Catholic men to shame in the area of social reform. The male of the species he judged too infected with the virus of materialism to stir.[109]

Just as Spalding had been an apostle of priestly culture, Ryan, who greatly admired Spalding, called for a clergy knowledgeable on economic issues. He urged that social problems be studied in seminaries. He understood that individuals' economic status often dictated their views about the "morality of some of the most important activities." Among these, he listed the ethics of trusts, trade unionism, and the relationship between profits and wages.[110]

As an active member of a number of nondenominational reform

organizations, Ryan was upset that so few Catholics followed his lead. He would not accept the excuse that Catholic participants would be met with prejudice; he thought this a convenient front to hide indolence and incompetence. Ryan did not deny that bigotry existed, but he argued that the only effective way of overcoming it was through self-assertion, knowledge, efficiency, and fair-mindedness.

Although Ryan has been recognized as the leading Catholic progressive of his day, he did not battle alone. A handful of priests and laymen had entered the fray, among them the Ohio priest Peter Dietz. He, too, was concerned with the systemic causes of poverty. In 1901, he organized the American Federation of Catholic Societies as a national vehicle to coordinate social action.[111] Labor was Dietz's primary concern. He urged the church to identify with the cause of the worker and organized the "Militia of Christ for Social Service."[112] Among its membership were Catholics who held important positions in the trade union movement.

As broadly involved as Ryan, Dietz initially cooperated, then came into conflict, with Frederick P. Kenkel, a Saint Louis layman who dominated the German Catholic *Central-Verein* from 1908 to 1952.[113] Kenkel, whose parents were highly cultured and materially well-fixed, grew uncomfortable with the alienation of contemporary society. Unlike Ryan, who made "sane individualism" his platform, Kenkel longed for a society joined in organic unity. A thorough romantic, he looked to the Middle Ages as the climate most congenial to spiritual needs, though Kenkel did have a pragmatic streak.

In 1910, as a seasoned editor, Kenkel took full charge of the *Verein*'s magazine, *Central-Blatt and Social Justice*. Within a few years, the *Central-Verein* gained a reputation as the most socially conscious of American Catholic organizations. Ryan was impressed.[114] Both he and Kenkel had been influenced by the work of the German priest Heinrich Pesch.[115] Kenkel envisioned a Christian corporate order in which the economic interests of individuals would be subordinated to the needs of society. The *Central-Verein* adopted Pesch's theory of "solidarism." The fundamental thesis was that human beings are social animals with a free will to be used in promoting societal life. Individuals were held responsible for financial success. If they failed, the aid of relatives and friends was to be solicited. Only as a last resort could the State be expected to provide "energetic assistance."

Pesch and the *Verein* hoped that individuals would voluntarily limit their freedom in the interest of the common good. The ultimate goal of "solidarism" was a healthy middle class of independent producers. Fundamental to that dream was the creation of Catholic labor organizations similar to the guild system that flourished in medieval Europe. For that reason the *Verein* favored the American Federation of Labor. As in the guilds, membership was determined by vocation, not money or class.

Although Kenkel was not primarily concerned with the inequalities created by industrial capitalism, he did adopt a melioristic approach to social reform for a period. Prior to World War I, the *Verein* set up an office in Saint Louis, one of the cities in the German triangle that extended to Cincinnati and Milwaukee. The office coordinated social reform work. Under its aegis were day nurseries, lecture tours, and social study courses. A news service prepared items of a religious and reform nature for the Catholic press.

Verein members were urged to support a variety of progressive measures, including strict regulations of women's and child labor and industrial safety legislation. The *Central-Blatt* discussed the causes of unemployment and plans for insurance against such a calamity. It examined the problems of migrant workers and championed legislation guaranteeing a minimum wage. Workmen's compensation was urged as a protection against injury and disease sustained on the job. Kenkel's overall vision was utopian, but he was shrewd enough to realize what was immediately possible with the available resources. He was also convinced that people needed to realize how deficient the social order was before they would look for alternatives. There was, however, a fundamental weakness in Kenkel's and the *Verein*'s vision. In the quest for organic wholeness, they oversimplified the real complexities of modern society.

The German-American community was dealt a mighty blow when their Fatherland was defeated in World War I. The conflict had been precipitated by the assassination of Archduke Ferdinand at Sarajevo on June 28, 1914. The United States initially declared itself neutral, but strong ethnic loyalties dictated sympathies with either the Triple Entente of France, Great Britain, and Russia or the Triple Alliance of Germany, Austria-Hungary and, for a time, Italy. The Catholic Irish-Americans were an exception. They bore an age-old enmity against the English and were not particularly enthusiastic about either side. On the contrary, the German-American Catholics, with strong cultural ties and a very national sense of religious community, clearly favored the Central Powers. Shortly after the start of the war, a Pittsburgh chapter of the *Central-Verein* opened its meetings with a spirited rendition of "Deutschland über Alles," followed by a rousing cheer for the Fatherland. After Germany's defeat, as the organization's historian observed, the *Verein* was never again the same proud and fruitful German-American organization that it had been prior to 1914.[116]

Two years after the war had begun, Ryan published what is considered to be his best work, *Distributive Justice;* this demonstrated a mastery of economic data gathered from England, Germany, France, and America and provided a synthesis of moralists' and economists' thought. In his treatise, Ryan returned to the subject of a living wage, a theme that constantly occupied him. He did not argue for an equal amount of income for every individual. What he championed was the right to a decent livelihood based on the dignity of personality. This he thought was as fundamental as the right to life. Ryan understood that it was not opposition to the theory of a living wage he had to combat, but what constituted that wage in practice. As the Catholic ethicist saw it, a living wage should supply food, clothing, and shelter of the quantity and quality necessary to support health and elemental comfort. It should also be adequate to provide the environmental protection of morality and religion. Just compensation would allow workers a measure of contentment and security against sickness, accident, and old age. It should afford means and opportunities for recreation, social exchange, and education. The leisure to sustain church membership and conserve health and strength was integral. Workers should also have the possibility of exercising their "higher faculties," at least to some measure. It was the state's duty to enact legislation whenever any significant group was earning less than a living wage. Legislation, rather than organization, was a faster and more expedient way to attain the ideal.

For Ryan, distributive justice was primarily a problem of income derived from the process of production. There were four factors involved: landowners, capitalists, businessmen, and laborers. In balancing the claims of each party, the presumption always had to favor the laborer's right to just compensation.

Ryan saw glaring defects in the capitalist system. He enumerated the chief offenders: monopolies that manipulated market prices, excessive gains gotten at the expense of labor, and exclusion from the land because of greedy speculation for profit and not use.

On the issue of distributing superfluous wealth, Ryan had very clear ideas. Scripture, theologians, and the official teaching of the Catholic church demanded, as a strict moral obligation, that the rich give out of their abundance to the poor. Ryan realized that this charity was no substitute for justice, but he saw it as a concrete example of Christian love, a necessary propaedeutic to advance Americans along the road to strict justice.[117]

Like Kenkel, Ryan envisioned a reordering of society, but, unlike the Midwest reformer, the Minnesotan did not want to roll back the hands of time. Ryan's ideal was an industrial society in which labor shared in ownership, management, and profits, an idea whose time had not yet come.[118] In Ryan's way of thinking, the advantages were obvious. Workers would have the incentive necessary to eliminate waste and to improve production and their working conditions. Such a program would be an effective alternative to the socialistic impulse "entirely natural" in a democratic society, where workers were not content to be mere vassals to the "feudal lords of industry." In an industrial democracy where the majority of workers were also owners of capital, society would be more progressive and more enlightened than those societies existing under either socialism or capitalism.

Ryan ended his study *Distributive Justice* with an admonition: the rich must cease to put their hope in things material; the middle class and the poor must not envy or emulate the wealthy. The ideal Ryan suggested was a life not dissimilar to that of his youth, one of simplicity in which wants were few, aspirations were noble, and a religious spirit prevailed. Ryan reiterated his belief that the only key to a permanently just social order was the "revival of genuine religion."[119]

While Ryan was worrying about a just social order, Americans grew increasingly concerned about international affairs. After a series of provocative attacks by German submarines on American merchant ships, the United States declared war against Germany on April 6, 1917. Americans, Catholics among them, subordinated ethnic loyalties and rallied around the flag. Actually, Catholics served in the armed forces in proportions higher than their numbers warranted.

In 1917, the National Catholic War Council was established. It was a major organizational step for a church that lacked national structure. The following year, the NCWC was recognized by the government as an accredited war agency. For the first time the Catholic church made a commitment to social and political action, and at the same time made its presence felt in Washington, D.C. The NCWC cooperated with other denominations in the war effort and the church identified itself with the nation, currently in a progressive mood.[120]

Several months after the armistice was signed on November 11, 1918, the NCWC published what came to be called "the Bishops' Plan for Social Reconstruction." It was signed by the four members of the Administrative Committee: chairman Bishop Peter Muldoon of Rockford, the most progressive of the American hierarchy; and Bishops Joseph Schrembs of Toledo, William Russell of Charleston, and Patrick Hayes of New York. Actually, the plan had been hastily composed by John Ryan, who had studied over sixty reconstruction programs suggested by various American and European religious and secular groups. In "the Bishops' Plan," Ryan reiterated themes from his earlier works, and also urged that certain wartime measures be continued. He wanted to retain the United States Employment Service, which matched workers with jobs nationwide and the National War Labor Board, which represented capital, labor, and the public. Ryan saw the latter as a tool for social justice that he did not want jettisoned in peacetime. He advocated housing for urban laborers modeled on government projects built for war workers and urged women to leave war jobs that were harmful to their health or morality, but at no greater loss or inconvenience than was "absolutely necessary." Ryan repeated his plea for a legal minimum wage, close participation of labor with management, establishment of cooperatives and copartnerships, and the abolition of child labor.[121]

It has been observed, though not quite accurately, that "the Bishops' Plan" read like a blueprint of Franklin D. Roosevelt's New Deal.[122] Actually, the plan was designed to operate chiefly at the state level and only indirectly on the federal level. One author has rightly claimed that the bishops' program belonged more properly to the late progressive era in point of time and outlook.

Reactions to "the Bishops' Plan" were mixed. The press generally gave it a favorable reception.[123] Upton Sinclair called the program "amazingly radical" and thought that he had witnessed a "Catholic miracle."[124] Not surprisingly, big business was unhappy and condemned the plan as socialistic, a view shared by some conservative American bishops. German Catholics were annoyed that their own tradition of social thought had been overlooked. The capitalist Condé Pallen did not fault the Catholic church, but blamed "certain priests whose vision on social and economic issues are lauded by radicals and revolutionaries." The root of Pallen's disagreement with Ryan was the interpretation of *Rerum Novarum*. Pallen is said to have accepted its letter while Ryan caught its spirit.[125]

Ryan's own clerical career has been judged unique because of his orientation toward politics.[126] He has been faulted for his lack of a historical sense and his narrow approach to economics and morality.[127] To his credit, "the Bishops' Plan" had two significant effects. It broke the American Catholic church's long silence on social issues in a public and authoritative manner. At the same time, it also helped remake the image of the church in industrial society and forced it out of its past lethargy.[128]

World War I acted as a midwife to American Catholic identity. From it Catholics emerged with enthusiasm for ideals and a confidence in their own beliefs. They were sure that their own political and social philosophers had helped them understand the meaning of freedom and democracy based on natural rights in a way that no other group had.[129] In postwar America, many thought that progressive ideology was bankrupt, but Catholics were ready to embrace it.[130] The burst of reform energy was quickly spent. In the 1920s, new conflicts between Catholics and Protestants were sparked by Prohibition, the emergence of the Ku Klux Klan, and, toward the end of the decade, the presidential candidacy of Alfred E. Smith.

One permanent structure survived the war, though not without its own battle. The NCWC became the National Catholic Welfare Council. Cardinal William O'Connell of Boston, who had opposed "the Bishops' Plan" as socialistic, thought the NCWC infringed on the rights of local ordinaries. He and Cardinal Dennis Dougherty of Philadelphia tried to have the organization suppressed. Rome, at best suspicious of American independence, was especially wary of the term "Council" in the organization's name. Bishop Joseph Schrembs of Toledo, Ohio, defended the NCWC in Rome. Pius XI, who had already authorized the NCWC's dissolution, relented. He made it clear, however, that the organization was not a legislative body, nor did it have conciliar status. To underscore the point, "Council" became "Conference." In 1966 it metamorphosed into a two-tiered structure, the National Catholic Conference of Bishops and the United States Catholic Conference.[131]

O'Connell suffered a temporary setback, but it did not curb his wrath against Ryan. The Cardinal was leery of the priest, not because he condemned socialism, but because he endorsed much of socialism's analysis of society's ills and the remedies proposed.[132] By his own admission, one of the sharpest controversies in which Ryan was embroiled concerned child labor. In 1924, Ryan supported a proposed amendment to the federal Constitution that would regulate child labor. Many Catholics feared that the family would be "sovietized" and that control of children would pass to the government. They also worried that Congress would be empowered to dictate education for all children under eighteen and ring the death knell to Catholic schooling. Some claimed that Ryan was close to heresy in his support of the legislation.[133] Even his long and friendly rapport with Kenkel was strained over the issue. O'Connell put pressure on Archbishop Michael Curley, chancellor of the Catholic University, to curb Ryan, a faculty member. Although Curley did not share Ryan's position, he was furious at O'Connell. The chancellor informed O'Connell that Ryan was at liberty to express his opinions with academic freedom at the university.[134] As it turned out, the amendment was never passed for want of sufficient states' support.

Because John A. Ryan's social thought was based upon traditional neo-Thomism, it was not linked to modernism. Ryan provided new ways of adopting Catholic thought to modern industrialism. On the other hand, James Driscoll and his colleagues were attempting to fashion a modern apologetic. These two developments were to converge in the 1960s.

CHAPTER
6
The Path to Pluralism, 1920–1985

❦

$\mathcal{S}$ince the time of Saint Anselm (1033–1109), theology has been defined as "fides quaerens intellectum," faith seeking understanding. A dominating force in the theological enterprise during what one historian has called the third era of the Catholic church in America was neo-Thomism.[1] That era opened after World War I, and that era brought as well the enactment of legislation to restrict immigration. As a result, the Catholic church was able to stabilize, and the National Catholic Welfare Conference threw its energies into the Americanization of its members. For many outside the Catholic community, the Great War shook to its foundations the intellectual and cultural establishment of the nineteenth century. This has been characterized as a belief in a rational and predictable cosmos and in a moral structure within the universe.[2] Now progress no longer seemed guaranteed, and a mood of complexity and uncertainty prevailed. However, the revolt against formalism in literature and art and the pessimism of the period did not penetrate the American Catholic community. It has been argued that they consciously set out to shape a culture both American and Catholic. They hoped to preserve American idealism, which was being threatened on every side by relativism and skepticism.

Intellectually, Catholic Thomism shared a relationship with nineteenth-century American Enlightenment thinking and Scottish commonsense realism. Both affirmed reason and a belief in an objective moral order in nature. After World War I, American Catholics were

114

for the first time beginning to reap some of the material benefits of the American dream. They were therefore unwilling to share in any pattern of thought that might challenge or shatter that promise. It was the American Catholic community that kept alive the illusion of American innocence for a half-century after the nation had abandoned it.

Neo-Thomism as an objective rational system was enlisted to save the spiritual, intellectual, and human values that were being eroded within society. The fascination with the Middle Ages that characterized some Catholic thinkers stemmed from their conviction that the medieval heritage was one component of the general defense of Western values.[3]

Quite consciously, Catholics continued to build and populate their schools and other charitable institutions. They also set up parallel intellectual organizations to match almost every existing national group. Between World War I and World War II the influence of neo-Thomism as a Catholic philosophical and cultural vision came into its own. In 1921 Virgil Michel, O.S.B., warned that neo-Thomism would come to naught if isolated from modern philosophical movements. By and large that warning fell on deaf ears. Though neo-Thomists did not dialogue with pragmatism, idealism, or the emerging Protestant neoorthodoxy, it has been argued that neo-Thomism was not simply a monolithic form of "common sense philosophy,"[4] but existed in more sophisticated forms. During the decades of the 1930s through the 1950s, American Catholics were influenced by the French convert Jacques Maritain and his native countryman, Etienne Gilson. Gilson, whose work attracted Thomas Merton to the Catholic Church, applied a historical approach to Saint Thomas Aquinas's own philosophy.[5] In the process, he discovered the diversity of scholasticism. Maritain, who resided in America in the 1950s, stressed the central importance of the doctrine of the Mystical Body of Christ. This had tremendous implications for the laity. It increased their awareness of their duty to witness the Christian message to the modern world.

Neo-Thomism has been sharply criticized for its lack of historical consciousness and its closed-mindedness to other avenues of contemporary thought. It did, however, help American Catholics rediscover the sources of their own unity.[6] The movement also fostered a sense of self-confidence that was admired by a few outside the Catholic church. Carried to the extreme, this certitude bordered on arrogance. A year before his premature death in 1938, Virgil Michel, the moving spirit of the liturgical revival in the United States, sounded another warning. He sharply criticized the American Catholic Philosophical Association for its lack of challenging philosophical thought and an apologetics that betrayed an "irritating smugness of convictions."[7]

Two American Catholic prelates of the period were explicitly and

consciously Thomistic—the Dominican John T. McNicholas, O.P., and
Fulton J. Sheen. Appointed archbishop of Cincinnati in 1925,
McNicholas has studied the *Summa Theologica* of Saint Thomas
Aquinas at the Collegio San Tommaso in Rome. Sheen, who became
bishop of Rochester shortly after the Second Vatican Council, was
graduated from the Superior Institute of Philosophy of Louvain.
McNicholas's career has been identified as the "Thomistic Apogee."[8]
The Dominican had a clear distaste for modernity and saw Thomism
as offering a synthesis to a fractured world.[9] His aim was to have the
priests of Cincinnati become clear-thinking scholastics. To that end
he sent a record number, more than one hundred diocesan priests,
to European Thomistic centers.[10]

As a trustee of the Catholic University of America, he became
chairman of the Pontifical Commission for Ecclesiastical Studies in
1934. This brought him into conflict with the fifth rector of the university, Bishop James Hugh Ryan, who had been appointed six years
earlier. Ryan had restructured the institution along American lines
with distinct schools for graduates and undergraduates in the arts
and sciences. Ryan's emphasis on research was criticized. McNicholas
thought the Rector was secularizing the university and was trying to
make it "a little Harvard." Through his influence in Rome, Mc-
Nicholas had him transferred to the Diocese of Omaha, Nebraska.

As chairman of the Pontifical Commission for Ecclesiastical Studies, McNicholas brought the independent Sulpician Seminary in
Washington, D.C., under the control of the Catholic University as the
Theological College. He also negotiated the affiliation of ten seminaries
with the university. Described as obsessed with the "mind of the
church," which he equated with that of the Holy See, McNicholas
moved the Catholic University and its affiliates along the path of Roman centralization.[11] He and his Pontifical Commission reinforced
the notion that Roman ideas were normative.

With Edward Mooney of Rochester and Samuel A. Stritch of Milwaukee, McNicholas formed an episcopal troika that dominated the
National Catholic Welfare Council for many years.[12] The Dominican
member of the trio often acted against the wishes of the other members of the Catholic University's board of trustees. He was far removed
from any notion of episcopal coresponsibility and blind to John Lancaster Spalding's vision of a broad intellectual culture for priests.[13]

No attempt has been made to defend McNicholas as an intellectual,
but the opposite is true in the case of Fulton J. Sheen.[14] Sheen's doctoral dissertation, published as *God and Intelligence in Modern Philosophy* in the mid-1920s, made Sheen the first American who was
awarded the Cardinal Mercier Prize for International Philosophy. For

twenty-five years the famous orator held the chair of Apologetics at the Catholic University. His message was a blend of scholasticism, synthesis, and social teaching. One author has called him the most successful representative of "everyman's Thomism."[15]

It has been argued that Sheen consciously chose to be a popularizer and always considered himself an intellectual, though not part of the intelligentsia. That group, he argued, is separated from the people. "The true intellectual," Sheen wrote, "is never separated from the masses."[16] Beyond question is the power of his personal appeal. As both a radio and a television celebrity, he enjoyed an audience estimated in the millions.[17]

Those who remember watching Sheen on television may need a historian to remind them that the prelate was not simply against communism but for social justice. His television theatrics were an embarrassment to some American Catholics, but his anticommunism helped them identify with the mood of the nation and with the religious revivals of the 1950s. One historian has remarked that it is difficult to exaggerate what Sheen accomplished for the American Catholic church or to calculate his contribution to the general public.[18] There is truth in the judgment that Sheen's early promise as a potential American Jacques Maritain remained unfulfilled. He exploited his gift for clever rhetoric and let scholarship slide.[19] As bishop of Rochester he did show his commitment to providing an intellectual climate for Saint Bernard's Seminary; he broadened the scope of the curriculum, tried to make the institution an ecumenical model, and as a part of his agenda initiated a Catholic-Marxist dialogue. Unfortunately, Sheen's tenure in Rochester was racked by controversy, but he did succeed in forging a lasting spirit of ecumenical cooperation between Saint Bernard's and Colgate-Rochester Divinity School.[20]

During the years when Sheen was reaching millions of homes, a definite shift was taking place within the Catholic community. Thousands of its members had returned home from the Second World War. They were attending college in record numbers under the provisions of the so-called G.I. Bill of Rights, technically called the Servicemen's Readjustment Act. Over 50 percent of those who taught philosophy in these Catholic colleges and universities identified themselves as Neo-Thomists.[21] The historical recovery of Thomism had been advanced in many of these institutions. *The Modern Schoolman*, the first journal dedicated to scholasticism, appeared in 1925 and was followed by the Jesuit journal *Thought* the next year. *The Thomist* made a later debut in 1940. The Dominican Walter Farrell, whose *Companion to the Summa* helped popularize the theological writing of Saint Thomas Aquinas, was its moving spirit. The journal was, in part, a response to the "growing interest in Thomistic studies manifested today even outside the church"—so note the minutes of the journal's first board meeting, held on February 17, 1938.[22]

Almost two decades earlier another journal had already entered the growing field of Catholic literature. *The Commonweal* was born in 1924 during a period of national and international stability. It was also a decade that had retreated from the ideal of social melioration. Initially, *The Commonweal* represented an upper-class Anglo-American Catholicism, and some of the journal's early backers had roots that traced back to the founding families of Maryland. Though never intended as an exclusively lay journal, within a few years it became recognized as the voice of the Catholic laity.[23] The editor was Michael Williams, a native of Nova Scotia, a seasoned journalist. Unlike the early magazine staff who were heavily represented by Ivy League alumni, Williams, called a "maverick genius," was the graduate of no college. Several years later, George Shuster joined the staff, and for thirteen years Williams and Shuster dominated the journal.[24] Shuster, born of German parents in Wisconsin, was a professor of English at Notre Dame from 1919 until he joined the staff of *The Commonweal*. He was appreciative of Thomism's deep passion for reality, but he opposed what he considered abuses in neo-Thomism's abstraction and "unearthly formalism." Because of this cool approach, he has been called "a romantic in a pasture of logicians."[25]

Shuster wanted to help Catholics feel at home in American thought. He admitted to being elitist in deliberately patterning *The Commonweal* on the sophisticated *New Republic*. Though *The Commonweal* was dedicated to advocating the "Catholic outlook on life and the Catholic philosophy of living," it provided a forum for those of different beliefs or no belief at all.[26]

A vocal critic of the intellectual climate of the American Catholic community, in 1925 Shuster goaded his coreligionists to shake off their mental torpor. Many angrily rejected his suggestion that their church had produced no scholars nor public-spirited citizens. Three years later, a Catholic candidate was nominated for the first time by a major political party to run for the highest office in the land. Alfred E. Smith had been the governor of New York and had successfully won that elected position four times. One of the issues in the presidential race was Smith's opposition to enforcement of the Eighteenth Amendment, which had established prohibition. The religious factor surfaced when the *Atlantic Monthly* published an article by a prominent New York lawyer, Charles C. Marshall. He questioned whether a Catholic could in conscience uphold the Constitution with its provision for civil and religious freedom.[27]

The editors of *The Commonweal* maintained an official position of neutrality during the campaign. They did, however, print a refutation of Marshall's article written by Father John A. Ryan, professor at the Catholic University. He and Moorhouse F. X. Miller, S.J., had published *The State and the Church* in 1922.[28] The book created quite a stir and has rightly been called "one of the most frequently employed [against Catholics] and scare exciting ever penned by American Catholics."[29] Taking a position almost unheard of among their native co-religionists, the two priests supported the contention of Pope Leo XIII that the state must recognize the true religion, namely the Catholic church. The authors pointed out that this only applies in Catholic countries. They recognized the protective provision of religious liberty found in the constitutions of most modern states. However, they argued, one "cannot yield up the principles of eternal and unchangeable truth." If however, they continued, non-Catholic sects would decline to such a point, the political proscription of them might become feasible and expedient.[30] When *The State and the Church* became a campaign issue, the strongest reassurance that Ryan could offer to the public was that the realization of a Catholic majority in the United States was so remote a possibility that no practical person would give the idea a second thought.[31]

Indeed, quite a few Americans were disturbed. In a book-length response by Winfred E. Garrison, *Catholicism and the American Mind*, the author articulated what was bothering a number of Protestants. Garrison concluded that *The State and the Church* was "much more interesting than anything a non-Catholic could say about Catholic intolerance, and much more convincing."[32]

Smith was soundly defeated by the Republican candidate, Herbert Hoover. In the aftermath, Ryan tried to distance himself from the defeat. He claimed that the only argument in the election that might enjoy any real plausibility, the danger that a Catholic majority might work for union of church and State, got little attention.[33]

A number of factors, the religious factor included, combined to defeat Smith. He was against Prohibition and had a connection with machine politics. At a time when anti-Catholicism ran high, his religion was not a positive factor in some polling places. His defeat had a chilling effect on a generation of Catholic children who grew up with the suspicion that it was useless for them to aspire to the highest office in America. Catholics were hurt, and Father Gillis, editor of the *Catholic World*, could only resolutely remark, "We shall not wither up and blow away."[34] Soon more than the Catholic community was aching. The world was shocked and unprepared for the Wall Street crash of 1929 and the bitter worldwide economic depression that set in. The Bishops' Plan for Social Reconstruction, which had languished during the 1920s, achieved a new relevancy. Its author, John A. Ryan, a social liberal and theological conservative, rose to some prominence. Writing forty years after Leo XIII's labor encyclical, *Rerum Novarum*, Pope Pius XI issued *Quadragesimo Anno* in 1931. Like his predecessor, he supported the rights of modern industrial labor. His encyclical prompted Joseph M. Corrigan, the rector of the Catholic University, to remark, "This is a great vindication for John Ryan."[35]

The decades of the 1930s and 1940s have been called an extremely fertile period for American Catholics. They were exposed to an array of Catholic thinkers who expressed new and more mature understandings of Christian doctrine and its relationship to the problem of modernity. It was through the efforts of the social philosophers John A. Ryan and Paul Hanly Furfey that so-called Catholic social justice courses found their way into the college curriculum.[36] Virgil Michel's *Orate Fratres*, now *Worship*, was the leading journal of the liturgical movement, which was deeply in touch with the social emphasis of the period.

As Catholics, along with other Americans, joined the ranks of the unemployed, Ryan continued to examine the principles of social ethics and to argue that the state was obliged by the norms of distributive justice. Using Thomistic principles, Ryan pushed ahead for practical applications. After some initial doubts, the Catholic priest endorsed the New Deal of Franklin Delano Roosevelt. He welcomed the relief for unemployed, the Agricultural Adjustment Act, the National Industrial Recovery Bill, banking reform, and the Tennessee Valley Authority.

Ryan's support for the New Deal brought him into a classic confrontation with another popular Catholic priest, Father Charles Coughlin of the Shrine of the Little Flower in Detroit. At first an F.D.R. supporter, Coughlin became enraged when America entered the World Court. During Roosevelt's campaign for reelection, Coughlin—the "radio priest," a superior orator with a vast listening audience—accused the president and his administration of being communists.[37] Ryan took to the airwaves to defend Roosevelt and to dispel the red scare.

From the beginning, the editors of *The Commonweal* kept a wary eye on Coughlin. They were convinced that he was more a demagogue than an intellectual. After the Coughlin-Ryan exchange, the journal praised the latter for his appeal to reason and condemned the former for his lack of logic.[38] However, Archbishop Michael Curley, Ryan's superior, was annoyed with his public stand. One source, the *Catholic Review*, published the opinion that both Coughlin and Ryan had made spectacles of themselves.[39]

The heart of the issue was Coughlin's monetary theory. Before his disaffection, Coughlin was far more politically involved with Roosevelt and the New Deal than Ryan ever was.[40] Hurt because F.D.R. ignored the radio priest's proposed fiscal policies, Coughlin turned venomous.[41] He continued to preach his theory that monetary ills were a result of a conspiracy of international bankers. He became stridently anti-Semitic and was silenced from broadcasting under government pressure after the country entered the Second World War.[42]

History will forever identify the embodiment of anti-Semitism in the person of the maniacal Adolf Hitler. In 1936 *The Commonweal* editors joined with individuals of other denominations who called for either a boycott of the Olympic Games scheduled for that year or a change of location from the slated city of Berlin. Not all were gifted with the same clarity of vision to perceive Hitler's true colors at that time. For his part, George Shuster was publicly rebuked by the bishop of New York, Francis McIntyre. The editor of *The Commonweal* also found himself on the receiving end of bags full of hate mail, many of which, it has been suggested, were written by Coughlin supporters.[43]

The Spanish Civil War, which erupted that same year, provoked a more heated debate between Catholics and non-Catholics in the United States than in any other country.[44] Both sides were generally ill informed of the causes that unleashed a fury devouring the lives of nearly seven thousand priests and religious and untold numbers of lay people. Most were victims simply because they were Catholics. The fury has been judged as a visible indictment of centuries of misguided Catholic attempts to tailor the essence of Christianity to fit narrow parochial ends. Some Spanish Catholics who survived the bloodletting protested the brutality of the counterattack led by Francisco Franco, who was backed by Nazi Germany and Fascist Italy; however, a majority remained silent during the ruthless bombing of Madrid. They and the bulk of Catholics in the United States supported a regime characterized as one built on oppression and special privileges.

The Jesuit editors of *Thought* reprinted articles from the Society's popular journal, *America*. It had taken the lead in supporting Franco and argued that his counterforces were both democratic and Christian. Most Catholic journals seemed to agree. Only *The Catholic Worker*, the fledgling newspaper under the leadership of Peter Maurin and Dorothy Day, argued against any use of force in Spain and for Christian pacifism.[45] The staff of *The Commonweal* was severely divided over the war. George Shuster had openly depicted Franco's regime as reactionary and militaristic. He challenged the notion that the Spanish allies, Hitler and Mussolini, were saving Europe from the communists. His view was decidedly unpopular and subscriptions fell to the degree that the future of the journal was in jeopardy. Michael Williams, with what has been called "a marvelous combination of pragmatism and morality," threw *The Commonweal*'s support in favor of Franco. To save his intellectual integrity, George Shuster relinquished his post as the managing editor of the journal.[46] Carlton J. Hayes, a distinguished professor of history at Columbia University, a convert to Catholicism, and a member of *The Commonweal*'s board of directors, worked quietly behind the scenes to tone down excessive pro-Franco nationalism during the controversy.[47] At times that effort proved impossible. With his sense of the dramatic and the symbolic and with his unbounded enthusiasm, Michael Williams orchestrated a pro-Franco rally in Madison Square Garden on May 19, 1937. However, the attendance was only half of what the mercurial Williams had anticipated, and the lack of enthusiasm left him crushed. Hayes had been totally opposed to the rally and had distanced his name from it. Within a year, the board of directors, at the injunction of Hayes, removed Williams as editor. The Garden event was only one of a series of factors that led to the decision. Williams, always a colorful and controversial character, was a sick man plagued by a host of emotional problems as well as alcoholism. After a prolonged illness, he died in 1950. In retrospect Williams has been judged a first-rate journalist and reporter. *The Commonweal*, for which he labored fifteen years, has been called perhaps the most significant lay enterprise and achievement of American Catholicism.[48] A mark of its distinction is the fact that Carlton J. Hayes served as Roosevelt's World War II ambassador to Spain.[49]

It has been argued that the Catholics of the 1920s needed and cultivated the myth of American innocence as a mark of their distinctiveness.[50] It gave them a sense of unity and security against the larger culture by which they had been rejected. The fact that this self-imposed and conspicuous isolation from the mainstream of contemporary literature continued relatively unabated until the 1950s has come under scrutiny and harsh judgment.

George Shuster of *The Commonweal* has been singled out as the "one authentic hero" in an otherwise lackluster story of American Catholic literary attitudes during the period under discussion.[51] He recognized the "problem" was created by the great American literary figures who either publicly rejected their Catholicism or agonized over it and distanced themselves. Among the former groups were Theodore Dreiser, Ernest Hemingway, and James T. Farrell; prominent among the latter were F. Scott Fitzgerald and Eugene O'Neill.[52] For O'Neill in particular, the exploration of Catholic culture was both painful and profound. Considered the most distinguished of American Catholic writers, he had to live apart from the church to be able to write at all.[53] Shuster did not accept the thesis that religion and art are incompatible. What these artists rejected was not the authentic Catholic spirit but American Catholicism, which they understood as little more than middle-class primness. In his study entitled *The Catholic Spirit in America*, published in 1927, Shuster identified Ralph Waldo Emerson and Walt Whitman as the first to speak of America as an intellectual concept rather than a mere geographical entity. They dipped into the wells of the Catholic spirit and shared the vision that humans need not be enslaved by culture but can transcend it. Shuster was pained by the dearth of creative American Catholic literature. "Our books are dull and asleep," he told his readers; "our young men follow other gods." Shuster placed the blame squarely on the shoulders of the majority of American Catholic writers who insisted on identifying art with apologetics. He upbraided the Catholic reading public who were blind to the "beautiful and mystical insight" presented by some contemporary writing because they did not approve of the view of life presented.[54] What Shuster's associate, Carlton Hayes, considered an obligation for American Catholics was never realized, not even acknowledged, by most of his coreligionists. Hayes urged that they contribute more than their numerical quota of first-rate artists and critics to American culture and civilization. Because Catholics remained closed to the remarkable power of contemporary literature, they not only lost touch with the American mainstream but even with their own Catholic heritage. It has been pointed out that two American Catholic poets of some stature, the converts Thomas Merton and Robert Lowell, remained anomalous to their coreligionists for a generation.

Part of the failure of American Catholic literature has been traced to the literary critics of *The Commonweal* and *America* as well as to the formation of the Catholic Poetry Society.[55] *The Great Gatsby*, F. Scott Fitzgerald's powerful novel of 1925, was judged "mediocre" by *The Commonweal* and inferior by *America*.[56] The Catholic Poetry Society had been established to harbor its own poets against "the strange bedfellowship with our contemporary Sandburgs," so that they would not be "yoked with the wildest opposites."[57]

One aesthetic area in which Catholics did exercise influence was the film industry. In the early days of talking pictures, the industry was supposed to regulate itself, though it rarely did. By 1934, the National Catholic Welfare Conference established the National Catholic Office for Motion Pictures, popularly called the Legion of Decency. It enlisted millions of Catholics who solemnly pledged to avoid movies not approved by the Legion. Because of the potential economic backlash, movie moguls capitulated to Catholic demands for a long time. Those outside the church resented this infringement on their freedom and the Legion was a source of Catholic-Protestant tension until its eclipse in the 1960s. The most celebrated, but certainly not the only film to evoke mass demonstrations against theater owners who showed "condemned" films, was Roberto Rossellini's film, "The Miracle." A court battle was fought and won to suppress the film, but it was a pyrrhic victory, for the decision was overruled by the Supreme Court in 1952. The Justices pointed out that it was not "the business of government in our nation to suppress real or imagined attacks upon a particular religious doctrine."[58] One of the Justices quoted an editorial that had been published by *The Commonweal* in the midst of the brouhaha. It claimed that Catholic pressure to censor movies made those outside the church "feel as if they were being treated like children by an alien force that didn't give two cents for their personal liberty."[59] The issues gave substance to Paul Blanshard's 1949 blockbuster, *American Freedom and Catholic Power*, which argued a fundamental incompatibility between the two concepts and, at the same time, capitalized on his target's lack of historical sensibility.[60] Walter Kerr, drama critic for *The Commonweal* during the 1950s, wrote that the Catholic taste in motion pictures had been identified with the well-meaning second-rate.[61] It was "frozen at the 'unobjectionable' or purity with popcorn level, a level which if pursued down the ages would have called into question nearly every literary or dramatic masterpiece ever produced."[62]

Despite its insistence on a rigorous, almost puritanical attitude toward sex and the depiction of raw passion, Catholic periodic fiction of the period displayed what has been judged as an alarming surrender to the seduction of contemporary culture.[63] Though Catholic short stories of the period have been judged literarily wretched, they are important as a historic indicator, for they reached a wider audience than did church teaching by the end of the 1950s. From the 1930s to the 1950s Catholic writers began to espouse the American Protestant myth about the dangers and destructive power of the cities. Life in the country was extolled as the ideal way to preserve faith and community. The irony of the situation rests in the fact that most Catholics of the period were urban dwellers. It was there that they had to work out their salvation.[64]

One Catholic short-story writer of the period had the distinction of being featured in both the secular and the Catholic press in the mid-1930s. Harry Sylvester, a Brooklyn-born son of a Catholic mother and a Jewish father, was graduated from the University of Notre Dame in 1930. A talented essayist and crafter of short stories, he is reported to have been the highest-paid fiction writer for *Collier's Magazine* since the famous Damon Runyan.[65] Sylvester's writing was a harbinger of the change that was beginning to occur within American Catholicism.

He wanted Catholics to break down the ghetto wall and engage constructively in contemporary society armed with the papal social teaching. Sylvester was critical of the legalistic mind-set of his co-religionists and of their bourgeois spirit. He lambasted their sexual prudery, and rebelled against the dichotomy he saw between Catholic belief and Catholic practice. His best novel, *Moon Gaffney*, was published in 1947. In the story, Aloysius "Moon" Gaffney is a minor Tammany Hall figure who opts to follow the inspiration of the papal encyclicals on social justice and of Catholic radicals inspired by the Catholic Worker movement. In the process Moon falls out of favor with his friends, his church, and the political machine. Gaffney ends up as a labor lawyer defending blacks and communists. Sylvester himself broke with the church in the early 1950s.

John F. Powers, another writer influenced by the Catholic Worker movement, drew some attention from non-Catholic critics for his control of the techniques of storytelling. Born in Jacksonville, Illinois, in 1917, he was educated by the Franciscans in Quincy College in Illinois. Of his first ten short stories, eight had strong social themes. He fearlessly depicted the injustices committed by Catholics against blacks and Jews.[66] A deliberate craftsman, Powers had his stories published in *The New Yorker* in the 1950s and the 1960s.[67] He frequently wrote on the improbable life of the parish priest with both compassion and sharp criticism. In 1962, he received the National Book award for his first novel *Morte D'Urban*. Powers's use of "Catholic decor" was the device he employed for unmasking scandal. The central problem with which Powers grappled has been defined as the question of stewardship, an issue that has plagued the American Catholic church since the nineteenth century. Different answers have been given to the interpretation of material wealth as a blessing or a curse.

In the novel, Father Urban, Powers's most complex and compelling character, attempts to win rich and powerful friends to help bring his religious order into the American mainstream. Eventually, Urban realizes that most attempts at stewardship are morally compromising. At the end of the novel, Urban's conversion demanded that he become a secular loser.[68] The force behind Powers's mature work has been identified as dialectical tension between the actual and the ideal, between secularism and divinity.[69] After twenty-five years, Powers completed his second novel. He admits that the use of "Catholic decor" is not easily employed in contemporary society. Two convictions, however, have remained constant for Powers. Stewardship is still a problem for the Catholic church in America, which continues to identify the church with national expansionism. All Christians, like his earlier character, Father Urban, are under the obligation to endure material loss over spiritual loss.[70]

Flannery O'Connor entered the small field of American Catholic writers of distinction in the 1950s. Born in Savannah, Georgia, in 1925, she completed two novels before her death thirty-nine years later.[71] She is best remembered for her short stories, and her third published collection, *Completed Stories*, printed posthumously in 1971, was selected for the National Book Award in fiction a year later.[72] Her stories were set in the rural Bible Belt as a foil against which she satirized secularism. She was convinced that the religious impulse had been "bred out of certain sections of the population like the wings have been bred off certain chickens."[73] Her work is known for its use of unusual characters and extreme situations. She wanted to write what has been called prophetic fiction. Her protagonists were usually uninterested in the spiritual dimension of reality. Through the use of the unexpected or even the grotesque, she prepares her characters for their moment of grace in the real world. O'Connor chose her method deliberately. She believed that her technique was necessary. "To the hard of hearing you shout, and for the almost-blind you draw large and startling figures," she said.[74]

O'Connor was critical of what she called the "Catholic smugness" characteristic of the period. She complained about the "vapid Catholicism" in which she had been reared. She believed that "you have to save yourself from it some day or dry up."[75]

Creators of fiction were not the only ones who sent signals that all was not well in the American Catholic church. In 1952, Walter Ong, a young Jesuit scholar, pointed to his native coreligionists' failure to grasp intellectually their real part in the "historical process as a historical process." He chided them for their romantic fascination with and their illusions about their medieval heritage. As a case in point, the Jesuit pointed to American Catholics' "magnificent educational system," which they mistakenly understood as a "recovery effort" of past glories. Not even during the height of the Middle Ages, Ong argued, had the church been even remotely connected with such a massive educational effort.[76]

The year before, Paul Blanshard had launched a second attack against the Catholic church. *Communism, Democracy, and Catholic Power* was a *tour de force* in which the author equated Catholicism with communism and declared that both systems produced "heroes and martyrs of sublime courage."[77] Unlike his Catholic contemporaries, Ong did not see Blanshard's works as a "recrudescence of the mad Protestant anti-Catholicism manifested periodically," though ever decreasingly. He saw that Blanshard's books were raising the same disturbing questions that were precipitating a crisis in the American Catholic mind of the day. At issue was "the place of the church in terms of America's place in history." Ong almost welcomed Blanshard's capitalization on American Catholic weakness, lack of a well-developed historical sensibility. Because of his attacks, Blanshard had forced Catholics to plunge into history.[78]

The Jesuit John Courtney Murray had begun to study the problem of church–state relations in the mid-1940s. Much of the opposition that members of the Catholic church had encountered questioned their real intent and political aspirations should they become a majority. The fears Blanshard articulated about Catholic abrogation of non-Catholics' civil liberties were real and needed to be addressed. As Murray assessed the situation, Blanshard represented not the old Protestant nativism but the premise that a democracy required a naturalist, secularist philosophy. This emphasis, that religion had no place in secular life, Murray saw not as freedom *of* religion, but freedom *from* religion that would lead to tyranny.[79] Nonetheless, Murray held out the hope in the late 1950s that America's four "conspiracies," the Protestant, Catholic, Jewish, and secularist, could "conspire into one conspiracy that will be American society—civil, just, free, peaceful, one."[80]

It was not simply those outside the church who created problems for American Catholics. Early in 1950 a Catholic graduate of Marquette University capitalized on the Soviet scare that had been unleashed by a confluence of events. In the face of Cold War paranoia which had developed between the American-Russian superpowers, Senator Joe McCarthy promised to be tough on communist infiltrators in the United States. What he unleashed, however, was a witch-hunt often based on flimsy or shabby "evidence." McCarthy saw communists everywhere—in the State Department, in the armed services, and in the entertainment industry. The results were painful. Reputations were threatened or lost. Actors and musicians were blacklisted and were often out of work.

The bulk of the Catholic press backed the senator and his tactics. The most vocal anti-McCarthy Catholic was John Cogley of *The Commonweal*. Many of his coreligionists angrily rose to the senator's defense. By the end of 1954, McCarthyism had run its course. Fully 66 percent of his fellow senators had voted to censure him after his activities had been investigated.[81]

McCarthy's rantings and bombast had bordered on the irrational. Unfortunately, many outside the Catholic church branded his fanaticism as characteristic of his antidemocratic church. After the dust had settled, Walter Ong sent forth another signal of the wave of the American Catholic future. Rather than retreat from the world that had been the stance of American Catholics during its "Age of Innocence," the Jesuit called for a dialogue with the secular community that would be based on personalism. Respect for the human person, Ong argued, was the basis of democracy. Dialogue was a way of preserving unity and preserving difference. The promise of a free society is realized, Ong argued, not by love for a vague secularist, abstract humanity, but by love for concrete individuals.[82]

John Courtney Murray continued to grapple with the problem of religious freedom. He sought to provide a theoretical base for what had been the almost universal declaration of American Catholics from the time of John Carroll onward. They would never, even if in the majority, change the American Constitution's provision for the separation of church and State. Murray had accepted the principles of America's "Religion of Civility" and went out of his way not to offend.[83] As a result, he gained Protestants' and secularists' respect as a clear and formidable articulator of Catholic positions.[84] Actually, the fiercest opponents to his work came from his theological colleagues who had a powerful ally in Rome.

In the late 1940s and early 1950s Murray was involved in a scholarly debate carried on in two important Catholic journals. Joseph Fenton, editor of the *American Ecclesiastical Review,* and his ally, the Redemptorist Francis J. Connell, were lineal descendants of John A. Ryan and Moorhouse F. X. Miller. Echoing the papal position that the Catholic church was the only true church, they argued that it had a right to protection and support by the civil government. They believed that what they supported was the unerring teaching of the Catholic church. Murray responded in the pages of *Theological Studies,* a journal that he had helped establish. The traditionalist thinking represented by Fenton and Connell rested on the century-old "thesis-hypothesis" argument. As Murray understood it, the "thesis" or "ideal" relationship was one in which the Catholic faith was the majority faith and Catholic principles could, without qualification, be applied. The "hypothesis" relationship applied where the church was a minority faith, as in America, and the church gave up its right to legal establishment. This situation, of itself, was a tolerable evil.[85] In terms of religious freedom, what the "thesis-hypothesis" position implied was tolerance wherever it was necessary and intolerance wherever it was possible. Murray, with a keen historical sense and a perspective based on Thomistic natural law and American political theory, argued that the proponents of the "ideal" situation operated with a methodology that transformed concrete, historical facts into immutable and transhistorical principles. Little or no recognition was given to historical determination. This approach stood in sharp contrast with his own methodology.[86] Murray saw the problem of separation of church and state as a historically conditioned reality, not a metaphysical problem.

In 1954, the same year that the less-than-intellectual Joe McCarthy was unmasked, Murray, the theological sophisticate, came under an ecclesiastical cloud. Over a decade earlier, he had locked horns with one of his adversaries, the Redemptorist Francis Connell. Connell, among others, thought that the theology taught to lay college students should emphasize the "demonstrability of truth from the revealed word of God" as it was in seminaries. Murray advocated an approach that emphasized the "livability of the word of God," which would be appropriate to lay life "and serve as an antidote to secularism."[87]

Those who now opposed Murray at home had a powerful ally in Rome. The head of the Supreme Congregation of the Holy Office, Cardinal Alfredo Ottaviani, charged with defending Catholic orthodoxy against deviants, insisted on the "traditional" interpretation of the "thesis-hypothesis" theory of church-state relations. The July 23, 1953 edition of the *New York Times* carried his defense as a front page story.[88] Less than a year later Murray suggested that the Cardinal's position was not in harmony with that of the reigning pontiff, Pius XII. Subsequently, the American Jesuit was required to submit all of his work on the church–state issue to his superior general in Rome. As a result, Murray put down his pen and the issue remained unresolved.[89]

Meanwhile, the Catholic laity, theologically better educated than ever, were demanding a voice in running their own institution. The call came from both the left and the right. It was one issue on which the liberals typified by *The Commonweal* and the conservative view embodied in William Buckley, Jr., could join in common cause. Although Buckley's journal, the *National Review*, was never labeled a Catholic journal, most of its early contributors were Catholic; though at odds with their liberal coreligionists on a number of issues, they could agree on the historical and dogmatic meaning of Catholicism. This state of things would soon change.

Before that paradigmatic shift occurred, several other figures must be considered. Gustave Weigel joined his Jesuit friends in the 1950s by suggesting that religion must recover its prophetic function. It must take a stand against the current secular climate. The churches cannot merely accommodate themselves to the demands of culture as they had on the question of atomic power and the devastation of Hiroshima and Nagasaki during World War II. Even Russia had appealed to religion during that period in its titanic struggle with Germany. The Jesuit felt that America was asking religion to solve its problems, a work not consonant with the churches.[90]

Despite the prophetic stance which the Catholic church would later struggle to adopt, Weigel is best remembered for his work in ecumenism. He stoutly defended his church's refusal to join the World

Council of Churches, but he ardently strove to understand the Protestant mind.[91] There had been little by way of ecumenical exchange on the part of the American Catholic community in over half a century. The one exception was the Church Unity octave held annually from January 18 to January 25. It had been established by the Episcopalian Father Paul Wattson before he entered the Catholic church in 1909. The Society of the Atonement which he had founded took as its special vocation the reunion of Christendom.[92]

For Wattson and for Weigel, reunion meant a return to Rome. The Jesuit understood, however, that their "solution" to the problem would be unacceptable to most of those Protestants who were loyally committed to the Reformation and to those who found failure in both traditions. However, a compromise solution would be unacceptable to everyone.

The official position of the Roman Catholic church in the late 1940s and early 1950s was one of censure. *Humani Generis*, issued by Pope Pius XII in 1950, warned against "a false use of the historical method . . . in dealing with the problems of philosophy or with doctrines of the Christian religion."[93] Consequently, American Catholics were intimidated and kept themselves aloof from entangling alliances. It was Weigel's friend John Courtney Murray who drew him into ecumenism. In 1948, Murray invited Weigel to become a specialist in Protestant thought for *Theological Studies* after the latter had returned from an eleven-year teaching assignment in Santiago, Chile.[94]

As a systematic thinker, Weigel searched for a unifying principle by which he could address the myriad forms of Protestantism. He realized that there was a fundamental methodological difference between Catholic and Protestant conceptions of religious truth. Protestants believe that they can know the practice of the Apostolic church through scriptures illuminated by the guidance of the Holy Spirit. Then the divine message is "judged" in accord with one's experience and assumptions about God. Catholics do not "judge" the divine message, but "receive" it as interpreted by the "ever-living magisterium." Weigel admitted that Catholic dogma developed or "evolved." Its core content, however, remained unchanged. New circumstances and the import of historical forces sharpened awareness, and consequently, deeper and wider levels of meaning came to be expressed. In the early 1960s Weigel judged that the existing historical moment, in which a stable ecumenical framework was being attempted, was itself unstable. He believed that scientific, materialistic humanism, the basis of both communism and contemporary democracy, was not capable of the vision necessary to construct a "soul saving" society. It was not capable of instructing humanists how to use science constructively as long as the naturalist's goal continued to be simply the fulfillment of the individual's instinctual drives. For survival, only the "universal submission of man to an absolute, commanding, personal God, transcendental and infinitely greater than man," would suffice.[95]

Because he sensed the urgency of the times, Weigel was anxious to involve Catholics in the ecumenical dialogue underway in America. However, on the question of dogma he has rightly been called an "uncompromising ecumenist." His own theological writings on Protestantism bear the general negative tones of the day. Because of his innate graciousness, genial personality, and warm heart, however, he was able to escape in practice the narrow confines of this theory. He worked untiringly to chart a course for the churches to "converge." Through mutual understanding and dialogue, he wanted churches to move closer and closer together. After he and the Paulist editor of the *Catholic World*, John B. Sheerin, attended the North American Faith and Order Study Conference in 1957, Weigel realized that unity already existed. The two were the first Catholic informal observers ever to attend the meeting. Afterward, he wrote, "Christ Himself made all ontologically one by his saving work. . . . The work, then, of the divided churches is to manifest even more visibly this basic unity which is there."[96]

Weigel's concern for ecumenism was given official reinforcement during the pontificate of Pope John XXIII. As apostolic delegate to Bulgaria, Angelo Roncalli spent ten years in Sophia and an equal number of years in Istanbul. This gave Roncalli the advantage of approaching ecumenism from his personal experience with Orthodox Christianity. In 1959 he announced that he intended to convoke an ecumenical council. His decision, he said, was born of an "inspiration which struck Us in the humility of Our heart, like an unexpected and irresistible command."[97]

John XXIII worked for peace and justice in the frigid climate of the Cold War, which had developed between Russia and the United States during the 1950s. Out of his concern for unity and peace, the pope also worried about "our dear separated brothers." He seemed anxious, as one author put it, "to provide for and succor the whole of humanity; he seemed less preoccupied with the visible church than with the world as a whole. Here, indeed, was a revolution."[98]

A revolution on a smaller scale was also taking place in America. For the second time a Catholic was making a bid for the presidency. He, too, was running on the Democratic ticket, but the similarities between John F. Kennedy and Alfred E. Smith ended there. Kennedy was a young senator from Massachusetts, the son of a wealthy Harvard alumnus who had been Roosevelt's special ambassador at the coronation of Pius XII in 1939. Also a Harvard graduate, John F. Kennedy felt estranged from his articulate coreligionists with Catholic educational backgrounds. He told John Cogley, who left *The Commonweal* to work with the Kennedy campaign, "It is hard for a Harvard man to answer questions in theology." On the trail he was not left to his own devices. Cogley, the son of working-class parents, was there to help. He had been the first layperson to matriculate in the Theology school of the University of Fribourg, Switzerland.

It came as no surprise that the question of the candidate's religion became an election issue. Kennedy met the challenge in a nondefensive, coolly detached, and urbane style. Perhaps the most critical moment of his campaign was his nationally televised appearance before the Ministerial Association of Greater Houston, Texas. To ensure that his address would not offend Catholic sensibilities, his speech was read over the phone to John Courtney Murray. His staff prepared him for any questions that might come from the audience.[99]

In 1960, Kennedy was narrowly elected president, and that same year, John Courtney Murray published his famous *We Hold These Truths: Catholic Reflections on the American Proposition*. It was the fruit of fifteen years of reflection and rated the cover story of *Time* magazine. Four years later, when a Georgetown undergraduate asked Murray to autograph his copy, the distinguished scholar graciously complied, remarking, with just the right touch of self-deprecation, "Is that still knocking around?"[100] In his writings, Murray strove to develop a statement on religious freedom that was based on natural law and would be applicable universally. To answer his critics, the Jesuit insisted that his position on church–state relations was the original teaching espoused by Saint Augustine and based on the two-cities concept, those of God and man. This distinction was lost when "Christian" states were established that merged political and religious functions in the same society.[101]

The central theological concern for Murray was to emphasize the changelessness of the church's sociopolitical doctrine, yet adapt these to the actual historical situation. As he saw it, the principles of Catholic teaching on church and state were known only in historical exchanges. Murray concluded that the traditional Catholic arguments for religious liberty were essentially irrelevant to the question of the civil right to religious freedom. That is a juridical matter because the government is incompetent to judge the truth or error of one's convictions. It is, however, not only proper but necessary that a political society guarantee the immunity of its citizens from coercion in religious matters.[102] The "ideal" of the union of church and State, which the Vatican had clung to so tenaciously, Murray concluded, was not Catholic doctrine. It simply represented an outmoded way of thinking dictated by the circumstances of Continental history.[103] Murray's line of reasoning did not please those few American traditionalists who held the "thesis-hypothesis" theory or the secularists who were uncomfortable with this notion of "concordia" or harmony between church and state, which allowed for cooperation.

Like some other important theologians who were later invited to the Second Vatican Council as *periti* or official experts, Murray was not asked to attend the opening session. In fact, he and three liberals were banned from lecturing at the Catholic University in the spring of 1963. The reason given was that they presented a certain point of view still being deliberated at the council. Actually, the rector's position had been urged by the apostolic delegate, Egidio Vagnozzi.[104] The issue became somewhat of a "cause célèbre" in America and Europe. Murray shared the limelight with his friend, Gustave Weigel; the liturgist from Saint John's Abbey, Godfrey Dieckmann, O.S.B.; and the young Swiss theologian Hans Küng. Several years later it was claimed that the affair "marked not only a new high point in the intransigence of the conservatives but also a turning point in the history of freedom in the Catholic Church in America."[105]

In April of the same year, Murray was invited to attend the council as a *peritus* to Cardinal Francis Spellman of New York. When the Jesuit arrived in Rome, he discovered that the question of religious liberty had been dropped from the council's agenda. However, with help from the cardinal, the American bishops were persuaded to demand that the issue be restored. It is generally recognized that without American intervention, the church–state question would have been ignored.[106] On September 25, 1965, a vote was taken in the one area of significant American input. *Dignitatis Humanae Personae*, the declaration on religious freedom, had behind it two centuries of American experience in a religiously pluralistic society. The document declared that the right to religious freedom was rooted in the very "dignity of the human person."[107] The "thesis-hypothesis" position was quietly buried.

Murray, the principal architect of the document, suffered the loss of his close friend Gustave Weigel early in 1964. Weigel had acted as an interpreter for the English-speaking ecumenical observers whom John XXIII, in a historic gesture, had invited to the Council. Neither he nor the pope lived to see the council close. Weigel did live long enough to see progress made toward convergence. Catholics were bringing Scripture to their tradition and Protestants were bringing tradition to their Scriptures. As a result, he said, "For the first time in hundreds of years Catholic theology is relevant to the Protestant theology and also the other way around."[108]

Writing in the early 1960s, an astute American Catholic historian observed that the previous decade had produced a new kind of literature within his native church, that of self-analysis.[109] The works fell into three categories: descriptive, sociological, and philosophical. Henry J. Browne's essay took the descriptive approach with the same kind of honesty that marked all the contributions to *The American Apostolate*, released in 1952. Leo Ward, C.S.C., the editor, admitted that relatively few persons were immersed in the works outlined in the book. He was highly critical of Catholic education, which he felt had yet to take intellectual excellence as its end. Consequently, he could not justify including a chapter on the subject in his collection. To do otherwise would have been "immature," Ward wrote, since Catholic educators were "ignorant as any secular lamb . . . on the place of science in society and in a university."[110]

In the same vein, Browne noted that because of the labor encyclicals, some Catholics had made their mark in Congress and in government. He judged, however, that the average Catholic was less zealous in social reform than his or her Jewish counterpart. Browne offered his own critique of Monsignor John Tracy Ellis's devastating exposé, unleashed in 1955, of American Catholics' dreary performance in areas intellectual. The main thesis found wide agreement but Browne called for more scientific and statistical thoroughness to check the facts. He made the same observation about Thomas O'Dea's 1958 study, *American Catholic Dilemma: An Inquiry into the Intellectual Life.*

Browne pointed to a problem that he felt had not been addressed in the discussion erupting in the wake of Ellis's salvo. This was the fact that many talented and promising young scholars regularly left Catholic academic circles out of economic necessity. He recognized that Catholics were dissatisfied with "their small role in the leadership of American intellectual pursuits in general and their lack of import on American society." Now Catholics were mature enough to blame themselves. However, Browne felt that most Catholic newspapers and sermons continued to reflect a genre popular a half-century earlier. Then Catholics consoled themselves by counting up the number of Catholics who explored America and fought or died for it. All in all, Browne concluded, their cultural contributions were "not a matter of boast."

On the credit side, Browne's essay pointed to "officially sponsored art . . . which was not bad."[111] Indeed, the Grailville School of Music had in the 1950s produced several recordings of liturgical and folk music that were admired by Catholics and won praise from the *New York Times.*[112] Begun in Holland in 1921, the Grail movement was a lay organization for women. It arrived in America in 1940. After a rather shaky beginning in the archdiocese of Chicago, Archbishop John T. McNicholas, O.P., of Cincinnati helped the pioneer foundresses purchase a farm, which they renamed "Grailville." There they attempted to be "the Mystical Body in miniature." Their vision was one of "religious search, social transformation, and the release of women's energy throughout the world." This would be translated into Catholic action. The women of Grailville staunchly condemned the American use of the atomic bomb in World War II. They were admired by people as diverse as the American social worker Dorothy Day, the English novelist Evelyn Waugh, and the French theologian Jean Daniélou. What happened to Grailville only one day after the opening of the Second Vatican Council is paradigmatic of the shift that had subtly occurred in the American Catholic psyche in the 1950s and would accelerate dramatically in the late 1960s and early 1970s. On that day Grailville opted to receive women from all spiritual backgrounds but remain rooted in Roman Catholicism. They admitted that they had failed to intersect with American culture. In fact what they had built was a parallel or substitute culture.[113]

The 1960s opened on a more optimistic note for a group of young American Catholics called "Jubilee" or "Commonweal" Catholics. They were college-educated liberals who were avid readers of the two independent Catholic publications providing their sobriquet. They also were influenced by the writings of French theologians like Henri de Lubac and Yves Congar, who had tackled the problem of a theology of the laity. These young American Catholic intellectuals had worked out, through neo-Thomism or the new Transcendental Thomism espoused by the German theologian Karl Rahner, an intellectual approach to Catholicism. They sought to recover a new identity in the broad cultural climate of the Catholic tradition. In particular, they were enthusiastic about papal encyclicals such as *Mater et Magistra* (1961) and *Pacem in Terris* (1963).[114] In both encyclicals, the pope pointed to the widening inequities between the first and the third world as the major social crisis of the age. Because of changed and complex historical circumstances, he urged public authorities "to intervene in a wide variety of economic affairs" to reduce the imbalance in the distribution of the world's wealth, goods, and services. No longer was atheistic communism the sole object of papal criticism, but liberal capitalism was judged and found wanting. *Mater et Magistra*, the first of John's encyclicals, caused quite a stir in America and provoked the first public dissent to an encyclical in living American Catholic memory. The conservative Catholic William F. Buckley represented the dissent in his response, "Mater, si; magistra, no."[115] Subsequent popes have reinforced the "fundamental option for the poor" enunciated at the Second Vatican Council and have been intensely critical of Western cultural imperialism.

A new Catholic quarterly emerged during the 1960s and for a decade became the most influential journal in the English-speaking Catholic world. *Continuum*, under the leadership of Justus George

Lawler, espoused a religio-political position of nuclear pacifism. It was a position based not on logic but on a series of "converging probabilities," in the words of the editor. More than most journals, *Continuum* writers were extremely critical of their fellow American Catholic, John F. Kennedy. They denounced the buildup of a massive deterrence force that he had initiated. They judged the strategy of the Cuban missile crisis to be immoral.[116]

Shortly after that crisis, Nikita Khrushchev, leader of the Russian Communist party, showed his appreciation for the helpful role that John XXIII's public statements had played at that time. Earlier the Russian had spoken about "peaceful coexistence" between the superpowers, and John XXIII made an overture to Khrushchev in 1963. A way for dialogue between Communism and Catholicism was initiated at the highest levels. By the end of the year the pope was dead, and America's first Catholic president had been assassinated. Later, Khrushchev was removed from office by his party.

In 1965, the year that the Vatican Council closed, the United States found itself more deeply involved in an undeclared war on Communist North Vietnam. In early February, President Lyndon B. Johnson ordered round-the-clock bombings on targets in the Asian country. Several days later, a large group of dissenters released a "declaration of conscience" pledging total noncooperation with their U.S. government's North Vietnam policies. Among the hundreds of signers were Martin Luther King, Jr., Linus Pauling, Benjamin Spock, and two Catholic priests. *The Commonweal* praised the priests, Jesuit Daniel Berrigan and his Josephite brother Philip, for their courage to be the first Catholic priests to criticize their government's policy in Asia. The journal predicted a great deal of fallout, and there was.[117]

Daniel shared the spotlight with his Trappist friend, Thomas Merton, as American Catholicism's premier poets. In 1967 Merton published the study *Faith and Violence*, in which he tried to work out a theology of resistance. He urged nonviolence as the demand of the Christian conscience.[118] Catholics, some influenced by these men and by Dorothy Day's *Catholic Worker*, became conscientious objectors in record numbers. By 1971, the American Catholic hierarchy had measured the conflict in Vietnam against the traditional Catholic "just war" theory. It failed the test of proportionality and the war was condemned as immoral. This was a certain sign that the church had entered a period of "creative inculturation," to borrow the phrase.[119] The Catholic church felt enough at home to build on the positive values of American culture while challenging values that it perceived to be dubious or wrong. Two recent statements issued by the United States Catholic bishops reflect this phase. In 1983 they released *The Challenge of Peace: God's Promise and Our Response*. In a sense, the process of preparing the document was as important as the product. The bishops based their letter on extended interviews with a wide variety of experts and subjected their drafts to constant revision. The letter itself bore a tone of humility with the recognition that it was not the last word on the complex subject of the nuclear arms race. It was addressed not only to Catholics but also to the "wider political community." The bishops acknowledged that the nonviolent witness of both the black Baptist minister Martin Luther King and the unflinching Catholic lay activist Dorothy Day had a profound impact on the life of the church.[120] Day herself had testified before a panel of bishops in 1975 at a hearing on the meaning of liberty and justice from a Catholic perspective.[121] She was the heir to her spiritual mentor Paul Maurin's personalist philosophy; both had a radical commitment to nonviolence and evangelical poverty. Day died three years before the *Challenge of Peace* was released. The cause for her canonization was begun shortly after.

The bishops' statement evoked mixed reactions. Some conservative Catholics were vocally upset because they believed it divided Catholics at a time when keeping the faith at all was difficult. Some pacifists, on the other hand, were disappointed with the bishops' strictly conditioned acceptance of nuclear deterrence as an interim measure toward a nuclear-free world.[122] The second pastoral letter issued by the American hierarchy in the 1980s addressed Catholic Social Teaching and the U.S. economy. Like the letter on peace, the same broad consultative process and revision of drafts was followed. Some lay conservatives now believe that the bishops should teach general principles but not involve themselves in the specifics of economic policies. Catholics of a more liberal stripe sharply disagree.[123]

Many who composed the Catholic left in the antiwar movement had been deeply involved in the struggle for racial justice led by the charismatic Martin Luther King, Jr., in the mid-1950s and 1960s. The movement was interracial and interdenominational. Its culminating demonstration was the convergence of twenty-five thousand people from across the nation at Selma, Alabama, in March of 1965. Three years later the prophet of nonviolence fell to the bullet of an assassin. Martin Luther King's dream for a just society today remains unfulfilled.

Priests and religious sisters and brothers had left their rectories and convents in the fifties and sixties to protest and demonstrate. By the late 1960s and through the 1970s they were leaving them permanently in record numbers. Some of the Catholic laity found this profoundly disturbing: if "professional" religious, respected theologians, priests—and even two bishops—had abandoned their church vocations, was anything left sacred? One intellectual felt personally devastated in the aftermath of Vatican II. What seemed threatened was the "utter decomposition . . . [of] faith itself."[124] Another performed a post-mortem on the rebirth promised by neoscholasticism and chided the Catholic intellectual community for having declared "irrelevant its own richest flowering."[125] Other intellectuals interpret the results differently. One welcomed the release from a philosophy intellectually confining.[126] Another wrote, "With the Second Vatican Council, a sense of history was recovered," which had rendered it (quoting Josef Ratzinger) "impossible to ignore the critical historical method" in matters of all church teachings. History's role is to aid in the discernment of authentic tradition.[127]

Perhaps no single group in the American Catholic church has been more revolutionized through the discovery of their authentic tradition than the women religious. Responding to a mandate issued in 1966 by Pope Paul VI, they have reexamined their rules and customs in the light of the Gospel, the "charism" of their founders, and the human conditions of the modern world. As a group, they are now probably the best-educated American Catholics. Among their numbers are theologians, doctors, lawyers, psychologists, sociologists, and anthropologists, and the list continues. Deeply in touch with their spiritual roots, many have made the "fundamental option for the poor," in all its multiple ramifications, the focus of their ministry. The transformation from docile "good Sister" to public "prophetic woman" has been, in many ways, traumatic and dramatic. One author has envisioned them as the midwives of the future.[128]

In the post–Vatican II theological renewal, American Catholic scholars have made an untiring effort to exploit the best in their own tradition. Avery Dulles, David Tracy, Monika Hellwig, Rosemary Radford Ruether, Richard McCormick, S.J., Charles Curran, and others have made their theological mark. However, Curran again ran afoul of the Congregation for the Doctrine of the Faith, formerly the Holy Office.

Curran, a moral theologian, was at the center of a swirl of controversy almost twenty years earlier. The decade of the 1960s has been called a "watershed" for the Protestant "nation with the soul of a church."[129] American Catholics certainly shared in the traumas of the decade. However, their own particular watershed, according to a Catholic sociologist, was precipitated by *Humanae Vitae* in 1968.[130] In the papal encyclical, Pope Paul VI had rejected the majority findings of a Vatican commission established to study the question of contraception and repeated the traditional ban on every artificial form of contraception. This set up a string of protests, with most of the activity centering at Catholic University. Then, as now, the matter at issue was the scholarly freedom to dissent from noninfallible teachings of the official magisterium of the church. An outcome of such restriction, Charles Curran's threatened removal from the faculty of the Catholic University of America, raised serious concerns; the president of the university pointed to the danger connected with suppressing freedom of theological inquiry. The entire church, including dedicated Vatican authorities, would be denied access to creative theological insights of loyal scholars. Consequently, the church "will not grow in its understanding of the full implications of the gospel of Christ."[131]

Other challenges currently face the American theological community. There seems to be a trend on the part of Catholics to escape the complexities of the current age in a new and nonviable fundamentalism. Part of the problem is that they have not been helped to find answers to new questions in a way that they can recognize. The difficult task is one of maintaining the unity of the church universal while dealing honestly, openly, and humbly with particular questions.[132] This presupposes open lines of communication on all sides.

The role played by the Canon Law Society of America in implementing the ecclesiology elaborated during the Second Vatican Council has been considered distinguished. These male and female church law specialists studied, among other things, the application of due process. They elaborated "American procedural norms," which were approved by the Vatican in 1970. These facilitated the process for Catholics seeking marriage annulments. The newly revised code of canon law promulgated in 1983 does not, however, reflect American canonists' concern for the protection of human rights and freedoms within the church.[133] Among other scholarly societies, extensive ecumenical cooperation has developed. Scholars of all faiths belong to the Catholic Biblical Society and the Society of Biblical Literature. Catholics and Protestants have served as presidents of societies that a generation earlier had been either exclusively Protestant or exclusively Catholic. Catholic schools play an important role in the theological consortia in Berkeley, Washington, Chicago, and Boston.[134]

A scholarly dialogue among Catholics, Protestants, and Jews in America was initiated in the late 1950s. Philip Scharper, a Catholic editor at Sheed and Ward, proposed a symposium in which Protestants and Jews would give an honest appraisal of American Catholicism. The result was *American Catholics: A Protestant-Jewish View*, published in 1959. It contained essays by four Protestant and two Jewish scholars.[135] In the 1960s Scharper brought to his Catholic readers the new European theological pace-setters, the German Karl Rahner, the Dutch Edward Schillebeeckx, and the Swiss Hans Küng. In the next decade, he and Maryknoll Father Miguel d'Escoto launched what many considered a risky publishing venture, Orbis Books, which presented a forum to new theological voices from the third world such as Gustavo Gutierrez, Jon Sobrino, and Leonardo Boff. Though methodological questions have been raised about liberation theology's perspective, which addresses the cries of the hungry and oppressed, it seems already to have altered the theological landscape of many Catholic seminaries and institutions of higher learning.[136]

Those institutions themselves have gone through profound changes in the last twenty years. Novitiates, seminaries, and colleges have closed. What happened in the Pacific Northwest was not atypical of moves across the United States. In May 1976, Saint Edward's minor seminary of the Seattle, Washington, archdiocese was closed. The move was aimed at promoting "healthy adolescent growth" and realistic decisions about the priesthood. The next year Archbishop Raymond Hunthausen closed Seattle's Saint Thomas Seminary. There were too few students; the philosophy students would attend classes in local colleges and universities. The theology students were transferred to other seminaries.[137] In 1962 there were a total of 545 diocesan seminaries and religious seminaries and scholasticates in the United States. In 1985 that number was reduced to 318. During that same period the total number of seminarians dropped by a staggering 35,291. Slightly over 11,000 students were studying for the priesthood. In a ten-year period, from 1975 to 1985, 9 American Catholic institutions of higher learning closed, and the total number now stood at 242. In that same period, however, the student population attending those institutions increased by 127,697.[138] The number of sisters entering religious life in 1985, however, was only 15 percent of what it was in 1966.[139]

Such declines have allowed for a more mature and creative role for Catholic laity in the American Catholic church. Their numbers have increased dramatically in all divisions of education. In 1967 the University of Notre Dame became the largest religious organization in the world to be passed over to lay control, and one of the first. In 1985, the president of Notre Dame, Holy Cross Father Theodore M. Hesburgh, asserted that the university did not lose its Catholic character in the process. Hesburgh expressed confidence that Catholic higher education in the United States was "alive and well." He pointed to the growing excellence of its faculties and students, who were involved in a wide variety of basic Christian concerns. He believed that those graduated from these institutions carried these concerns "fruitfully, intelligently, and faithfully" into every avenue of their lives. He admitted that the story was not one of total success. However, he thought that the church and the world would be poorer without Catholic higher education.[140]

Writing that same year, Monsignor John Tracy Ellis was not so confident. He recognized Hesburgh as "facile princeps" of Catholic higher education and the foremost Catholic in the American national mind. However, thirty years have not changed the mind of the dean of American Catholic church history on several issues he raised in 1955. He pointed to the enervating character of the multiplicity of Catholic colleges and universities; the Jesuits alone operated twenty-eight of these. In Ellis's opinion, this diluted their pool of scholars. Ellis still believes that the American nation as a whole is concerned with material pursuits and does not place a high premium on intellectual excellence. He has maintained his position that Catholics disproportionately fit that description. Ellis admitted that he was disappointed but not discouraged. In a survey he conducted in 1984, the monsignor discovered that it was essentially the Catholic women's colleges that had excelled in doing the job of producing first-class liberal arts graduates.[141]

In concluding his monumental *Religious History of the American People*, the late Sydney E. Ahlstrom quoted from Frank Kermode's essay on eschatology and fiction, "It is one of the great charms of books that they have to end."[142] Written toward the close of the 1960s, Ahlstrom finished his work on a somber note. Two decades later there is even more reason for sobriety. There are glaring flaws in America's social fabric, one of the countries with the firepower capable of initiating global suicide. These are problems that face all Americans, Catholics among them. Within the Catholic church there is pain and frustration. Some of the frustration is born of the desire, typically American, for a quick solution to complex and time-conditioned problems; other problems are rooted in the church's failure to develop a full theology of Christian freedom for all its members. However, there has been progress in important aspects of Catholic life. Catholics are more richly sacramental and biblical. When asked if they would become more intellectual in the future, Ellis responded, quoting George Eliot, "of all forms of mistake, prophecy is the most gratuitous."[143] The historian is never the seer, but as a result of the profound cultural changes over the past three decades, we now have a clearer perspective of diversified challenges demanding the intellectual engagement of the American Catholic people.

Notes

Preface

1. John Tracy Ellis, "American Catholics and the Intellectual Life," *Thought* 30 (Autumn 1955): 351–88.
2. Thomas O'Brien Hanley, ed., *The John Carroll Papers*, 3 vols. (Notre Dame/London, 1976), 2:383. Georgetown opened in late 1791.
3. Annabelle M. Melville, *Louis William Du Bourg*, 2 vols. (Chicago, 1986), 1:103–122. It was in 1803 that Saint Mary's College accepted American students.
4. Thomas A. Becker, "Shall We Have a University?" cited in Frank L. Christ and Gerard E. Sherry, eds., *American Catholicism and the Intellectual Ideal* (New York, 1961), pp. 10–13.
5. John Gilmary Shea, "The Catholic Church in American History," cited in Christ and Sherry, *Intellectual Ideal*, p. 9.
6. Maurice Francis Egan, "The Needs of Catholic Colleges," in *Progress of the Catholic Church in America and the Great Columbian Catholic Congresses of 1893*, 2 vols. in one, 4th ed. (Chicago, 1897), pp. 103–105.
7. George Shuster, "Have We Any Scholars?" *America* 33 (August 15, 1925):418–420.
8. John Tracy Ellis, "No Complacency," *America* 95 (April 7, 1956):14–25. Here Ellis discusses the reaction to his article published in *Thought* in Autumn 1955.
9. Dolores Liptak, R.S.M., and Timothy Walch, "American Catholics and the Intellectual Life: An Interview with Monsignor John Tracy Ellis," *U.S. Catholic Historian* 4 (1985):190.
10. Thomas F. O'Dea, *American Catholic Dilemma: An Inquiry into the Intellectual Life* (New York, 1958), pp. 151–67.
11. Philip Gleason, "Catholic Intellectualism Again," *America* 112 (January 23, 1965):112–19.
12. Numerous articles have been published on the topic in the last three decades. John T. Noonan, Jr., stated in "American Catholics and the Intellectual Life," *Cross Currents* 31 (Winter 1981–1982):433–46 that the situation has improved. He also offered a frank discussion of the

reasons why Catholic intellectuals leave the church. In response to John Tracy Ellis's "Catholic Intellectual Life: 1984," *America* (October 6, 1984), one reader challenged his conclusion that Catholics were still not getting fellowships and grants in higher education in proportion to their numbers; see "Letters," *America* 152 (January 26, 1985):76.

Chapter 1   Enlightenment and Episcopal Leadership

1. Thomas McAvoy, "The Catholic Minority in the United States, 1789–1821," *Historical Records and Studies* 39 (1952):34.
2. Henry F. May, *The Enlightenment in America* (New York, 1976), p. 3. The discussion of the Enlightenment is based on John Herman Randall, Jr., *The Career of Philosophy*, 2 vols. (New York, 1966), 1:563–656, and Ernst Cassirer, *The Philosophy of the Enlightenment*, trans. Fritz C. Koelln and James T. Pettegrova (Boston, 1966), pp. 160–96.
3. Joseph P. Chinnici, O.F.M., *The English Catholic Enlightenment* (Shepherdstown, W. Va. 1980); idem, "American Catholics and Religious Pluralism, 1775–1820," *Journal of Ecumenical Studies* 16 (Fall 1979):727–46, and 729, n.5. The following discussion of the Catholic Enlightenment is based on Chinnici, pp. 729–33. See also Samuel J. Miller, *Portugal and Rome c. 1748–1830: An Aspect of the Catholic Enlightenment* (Rome, 1978), pp. 1–27.
4. Robert Gorman, *Catholic Apologetical Literature in the United States: 1784–1858* (Washington, D.C., 1939), pp. 58–61.
5. Mary Peter Carthy, O.S.U., *English Influences on Early American Catholicism* (Washington, D.C., 1959), p. 33.
6. Thomas O'Brien Hanley, *Charles Carroll of Carrollton: The Making of a Revolutionary Gentleman* (Washington, D.C., 1970), pp. 32, 262–63.
7. Thomas O'Brien Hanley, *Revolutionary Statesman: Charles Carroll and the War* (Chicago, 1983), p. 407. The following is based on Hanley's works.
8. Hanley, *Revolutionary Gentleman*, pp. 202–203.
9. Ibid., pp. 167–68.
10. For the journal Carroll kept during the tour, see Thomas O'Brien Hanley, ed., *The John Carroll Papers*, 3 vols. (Notre Dame, 1976), 1:6–26. [Henceforth called *JCP*.]
11. Ibid., 1:16; Annabelle M. Melville, *John Carroll of Baltimore: Founder of the American Catholic Hierarchy* (New York, 1955), pp. 25–30.
12. *JCP* 1:26.
13. Ellen Hart Smith, *Charles Carroll of Carrollton* (New York, 1971), p. 276.
14. *JCP* 2:409.
15. Hanley, *Revolutionary Gentleman*, p. 133.
16. *JCP* 1:32.
17. For a reprint of the debate, see Kate Mason Rowland, *Life and Correspondence of Charles Carroll, 1737–1832, with his Correspondence and Public Papers*, 2 vols. (New York, 1898), 1:250–96. Also see Peter S. Onup, ed., *Maryland and Empire 1773: The Antillon-First Citizen Letters* (Baltimore, 1974).
18. Hanley, *Revolutionary Gentleman*, pp. 262–64.

19. Thomas W. Spalding, in his article "John Carroll: Corrigenda and Addenda," *The Catholic Historical Review* 71 (October 1985):514, has identified Wharton as John Carroll's first cousin once removed.

20. *JCP* 1:82–144 carries Carroll's "Address to the Roman Catholics of the United States of America by a Catholic Clergyman"; quotation on 1:83, 167–68.

21. This point is made by James Hennesey, S.J., "An Eighteenth-Century Bishop: John Carroll of Baltimore," *Archivum Historicae Pontificae* 16 (1978):198–99; also by Chinnici, "American Catholics and Religious Pluralism," pp. 733–34.

22. *JCP* 1:86, 89–91, 105–106.

23. Chinnici, "American Catholics and Religious Pluralism," p. 743.

24. Carroll opposed mixed marriages and the practice of rearing the male and female children according to the religions of the father and mother, respectively, as breeding religious indifference: *JCP* 2:390.

25. *JCP* 1:140.

26. *JCP* 1:204, 276, 496; 3:290, 229.

27. *JCP* 1:311, 147–149, 149 n.1, 219, 225, 254–55.

28. Chinnici, "American Catholics and Religious Pluralism," pp. 737–41, presents the evidence.

29. In 1802 Carroll was finally satisfied with Berington's retraction of questionable points: *JCP* 2:384.

30. *JCP* 2:157.

31. Abelard told the story in his *Historia Calamitatum;* see J. T. Muckle, *Historia Calamitatum, Medieval Studies* 12 (Toronto, 1950).

32. *JCP* 1:253:54, 274.

33. Abelard is credited with introducing the dialectical method into scholastic philosophy.

34. Elizabeth Hamilton, *Héloïse* (Garden City, N.Y., 1967), p. 30.

35. *JCP* 1:254.

36. Eloise died as abbess of the Benedictine Abbey of the Paraclete. Abelard had died as a member of the same order in the Abbey of Cluny. They are buried side by side in the cemetery of Pére la Chaise, in Paris.

37. *JCP* 2:516; 3:124.

38. Melville, *John Carroll*, pp. 175–85 and *passim;* For Seton's correspondence to John Carroll, see Ellin Kelly and Annabelle Melville, eds. *Elizabeth Seton: Selected Writings* (New York, 1987), pp. 261–74.

39. Melville, *John Carroll*, p. 183.

40. *JCP* 1:312, 351; 2:53, 1:liv.

41. Hanley, *Revolutionary Gentleman*, pp. 24–25.

42. *JCP* 1:liv.

43. Hanley, *Revolutionary Gentleman*, p. 79.

44. Hennesey, "Eighteenth Century Bishop: John Carroll of Baltimore," p. 172.

45. Jay Dolan, *The American Catholic Experience* (New York, 1985), pp. 81–83, 91–92.

46. Gorman, *Apologetics*, p. 13, n.32.

47. Dolan, *American Catholic Experience*, pp. 94, 86.

48. Raymond H. Schmandt, "Catholic Intellectual Life in the Archdiocese of Philadelphia: An Essay," in *The History of the Archdiocese of Philadelphia*, ed. James F. Connelly (Philadelphia, 1976), p. 587.

49. *JCP* 3:lii; 1:52, 66–67.
50. Schmandt, "Catholic Intellectual Life," p. 587.
51. *JCP* 1:246.
52. Harold Buetow, *Of Singular Benefit: The Story of Catholic Education in the United States* (New York, 1970), pp. 35, 89.
53. *JCP* 1:315, 349.
54. John Gilmary Shea, *The Life and Times of the Most Rev. John Carroll, Bishop and First Archbishop of Baltimore* (New York, 1888), p. 312, n.1.
55. *JCP* 1:316, 338, 343–44, 350, 369. Carroll's reply is found in *JCP* 1:337–46.
56. Cited in Melville, *John Carroll*, p. 86.
57. *JCP* 1:432.
58. *JCP* 1:365–71; quotations on pp. 366, 368.
59. Patrick Carey, ed., *American Catholic Religious Thought* (New York, 1987), pp. 8–9.
60. Melville, *John Carroll*, p. 89.
61. Carey, *Religious Thought*, pp. 14–15 and *passim*.
62. Joseph Gurn, *Charles Carroll of Carrollton, 1737–1832* (New York, 1932), p. 138.
63. *JCP* 3:80–81.
64. Hanley, *Revolutionary Statesman*, pp. 145–55.
65. *JCP* 3:290; 1:454.
66. *JCP* 1:355, 360, 364, 372 n.1, 420, 425, 430, 435; A list of the patrons of Carey's bible may be found in Shea, *John Carroll*, pp. 375–76.
67. Eugene F. Maier, "Matthew Carey, Publicist and Politician (1760–1839)," *Records of the American Catholic Historical Society* 39 (June 1928):108.
68. Shea remarked in *John Carroll*, p. 376 n.1, that no one believed him when he claimed the early date of 1790 for the American publication of a Catholic version of the Bible.
69. Maier, "Carey," p. 85. The following is based on Maier.
70. Ibid., pp. 75, 88–89.
71. Henry N. Drewry, Thomas H. O'Connor, and Frank Freidel, eds., *America Is*, 2nd ed. (Columbus, Ohio, 1982), pp. 166–67.
72. May, *Enlightenment*, pp. 197–99.
73. Drewry et al., pp. 167–70.
74. Maier, "Carey," p. 91.
75. Schmandt, "Catholic Intellectual Life," p. 587, limits the designation to "intellectual" as understood to mean influencing the opinions of others through writings.
76. Maier, "Carey," p. 93.
77. Matthew Carey, *The American Museum, or, Repository of Ancient and Modern Fugitive Pieces, etc., Prose and Poetical* (Philadelphia, 1787, p. 1. [Henceforth called *Museum*.]
78. *JCP* 1:355, 361, 364.
79. *Museum*, 4 (July 30 1788), n.p.
80. Schmandt, "Catholic Intellectual Life," p. 588.
81. Maier, "Carey," p. 96.
82. Matthew Carey, *Philosophy and Common Sense* (Philadelphia, 1838), pp. i, ii, 64–73.
83. Maier, "Carey," p. 134.

84. Schmandt, "Catholic Intellectual Life," p. 588; Gorman, *Apologetics*, p. 25.
85. Maier, "Carey," p. 136; quotation cited on p. 155.
86. Ibid., p. 73. For an excellent study of the European roots of trusteeism and its American manifestations, see Patrick W. Carey, *People, Priests, and Prelates: Ecclesiastical Democracy and the Tensions of Trusteeism* (Notre Dame, Ind., 1987). The author discusses Matthew Carey's role in the Philadelphia struggle, pp. 112–203 *passim*.
87. Annabelle M. Melville, *Louis William Du Bourg*, 2 vols. (Chicago, 1986), 1:351.
88. Ibid. 1:352.
89. Edward J. Power, *Catholic Higher Education in America: A History* (New York, 1972), pp. 3, 19–21, 46–54.
90. Philip Gleason, "The Main Sheet Anchor: John Carroll and Catholic Higher Education," *Review of Politics* 38 (1976):585, citing Richard Hofstadter, *Anti-Intellectualism in American Life* (New York, 1963), esp. pp. 72ff., 90, 101ff., 105–106. See also James Hennesey, S.J., *John Carroll, American Educator*, bicentennial address at John Carroll University (Cleveland, 1987), pp. 1–12.
91. Gleason, "Main Sheet Anchor," 586–87.
92. Celestine J. Nuesse, *The Social Thought of American Catholics, 1634–1829* (Westminster, Md., 1945).
93. Celestine J. Nuesse, "Social Thought Among American Catholics in the Colonial Period," *American Catholic Sociological Review* 7 (March 1946):50.
94. *JCP* 3:441, 168–69; 2:122–23.
95. Smith, *Charles Carroll*, p. 272.
96. Gurn, *Charles Carroll*, pp. 189–91.
97. *JCP* 3:80.
98. Smith, *Charles Carroll*, pp. 271–72.
99. Martin E. Marty, *An Invitation to American Catholic History* (Chicago, 1986), p. 93.
100. Peter Guilday, ed., *The Life and Times of John England: First Bishop of Charleston, 1786–1842*, 2 vols. (New York, 1927), 1:124–82.
101. Leon A. LeBuffe, "Tensions in American Catholicism, 1820–1870, An Intellectual History" (Ph.D. diss., The Catholic University of America, 1973), p. 42.
102. Patrick Carey, *An Immigrant Bishop: John England's Adaptation of Irish Catholicism to American Republicanism* (Yonkers, N.Y., 1982), pp. 163–67.
103. Ibid., p. 93, citing Richard W. Rousseau, "Bishop John England and American Church–State Theory (Ph.D. diss., Saint Paul University, 1969), p. 376.
104. Gorman, *Apologetics*, p. 43.
105. Paul J. Foik, C.S.P., *Pioneer Catholic Journalism* (New York, 1930), pp. 75–76.
106. Gorman, *Apologetics*, p. 43.
107. *U.S. Catholic Miscellany* 2 (Jan. 7, 1824):1. [Henceforth *USCM*.]
108. Foik, *Pioneer Journalism*, pp. 86–89.
109. Gorman, *Apologetics*, p. 50.
110. Foik, *Pioneer Journalism*, pp. 90–91.
111. Gorman, *Apologetics*, p. 43.

112. Ryan Memorial Library Archives and Historical Collections at Saint Charles Borromeo Seminary, Philadelphia, England Box, England to William Gaston, Charleston, S.C., August 25, 1823. [Henceforth *RMLAHC*.]

113. Gorman, *Apologetics*, pp. 4–5, 24.

114. John England, *The Works of the Right Reverend John England, First Bishop of Charleston*, 7 vols., ed. Sebastian G. Messmer (Cleveland, 1908), 2:213–562; 3:9–103. [Henceforth *Works of England*.]

115. Gorman, *Apologetics*, p. 45. [The following section is based on Gorman.]

116. Ibid., pp. 46 n.25, 48.

117. *Works of England* 3:144–45, cited by Le Buffe, *Intellectual History*, p. 40.

118. *Works of England* 2:382, cited by Gorman, *Apologetics*, pp. 49–50.

119. *USCM* 2 (January 21, 1824):34–35; for the letter, see John Tracy Ellis, *Documents of American Catholic History* (Milwaukee, 1961), pp. 170–71.

120. Carey, *Immigrant Bishop*, p. 108.

121. *USCM* (January 28, 1824):51–52, 55, 57.

122. Carey, *Immigrant Bishop*, p. 60; Le Buffe, *Intellectual History*, p. 53.

123. Ibid., pp. 50, 53.

124. John England, *The Works of John England*, 6 vols., ed. Ignatius A. Reynolds (Baltimore, Md., 1849), 5:91–100. Attention has been called to the fact that Bishop Messmer's 1908 edition of England's works, though generally superior, omitted the constitution of the Charleston Diocese; Le Buffe, *Intellectual History*, p. 39 n.27.

125. Carey, *Immigrant Bishop*, pp. 114–15. [The following section is based on Carey.]

126. Ibid., pp. 116–17, 166, 139, 118 citing *Works of England* 5:105.

127. (Charleston: Gray and Ellis, 1824), p. 3.

128. *RMLAHC*, England Box, England to William Gaston, Augusta, Georgia, March 22, 1827.

129. England, *Constitution*, pp. 3–4, 9, 14.

130. *RMLAHC*, England Box, England to William Gaston, Charleston, S.C. December 1, 1837.

131. *Works of England* 2: 99–100, cited by Le Buffe, *Intellectual History*, p. 36.

132. *USCM* 20 (October 3, 1840):97–98.

133. Richard Cain Madden, "John England," *New Catholic Encyclopedia*, 15 vols. (New York, 1967), 5:353.

134. Gorman, *Apologetics*, p. 50.

135. *RMLAHC*, England Box, England to William Gaston, Hayetteville, January 27, 1826.

136. Anne Freemantle, ed., *The Papal Encyclicals in Their Historical Context* (New York, 1963), pp. 127–28.

137. Thomas F. O'Meara, *Romantic Idealism and Roman Catholicism: Schelling and the Theologians* (Notre Dame, 1982), p. 189.

138. Carey, *Immigrant Bishop*, p. 95.

139. Freemantle, *Papal Encyclicals*, p. 128.

140. *Works of England* 4:229, cited in Carey, *Immigrant Bishop*, p. 90.

141. *The Works of the Right Reverend John England*, 5 vols. (Baltimore, 1849). All other references to *Works of England* are to the Messmer edition.

142. Foik, *Pioneer Journalism*, p. 93.
143. Gorman, *Apologetics*, p. 65.
144. The following is based on Chinnici, "American Catholics," pp. 744–45.
145. Beutow, *Singular Benefit*, p. 49.
146. Chinnici, "American Catholics," pp. 744–45. For ultramontanism, see Richard F. Costigan, S.J., "Tradition and the Beginning of the Ultramontane Movement," *Irish Theological Quarterly* 48 (1981):27–46.
147. Carey, *Immigrant Bishop*, p. 164.

Chapter 2 Romanticism

1. John Tracy Ellis, *American Catholicism*, 2nd ed. rev. (Chicago, 1969), p. 51.
2. James Hennesey, S.J., *American Catholics* (New York, 1981), p. 102.
3. Edwin Berry Burgum, "Responses to Revolution," in *Romanticism*, ed. John B. Halsted (Englewood, N.J., 1965), p. 77.
4. Thomas F. O'Meara, *Romantic Idealism and Roman Catholicism: Shelling and the Theologians* (Notre Dame, 1982), p. 186; Gerald McCool, *Catholic Theology in the Nineteenth Century: The Quest for a Unitary Method* (New York, 1977), p. 67. McCool credits Möhler and John Henry Newman with introducing this approach.
5. Robert Gorman, *Catholic Apologetical Literature in the United States: 1784–1858* (Washington, D.C., 1939), p. 159.
6. John Herman Randall, Jr., *The Career of Philosophy*, 2 vols. (New York, 1965), 2:430; Crane Brinton, *The Shaping of Modern Thought* (Englewood Cliffs, N.J., 1965), p. 176.
7. Sydney E. Ahlstrom, *A Religious History of the American People* (New Haven, 1974), pp. 514, 615–21, 630.
8. Patrick W. Carey, "American Catholic Religious Thought: An Historical Review," *U.S. Catholic Historian* 4 (1985):129.
9. David J. O'Brien, "An Evangelical Imperative: Isaac Hecker, Catholicism and Modern Society," in *Hecker Studies*, ed. John Farina (New York, 1983), p. 87.
10. Orestes A. Brownson, *The Convert: or Leaves from My Experience* (New York, 1857), pp. 3–4.
11. Thomas R. Ryan, *Orestes A. Brownson: A Definitive Biography* (Huntington, Ind., 1976), p. 17, citing Per Sveino, *Orestes A. Brownson's Road to Catholicism* (1970), p. 307.
12. Brownson, *Convert*, pp. 35, 81, 94, 101, 122–23, 144–46, 157–58.
13. Leonard Gilhooley, C.F.X., *Contradiction and Dilemma: Orestes Brownson and the American Idea* (New York, 1972), p. 7.
14. Brownson, *Convert*, pp. 158–60.
15. Ryan, *Brownson*, p. 109.
16. Brownson, *Convert*, p. 179.
17. (Boston, 1836.)
18. Brownson, *Convert*, p. 183.
19. Orestes A. Brownson, *New Views of Christianity, Society, and the Church* (Boston, 1836), pp. v, 1–4, 6, 10–26, 31.
20. Brownson, *Convert*, p. 187.

21. Ryan, *Brownson*, p. 108.
22. Americo D. Lapati, *Orestes A. Brownson* (New York, 1965), pp. 19–21.
23. Henry F. Brownson, ed., *The Works of Orestes A. Brownson*, 20 vols. (Detroit, 1882–1907), 3:358–95. [Henceforth *Works of Brownson*.]
24. Brownson, *Convert*, pp. 139, 239, 247, 253. Brownson did not change his views in the twenty-year period separating his two publications.
25. England's letter to Forsyth, Sept. 29, 1840, in *U.S. Catholic Miscellany* 20 (Octber 3, 1840):97–98.
26. *U.S. Catholic Miscellany* 20 (September 12, 1840):6.
27. Alvan S. Ryan, ed., *The Brownson Reader* (New York, 1955), pp. 444–45.
28. Walter Elliott, C.S.P., *The Life of Father Hecker* (New York, 1891), pp. 1–35.
29. Joseph P. Chinnici, O.F.M., *Devotion to the Holy Spirit in American Catholicism* (New York, 1985), p. 26.
30. Joseph F. Gower and Richard M. Leliaert, eds., *The Brownson–Hecker Correspondence* (Notre Dame, Ind., 1979), pp. 8–10. [Henceforth *Brownson–Hecker*.]
31. "Doctor Brownson and the Workingman's Party," *Catholic World* 45 266 (1887):204–206. [Henceforth *CW*.]
32. *Brownson–Hecker*, p. 11.
33. Winthrop S. Hudson, *Religion in America*, 3rd ed. (New York, 1981), pp. 175, 188.
34. *Works of Brownson* 4:142–172; quotations on pp. 150, 153, 155, 169.
35. Brownson, *Convert*, p. 293.
36. *Works of Brownson* 4:165–66, 170–71.
37. *Brownson–Hecker*, 15; Elliott, *Life of Hecker*, pp. 76–100.
38. *Brownson–Hecker*, p. 14.
39. David O'Brien, Introduction to *The Oxford Movement in America*, by Clarence W. Walworth, rpt. (New York, 1974), pp. vi–viii, xii.
40. Gorman, *Apologetics*, pp. 53–61.
41. Hugh J. Nolan, *The Most Reverend Francis Patrick Kenrick, Third Bishop of Philadelphia, 1830–1851* (Philadelphia, 1948), pp. 372–75.
42. Francis Patrick Kenrick, *The Primacy and General Councils Vindicated in a Series of Letters Addressed to the Right Reverend John Henry Hopkins, Protestant Episcopal Bishop of Vermont* (Philadelphia, 1838), pp. 321, 353–54, 356.
43. The lay Catholic scholar John T. Noonan, Jr., in his "American Catholics and the Intellectual Life," *Cross Currents* 31 (Winter 1981–1982):439, has suggested that Kenrick, in comparison with someone like Henry David Thoreau, could be considered anti-intellectual.
44. Nolan, *Kenrick*, pp. 237–38.
45. James Hennesey, S.J., "A Prelude to Vatican I: American Bishops and the Definition of the Immaculate Conception," *Theological Studies* 25 (September 1964):413.
46. Leon A. Le Buffe, "Tensions in American Catholicism, 1820–1870, An Intellectual History" (Ph.D. diss., Catholic University of America, 1973), p. 133.
47. Nolan, *Kenrick*, p. 238.
48. Francis E. Tourscher, O.S.A., ed., *Kenrick-Frenaye Correspondence, 1830–1862* (Lancaster, Pa., 1920), p. 186.

49. Nolan, *Kenrick*, pp. 46, 241–44.
50. Mary Peter Carthy, O.S.U., *English Influences on Early American Catholicism* (Washington, D.C., 1959), p. 120.
51. Brownson, *Convert*, pp. 358, 368.
52. Hugh S. T. Marshall, *Orestes Brownson and the American Republic: An Historical Perspective* (Washington, D.C., 1971), pp. 289–90; Carthy, *English Influences*, p. 121.
53. Orestes A. Brownson, *Essays and Reviews* (New York, 1852), p. 368.
54. Marshall, *Brownson*, p. 291.
55. Carey, "American Catholic Religious Thought," p. 130.
56. Humphrey J. Desmond, "In Defense of Brownson," *The Acolyte* (March 1934), reprinted in Thomas R. Ryan, *The Sailor's Snug Harbor* (Westminster, Md., 1952), 152–60.
57. Carey, "American Catholic Religious Thought," p. 132.
58. Brownson, *Convert*, pp. 416–17.
59. Lapati, *Brownson*, p. 48.
60. *Works of Brownson* 1:v–xxviii.
61. *Brownson–Hecker*, p. 126, June 25, 1845.
62. (New York, 1857), pp. 421–23.
63. John P. Reidy, "Orestes Augustus Brownson: Conservative Mentor to Dissent," *American Benedictine Review* 21 (1970): 224–39.
64. *Brownson–Hecker*, p. 126, June 25, 1845; pp. 182–83, undated, c. June 1, 1855; 194, August 5, 1957.
65. *Works of Brownson* 18:330, cited in Carl F. Krummel, "Catholicism, Democracy, and Orestes Brownson," *American Quarterly* 6 (Spring 1954):20–22, 26.
66. Tourscher, *Kenrick-Frenaye*, pp. 292–93, February 28, 1849.
67. Orestes Brownson, "Temporal and Spiritual Power of the Pope," in *Works of Brownson* 12:22, 151–52. The series began in January 1853.
68. Lapati, *Brownson*, p. 94.
69. Tourscher, *Kenrick-Frenaye*, pp. 365–66, March 14, 1854.
70. Kenrick to Mr. George Allen, February 1, 1854, in a scrapbook containing 127 letters from Kenrick to Professor George Allen and his family. Collected in *RMLAHC*.
71. Reidy, "Conservative Mentor," p. 232.
72. Mary Rose Gertrude Whalen, C.S.C. *Some Aspects of the Influence of Orestes A. Brownson on His Contemporaries* (Notre Dame, Ind., 1933), pp. 90–93.
73. Gorman, *Apologetics*, p. 142.
74. Cited in Richard Shaw, *Dagger John: The Unquiet Life and Times of Archbishop John Hughes of New York* (New York, 1977), pp. 261, 305.
75. *Works of Brownson* 2:xxxiii, cited by Charles L. Sewrey, "Infallibility, the American Way and Catholic Apologetics," *Journal of Church and State* 15 (1973):293–302.
76. Whalen, *Influence of Brownson*, pp. 90–92.
77. Reidy, "Conservative Mentor," p. 233.
78. *Brownson–Hecker*, p. 187, Brownson to Hecker, August 29, 1855.
79. Gorman, *Apologetics*, p. 142.

Chapter 3   Isaac Hecker

1. Isaac Hecker, *Questions of the Soul* (New York: Co. 1855), 31–34, 108–114, 126–65.

2. John Tracy Ellis, *American Catholicism* 2d ed., rev. (Chicago, 1969), pp. 85–86, quoting Lincoln to Joshua F. Speed, Springfield, August 24, 1855, in Ray P. Bosler, ed., *The Collected Works of Abraham Lincoln* (New Brunswick, N.J., 1853), 2:322–23.

3. Joseph F. Gower and Richard M. Leliaert, eds., *The Brownson–Hecker Correspondence* (Notre Dame, 1979), 25–26. [Henceforth *Brownson–Hecker*.]

4. Archives University of Notre Dame, Brownson Papers, April 7, 1855, cited by Vincent Holden, C.S.P., *The Yankee Paul: Isaac Thomas Hecker* (Milwaukee, 1958), p. 193.

5. Isaac Hecker, *Aspirations of Nature* (New York, 1858), p. 197 and *passim*.

6. For a good summary of this controversy, see John Farina, "Isaac Hecker's Vision for the Paulists: Hopes and Realities," in *Hecker Studies*, ed. John Farina (New York, 1983), pp. 182–92.

7. "Aspirations of Nature," *Brownson's Quarterly Review* (October 1857), 459–503. [Henceforth *BQR*.]

8. *Brownson–Hecker*, p. 205, Hecker to Brownson, Rome, October 5, 1857.

9. Ibid., p. 201, Brownson to Hecker, New York, September 29, 1857.

10. Ibid., p. 31.

11. "The Present and the Future Prospects of the Catholic Faith in the United States of North America," (3d ser.) 8 (1857):385–408, 513–29; quotations on 385–87, 515–19.

12. Cited in Holden, *Yankee Paul*, p. 409.

13. In America it was carried in the *Freeman's Journal*, Dec. 12, 19, and 26, 1857, and Jan. 2, 1858.

14. Farina, "Hecker's Vision," *Hecker Studies*, pp. 183, 196, 201. Augustine Hewit, George Deshon, Francis Baker, and Clarence Walworth were the other former Redemptorists. Walworth did not become a Paulist.

15. Edward J. Langlois, C.S.P., "Isaac Hecker's Political Thought," *Hecker Studies*, ed. John Farina (New York, 1983), pp. 50–52, 63.

16. *Brownson–Hecker*, same to same, undated, Thursday [31 July 1845].

17. Robert W. Baer, "A Jungian Analysis of Isaac Thomas Hecker," *Hecker Studies*, ed. John Farina (New York, 1983), p. 157.

18. Ibid., p. 157 (citing diary entry for July 22, 1843); p. 158 (citing diary entry for August 26, 1843).

19. Diary entry for August 26, 1843, p. 12, from a biography of Hecker, manuscript graciously shared by David O'Brien while his biography of Hecker was in progress.

20. Cullen to Hecker, September 17, 1868, in ibid., pp. 15, 23.

21. *Brownson–Hecker*, p. 40.

22. William L. Portier, "Isaac Hecker and Americanism," *Ecumenist* 19 (Nov./Dec. 1980):10–12.

23. Robert Emmett Curran, S.J., "Prelude to 'Americanism': The New York Accademia and Clerical Radicalism in the Late Nineteenth Century," *Church History* 47 (1978):48–65. [The following is based on Curran.]

24. Ibid., pp. 49–55, 63–65.

25. For American participation, see James Hennesey, S.J., *The First Council of the Vatican: The American Experience* (New York, 1963).

26. Thomas W. Spalding, *Martin John Spalding: American Churchman* (Washington, D.C., 1973), pp. 285–86.

27. William L. Portier, "Isaac Hecker and the First Vatican Council," *The Catholic Historical Review* 71 (April, 1985):209, 218.
28. James Hennesey, S.J., *American Catholics* (New York, 1981), p. 169.
29. Spalding, *Martin Spalding*, pp. 286, 295–97.
30. Portier, "Hecker and Vatican I," pp. 209, 213.
31. Spalding, *Martin Spalding*, p. 306.
32. William B. Faherty, S.J., *Dream by the River: Two Centuries of Saint Louis Catholicism, 1766–1967* (Saint Louis, Mo., 1973), pp. 93, 97.
33. Reprinted in Raymond J. Clancy, "American Prelates at the Vatican Council," *Historical Records and Studies* (New York, 1937), appendix V, pp. 28, 93–131.
34. Faherty, *Dream*, p. 97.
35. 4th ed. (Baltimore, 1870).
36. Cited in Spalding, *Martin Spalding*, pp. 290, 316.
37. Hennesey, *American Catholics*, p. 169.
38. Portier, "Hecker and Vatican I," pp. 219–220. [The following is based on Portier.]
39. Ibid., pp. 219–22, 224, 226–27; Isaac Hecker to George Hecker, January 26, 1870, quotation on p. 220.
40. Anne Freemantle, ed., *The Papal Encyclicals in Their Historical Context* (New York, 1963), pp. 152–54.
41. Hennesey, *American Catholics*, pp. 170–71.
42. Spalding, *Martin Spalding*, p. 318.
43. Hennesey, *American Catholics*, p. 171.
44. Ibid., pp. 170–71; Spalding, *Martin Spalding*, pp. 322–25.
45. Faherty, *Dream*, p. 98.
46. Mary Augustine Kwitchen, O.S.F., *James Alphonsus McMaster: A Study in American Thought* (Washington, D.C., 1949), p. 194.
47. Charles L. Sewrey, "Infallibility, the American Way and Catholic Apologetics," *Journal of Church and State* 15 (1973):293, 301.
48. Here I am following the interpretation of Joseph A. Komonchak, "The Enlightenment and the Construction of Roman Catholicism," *CCIA Annual* (1985), pp. 31, 51 n.1, where the author notes that Roman Catholicism is not identical with the Catholic Church. For a somewhat similar view, see Edward Wakin and Joseph Scheuer, *The De-Romanization of the American Catholic Church* (New York, 1970).
49. James Hennesey, S.J., *Catholics in the Promised Land of the Saints* (Marquette, Wisc., 1981), p. 34.
50. *Brownson–Hecker*, Brownson to Hecker, Elizabeth, N.J., August 25, 1870, pp. 280–81.
51. Henry F. Brownson, *The Works of Orestes A. Brownson*, 20 vols. (Detroit, 1882–1907), 13:263–84.
52. Francis E. McMahon, "Orestes Brownson on Church and State," *Theological Studies* 15 (1945):178–90.
53. Brownson, "Church and State," cited in Alvan S. Ryan, ed., *The Brownson Reader* (New York, 1955), p. 369.
54. Hugh Marshall, S.J., *Orestes Brownson and the American Republic: An Historical Perspective* (Washington, D.C., 1971), pp. 284–85.
55. Mary Rose Gertrude Whalen, O.S.F., C.S.C. *Some Aspects of the Influence of Orestes A. Brownson on His Contemporaries* (Notre Dame, Ind., 1933), pp. 128–29, places the height of his popularity in the period 1851–1857.

56. Joseph P. Chinnici, O.F.M., *Devotion to the Holy Spirit in American Catholicism* (New York, 1985), pp. 27–29.
57. Farina, "Hecker's Vision," pp. 207–209; "The Church in View of the Needs of the Age." Propaganda Press was going to publish the essay but withdrew the offer. It was published in London by Pickering anonymously, and was translated into French by Mrs. Craven. It was published as a leader in *Catholic World* about the same time (1874); Walter Elliott, *The Life of Father Hecker* (New York, 1891), p. 397.
58. Published in New York, 1887.
59. Quoted by Walter J. Ong, S.J., *American Catholic Crossroads* (New York, 1959), p. 57.
60. Hecker, *Church and Age*, pp. 91–94, 39–41, 137, 215, 219.
61. Abbé Xavier Dufresne, "Personal Recollections of Father Hecker," *Catholic World* 67 (June 1898):333.
62. Hecker, *Church and Age*, pp. 39–41, 137, 215, 219.
63. Chinnici, *Holy Spirit*, pp. 32–33.
64. This quote was attributed to Hecker by John Ireland in his Preface to Elliott's *Life of Hecker*, p. xvi.
65. Hecker, *Church and Age*, p. 2.
66. Dufresne, "Recollections," pp. 335–37.
67. David O'Brien, "An Evangelical Imperative: Isaac Hecker, Catholicism and Modern Society," *Hecker Studies*, ed. John Farina (New York, 1983), p. 112.
68. Portier, "Hecker and Vatican I," pp. 226–27.
69. Hecker, *Church and Age*, p. 29.
70. O'Brien, "Isaac Hecker," p. 88; O'Brien does not intend this in a negative way.
71. Hecker, *Church and Age*, pp. 67, 81–87; idem, "The Mission of Leo XIII," *Catholic World* 48 (January 1889):10.
72. Archives of the Paulist Fathers, Hecker Papers, untitled and undated; Elliott later added the title "Notes concerning New Religious Institutes." It was composed sometime after April 1876.
73. O'Brien, "Isaac Hecker," pp. 108, 115.
74. Farina, "Hecker's Vision," pp. 204–215, for the conflict between Hecker's vision for the Paulists and that of other community members.
75. This was the title of Paulist Father Vincent Holden's biography of Hecker's early years. Holden died before the second volume was completed.

Chapter 4   The Catholic University and Americanism

1. John Tracy Ellis, *John Lancaster Spalding, First Bishop of Peoria: American Educator* (Milwaukee, 1962), p. 23. Ellis notes that it is tempting to see John behind his uncle Martin's proposal of a Catholic university.
2. *The Confessions of Saint Augustine*, trans. Frank J. Sheed (New York, 1943), Book 13, pp. 349–54.
3. Archives of the Archdiocese of Baltimore (AAB), 37-A-3, Spalding to Martin J. Spalding, Louvain (January 1, 1863), cited by David F.

Sweeney, O.F.M., *The Life of John Lancaster Spalding, First Bishop of Peoria, 1840–1916* (New York, 1965), pp. 55–56, 91.

4. Gerald A. McCool, S.J., *Catholic Theology in the Nineteenth Century: The Quest for a Unitary Method* (New York, 1977), pp. 19, 131–32.

5. John J. Wynne, S.J., ed., *The Great Encyclical Letters of Pope Leo XIII* (New York, 1903), pp. 34–57.

6. Sweeney, *Spalding*, p. 104.

7. Ibid., p. 19; David Killen, "Americanism Revisited: John Spalding and Testem Benevolentiae," *Harvard Theological Review* 66 (October 1973):414.

8. Michael V. Gannon, "Before and After Modernism: The Intellectual Isolation of the American Priest," in John T. Ellis, ed., *The Catholic Priest in the United States: Historical Investigations* (Collegeville, 1971), p. 318.

9. John Lancaster Spalding, "The Catholic Church in the United States, 1776–1876," *Catholic World* 13 (July 1876), reprinted in *Essays and Reviews* (New York, 1877), pp. 9–49, quotations on pp. 10, 46–48. [*Catholic World* will be cited henceforth as *CW.*]

10. John Lancaster Spalding, "Religion and Art," in *Essays and Reviews*, pp. 312, 345; John Lancaster Spalding, "Culture and Religion," in *Things of the Mind*, 6th ed. (Chicago, 1905), pp. 170–219; John Lancaster Spalding, "Religion," in *Religion, Agnosticism and Education*, 2d ed. (Chicago, 1903), pp. 7–57.

11. John Lancaster Spalding, "The Persecution of the Church in the German Empire," in *Essays and Reviews*, pp. 51–53.

12. Sweeney, *Spalding*, pp. 129–39.

13. See Robert Trisco, "Bishops and Their Priests in the United States," in Ellis, ed., *Catholic Priest in the United States*, pp. 111–272, for the long history of clerical dissatisfaction with the episcopal nominating process.

14. AAB 37-A-7, John Lancaster Spalding to Martin John Spalding, Rome, January 5, 1865, cited by Sweeney, *Spalding*, p. 160.

15. John Lancaster Spalding, "University Education Considered in Its Bearings on the Higher Education of Priests," reprinted as "Higher Education" in *Means and Ends of Education*, 4th ed. (Chicago, 1903), 181–232, quotations on pp. 209–216, 229–32.

16. Sweeney, *Spalding*, pp. 158, 166–71. Both Mary Gwendolyn and her sister Elizabeth were benefactresses to the university. Ultimately, both left the Catholic Church.

17. John Lancaster Spalding, printed as "University Education," in *Education and the Higher Life*, 8th ed. (Chicago, 1903), pp. 172–210, quotations on pp. 173–75.

18. Killen, "Americanism Revisited," pp. 422–25; here he traces the development of Spalding's understanding of the "spirit of the age."

19. Spalding, "University Education," pp. 191–92, 200, 210.

20. Ellis, *John Lancaster Spalding: Educator*, p. 84.

21. Patrick H. Ahern, *The Life of John J. Keane: Educator and Archbishop, 1839–1918* (Milwaukee, Wisc., 1955), pp. 1–10, 19.

22. Hecker was called Keane's "father in the spiritual life." Archives of the Paulist Fathers, Americanism Papers, O'Connell to Klein, Rome, Oct. 18, 1897. [Henceforth cited as *APF.*]

23. Joseph P. Chinnici, O.F.M., *Devotion to the Holy Spirit in American Catholicism* (New York, 1985), pp. 39–44.

24. John J. Keane, "Father Hecker," *CW* 49 (April 1889):7; see Thomas Wangler's "Bibliography of the Writings of Archbishop John J. Keane," *Records of the American Catholic Historical Society of Philadelphia* 89 (March–December 1978): 60–73 for a list of 232 publications by Keane. [This periodical will be cited henceforth as *RACHSP*.]

25. Charles Maignen, *Etudes sur l'américanisme, le père Hecker, est-il un saint?* (Rome, 1898), pp. 176–202 [henceforth *Père Hecker*]; several years previous, Maignen had published *Le souverainté du peuple est une hérésie* (Paris, 1892).

26. Sydney E. Ahlstrom, *A Religious History of the American People* (New Haven/London, 1974), p. 554.

27. John Tracy Ellis has traced the early history of the university in *The Formative Years of the Catholic University of America* (Washington, D.C., 1946).

28. John Tracy Ellis, *The Life of James Cardinal Gibbons*, 2 vols. (Milwaukee, Wisc., 1952), 1:406–408.

29. For a detailed account of the issue, see Henry J. Browne, *The Catholic Church and the Knights of Labor* (Washington, D.C., 1949). The Roman activities of Keane and Ireland are enumerated in Eduardo Soderini, *The Pontificate of Leo XIII*, trans. Barbara Carter, 2 vols. (London, 1934), 1:167–70.

30. Thomas Wangler, "American Catholic Expansionism: 1886–1894," *Harvard Theological Review* 75, no. 3 (1982):377–93.

31. Henry George, *Progress and Poverty*, (Author's Proof Edition, 1879. The market edition was published the following year by D. Appleton and Co., New York.)

32. For an account of McGlynn's support, see Margaret Mary Reher, "A Call to Action Revisited," *U.S. Catholic Historian* 1 (Winter–Spring 1981):54–60.

33. Frederick J. Zwierlein, *The Life and Letters of Bishop McQuaid*, 3 vols., 2nd ed. (Rochester, 1927), 1:1–83; Robert Emmett Curran, S.J., "Prelude to Americanism: The New York Accademia and Clerical Radicalism in the Late Nineteenth Century," *Church History* 47 (1978):58–59.

34. John Tracy Ellis, ed., *Documents of American Catholic History*, 2nd ed. (Milwaukee, Wisc., 1962), pp. 454–56, quotations on p. 454.

35. Robert Emmett Curran, S.J., "The McGlynn Affair and the Shaping of the New Conservatism in American Catholicism, 1886–1894," *Catholic Historical Review* 66 (April 1980):204.

36. David O'Brien, "An Evangelical Imperative: Isaac Hecker, Catholicism and Modern Society," in John Farina, ed., *Hecker Studies* (New York, 1983), p. 115.

37. Mary Augustine Kwitchin, O.S.F., *James Alphonsus McMaster: A Study in American Thought* (Washington, D.C., 1949), p. 166.

38. Colman J. Barry, O.S.B., *The Catholic Church and German Americans* (Milwaukee, Wisc., 1953), pp. 289–96 (reproduces Abbelen memorial) and 292–312 (Keane's and Ireland's countermemorial).

39. Thomas Wangler, "The Birth of Americanism: Westward the Apocalyptic Candlestick," *Harvard Theological Review* 65 (1972):424–25. Wangler identifies three factors provoking "Americanism": Ireland and Keane's meeting with Cardinal Manning, whom Wangler claims held the general lines of the Americanist program prior to the visit; several remarks by Leo XIII favorable to America; and the deplorable state of the Catholic church in Europe.

40. Published in Baltimore, 1892.

41. C. Joseph Nuesse, "Thomas Joseph Bouquillon (1840–1902), Moral Theologian and Precursor of the Social Scientists in the Catholic University of America," *The Catholic Historical Review* 72, no. 4 (October 1986):603–605.

42. *The Parent First: An Answer to Dr. Bouquillon's query, "Education: To Whom Does It Belong?"* (New York, 1891).

43. Vol. 6, no. 1 (1892), pp. 74–76. The entire question is covered in Daniel F. Reilly, O.P., *The School Controversy (1889–1893)* (Washington, 1943). Not included in Reilly's study are the Heuser Papers, which provide a number of insights on the issue.

44. Ryan Memorial Library Archives and Historical Collection at St. Charles Borromeo Seminary, Philadelphia, Heuser Papers, same to same, H H 165, 166, January 1892; H H 171, Woodstock, February 20, 1892. [Collection cited as henceforth *RMLAHC*.]

45. *RMLAHC*, Heuser Papers, H H 130, same to same, Catholic University (February 3, 1892). Heuser had established the *AER* in 1889 primarily as a vehicle for educating priests in the field of pastoral theology. Discussions in speculative theology did appear; however. Heuser was an advanced enough thinker to support a nontraditional interpretation of infants who died without baptism. He defended his position that they would enjoy the beatific vision in several issues of *AER*. See Francis J. Connell, "Dogmatic Theology in the American Ecclesiastical Review: 1889–1949," *The American Ecclesiastical Review* 121 (1949):315–16.

46. James A. Moynihan, *The Life of Archbishop John Ireland* (New York, 1953), pp. 79–103.

47. Curran, "Clerical Radicalism," p. 57.

48. Nuesse, "Bouquillon," p. 603.

49. Sweeney, *Spalding*, pp. 201–202.

50. Ahern, *Life of Keane*, pp. 125–128, 147.

51. Ellis, *John Lancaster Spalding: Educator*, pp. 81–83.

52. John Lancaster Spalding, "Progress in Education," in *Religion, Agnosticism and Education*, pp. 29–30.

53. John Lancaster Spalding, "The University and the Teacher," in *Opportunity and Other Essays and Addresses* (Chicago, 1901), p. 129.

54. Ellis, *John Lancaster Spalding: Educator*, pp. 80–81.

55. John Lancaster Spalding, "Women and the Higher Education," in *Opportunity and Other Essays and Addresses*, pp. 53–55.

56. John Lancaster Spalding, "Women and Education," in *Means and Ends*, p. 111.

57. Ahern, *Life of Keane*, pp. 151–58.

58. Wynne, ed., *Great Encyclical Letters*, pp. 325–26.

59. Ellis, *Gibbons*, 2:29–30, citing AAB, 93 R-4, Ireland to Gibbons, February 6, 1895.

60. William L. Portier, "Modernism in the United States: The Case of John A. Slattery (1851–1926)" (unpublished, American Academy of Religion, Roman Catholic Modernism Working Papers, 1986), p. 4.

61. For the circumstances surrounding O'Connell's dismissal, see Gerald

P. Fogarty, S.J., *The Vatican and the Americanist Crisis* (Rome, 1974), pp. 251–53.

62. Portier, "Modernism in the United States," p. 4.
63. Patrick H. Ahern, *The Catholic University of America, 1887–1896: The Rectorship of John J. Keane* (Washington, 1949), pp. 164–71, 187.
64. Sweeney, *Spalding*, p. 244.
65. Fogarty, *Americanist Crisis*, pp. 257–59, quotation on p. 257.
66. Moynihan, *John Ireland*, p. 75.
67. See Fogarty, *Americanist Crisis*, p. 260, for the work of Contessa Sabina Parravicino di Revel.
68. *Le Père Hecker, fondateur des "Paulistes" américains, 1819–1888* par le Père W. Elliott, de la même Compagnie. Traduit et adapté de l'anglais avec authorisation de l'auteur. Introduction par Mgr. Ireland. Préface par l'Abbé Félix Klein (Paris, 1897). [Hereafter called the *Vie.*]
69. Walter Elliott, *The Life of Father Hecker* (New York, 1891), p. iii.
70. The translation was done by Countess de Revilliax. She was called "la patiente et humble traductrice de votre livre" in a letter to Elliott, *APF*, July 13, 1897.
71. Fogarty, *Americanist Crisis*, p. 261.
72. Denis J. O'Connell, "A New Idea in the Life of Father Hecker," reprinted in Félix Klein, *Americanism: A Phantom Heresy* (Atchison, 1951), pp. 71–75.
73. Curran, "Clerical Radicalism," pp. 63–65; see also Elliott, *Life of Hecker*, esp. Ireland's Preface, p. xii, wherein it is recounted that the archbishop of Saint Paul spoke of the harm that "hair-splitting distinctions" of the casuists had done to America.
74. For Turinaz's reaction, see Klein, *Phantom Heresy*, pp. 65–70, 76–78.
75. Americo D. Lapati, *Orestes A. Brownson* (New York, 1965), p. 48.
76. John Richards Betts, "Darwinism, Evolution, and American Catholic Thought, 1860–1899," *Catholic Historical Review* 45 (July 1959):164–68, quotations on p. 194.
77. Published in London, 1871, pp. 243–89 cited in Betts, "Darwinism," p. 164.
78. Robert D. Cross, *The Emergence of Liberal Catholicism in America* (Chicago, 1968), p. 151.
79. Gannon, "Before and After Modernism," p. 315.
80. Betts, "Darwinism," p. 170.
81. Gannon, "Before and After Modernism," p. 316.
82. Portier, "Modernism in the United States," p. 2.
83. *AER*, February–July, 1891, cited by Connell, "Dogmatic Theology," p. 313.
84. John B. Hogan, "Clerical Studies II. The Natural Sciences," *AER* 5 (July 1891):2–4; ibid., 5 (August 1891):118–20, cited in Betts, "Darwinism," p. 175.
85. Wynne, ed., *Great Encyclical Letters*, pp. 55–56.
86. Joseph Pohle, "Darwinism and Theism," *AER* 7 (September 1892):161–76; cited in Betts, "Darwinism," pp. 175–76.
87. John Lancaster Spalding, "University Education," pp. 91–92.
88. Betts, "Darwinism," p. 177.
89. Wynne, *Great Encyclical Letters*, pp. 271–302, quotations on pp. 292–93.

90. Cross, *Liberal Catholicism*, p. 155.
91. Published in Chicago by McBride & Company.
92. Ibid., pp. 385–86.
93. Gannon, "Before and After Modernism," p. 317.
94. Series xvi, ix (January 4, 1897):201–204.
95. Gannon, "Before and After Modernism," p. 317.
96. "Gladstone on Evolution and the Gospel," *Literary Digest* 13 (June 25, 1896):403, cited in Cross, *Liberal Catholicism*, p. 151.
97. Keane to Zahm, September 28, 1898, Zahm Papers, quoted in Ahern, *Life of Keane*, p. 270.
98. John Tracy Ellis, "The Formation of the American Priest: An Historical Perspective," *Catholic Priest*, pp. 59–60, citing Zahm to Alfonso Gòlea, Notre Dame, May 16, 1899, *Literary Digest* 19 (August 12, 1899):200.
99. "Bible, Science, and Faith," p. 170, cited in Cross, *Liberal Catholicism*, p. 152.
100. Rome, November 27, 1898, cited in Gannon, "Before and After Modernism," pp. 317–18.
101. Fogarty, *Americanist Crisis*, pp. 269–71.
102. *Catholic World*, 66 (March 1898):721–30, reprinted in Klein, *Phantom Heresy*, pp. 286–95.
103. AJF Slattery Papers, Slattery to Keane, Baltimore, February 26, 1898, copy, quoted by Ahern, *Life of Keane*, p. 256 n.29.
104. John T. Farrell, "Archbishop John Ireland and Manifest Destiny," *Catholic Historical Review* 33 (October 1947):292.
105. Published in Rome, 1898.
106. Maignen, *Père Hecker*, p. 202.
107. Quoted in Ahern, *Life of Keane*, pp. 261–62.
108. Klein, *Phantom Heresy*, pp. 170–71.
109. Christopher J. Kauffman, *Tradition and Transformation in Catholic Culture: The Priests of Saint Sulpice in the United States from 1791 to the Present* (New York, 1988), pp. 63–65.
110. Quoted by Klein, *Phantom Heresy*, p. 170.
111. In accordance with Vatican policy, the letters and papers of Pope Leo XIII will not be accessible until the year 2003, one hundred years after the pope's death.
112. McCool, *Catholic Theology*, pp. 237–38.
113. *AASP*, O'Connell to Ireland, May 24, 1898, quoted in Thomas T. McAvoy, C.S.C., *The Great Crisis in American Catholic History: 1895–1900* (Chicago, 1957), pp. 206–208.
114. *APF*, Americanism Papers, O'Connell to Elliott, Freiburg im Breisgau, August 22, 1898.
115. *APF*, Americanism Papers, O'Connell to Elliott, December 10, 1898. For the basis of O'Connell's optimism, see Robert C. Ayers, "The Americanist Attack on Europe in 1897 and 1898," pp. 83–92 in *Rising from History*, ed. Robert J. Daley (New York, 1987).
116. Wynne, *Great Encyclical Letters*, pp. 441–53.
117. This is the burden throughout McCool's *Catholic Theology*; James Hennesey, S.J., draws the implications of the Thomistic Revival in "Leo XIII's Revival: A Political and Philosophical Event," *Journal of Religion* 58 (1978): Supplement, 5185–97.
118. Killen, "Americanism Revisited," p. 414.

119. Thomas E. Wangler, "Myth, Worldviews and Late Nineteenth Century American Catholic Expansionism," in Robert J. Daly, S.J., ed., *Rising from History* (New York/London, 1987), pp. 71–80, presents sketches of the various metaphysical bases of Hecker, Keane, Ireland, and O'Connell; William L. Portier, "Two Generations of American Catholic Expansionism in Europe: Isaac Hecker and John J. Keane," pp. 53–64, draws parallels between the two men's thoughts. For a review of the literature on "Americanism," see William L. Portier's "Isaac Hecker and *Testum Benevolentiae:* A Study in Theological Pluralism," in *Hecker Studies*, pp. 11–19.

120. James Hennesey, S.J., "A Prelude to Vatican I: American Bishops and the Definition of the Immaculate Conception," *Theological Studies* 25 (September 1964):410, n.7. It is stated here that no American held this view.

121. Ibid., citing Jules Morel, *Inquisition et libéralisme: Avec doctrinal soumis à M M. Louis Verillot, Albert Du Böys ex cie de Falloux* (Angers, 1857), p. 165.

122. Leo XIII, brief to the bishop of Grenoble, June 22, 1892. Here the pope appealed to the "âme naturellement chrétienne" of the many non-Catholic Frenchmen, cited in Albert Houtin, *L'américanisme* (Paris, 1904), p. 215.

123. See Margaret Mary Reher, "The Church and the Kingdom of God in America: The Ecclesiology of the Americanists," Ph.D. diss., Fordham University, 1972, 175–238, for the similarities and the distortions of Maignen's work with Hecker's and with *Testum.*

124. Published in Paris, 1892.

125. Maignen, *Père Hecker*, p. 176.

126. McCool, *Catholic Theology*, pp. 235–37.

127. Wynne, *Great Encyclical Letters*, pp. 107–134.

128. Pope Leo XIII was seventy-five at the time *Immortale Dei* was signed.

129. Wynne, *Great Encyclical Letters*, pp. 120–23, 118–20, 111; John Courtney Murray, S.J., "La Déclaration sur la liberté religieuse," *Nouvelle Revue Théologique* 88 (January 1966):62.

130. Murray, "Liberté religieuse," p. 54.

131. Wynne, *Great Encyclical Letters*, pp. 109–12, 120–22, 444–45.

132. John Ireland, *The Church and Modern Society* (New York, 1897), p. 35.

133. Wynne, *Great Encyclical Letters*, pp. 444–45, 452.

134. James Hennesey, S.J., "Papacy and Episcopacy in Eighteenth and Nineteenth Century Catholic Thought," *RACHSP* 77 (September 1966):185.

135. (Rome) preserved in the newspaper collection, *APF*, Americanism Papers.

136. Wynne, *Great Encyclical Letters*, p. 452.

137. Leo XIII reportedly told Ireland that the letter on Americanism had no application "except in a few dioceses in France." Ireland to Bellamy Storer, Rome, August 5, 1900, quoted by Maria L. Storer, *In Memoriam: Bellamy Storer* (Boston, 1923), p. 46.

138. For the opinion that some theological content of Hecker and the Americanizer, broadly understood, was censured, see Margaret Mary Reher, "Pope Leo XIII and Americanism," *Theological Studies* 34 (December 1973); idem, " 'Americanism' and the 'Signs of the

Times,' " in Daly, S.J., ed., *Rising from History*, pp. 93–100; Killen, in "Americanism Revisited," argued the same about Spalding; for the opposing view, see Portier, "Theological Pluralism," in *Rising from History*, 11–48; Thomas Wangler, "The Americanism of J. St. Clair Etheridge," *RACHSP* 85 (March–June 1974): 88–105; idem, "Catholic Expansionism," pp. 71–82.

139. McAvoy, *Great Crisis*, pp. 290–91.
140. This opinion was expressed by the Rector of the Catholic University of Paris, Père L. Péchnard, in his "The End of 'Americanism' in France," *The North American Review* 170 (March 1900):420–32; Houtin, in his *L'Américanisme*, attempted to vindicate the Americans involved.
141. McAvoy, *Great Crisis*, p. 344.
142. James Hennesey, S.J., "American History and the Theological Enterprise," *The Catholic Theological Society of American Proceedings* 26 (1971):113.
143. In 1968, Karl Rahner argued for legitimate plurality of philosophies in his "Philosophy and Philosophizing in Theology," *Theology Digest*, Sesquicentennial Issue (February 1968):17–29.
144. In his "Clerical Radicalism," 65, Emmett Curran accused the Americanists of jingoism and claimed that theirs was not a more Christian view of cultural pluralism.
145. Ahern, *Life of Keane*, p. 233.
146. Storer, *In Memoriam Bellamy*, pp. 85–87.
147. Jay P. Dolan, *The American Catholic Experience* (New York, 1985), p. 188.
148. Walter M. Abbott, S.J., ed., *The Documents of Vatican II* (New York, 1966), pp. 675–96.
149. Ibid., pp. 14–101, esp. pp. 24–65.
150. Ibid., pp. 137–188; John Ireland did not promote the vernacular.
151. Ibid., pp. 466–82.
152. *APF*, Americanism Papers, Elliott to Klein, Saint Paul's College, Catholic University, January 24, 1900.
153. *RMLAHC*, Heuser Papers, EH 26, same to same, June 6, 1909; EH 27, same to same, June 8, 1909.
154. Chinnici, *Holy Spirit*, pp. 84, 51.
155. Ellis, *John Lancaster Spalding: Educator*, p. 78.
156. Spalding, "Education and the Future of Religion," in *Religion, Agnosticism and Education*, pp. 156–60, 163–66, 191.
157. Sweeney, *Spalding*, p. 268; Killen, "Americanism Revisited," argues that Spalding was a theological Americanist.
158. Sweeney, *Spalding*, p. 277.
159. Houtin, *L'Américanisme*, p. 435.
160. This is the interpretation of Killen, "Americanism Revisited," pp. 442–43.
161. John Lancaster Spalding, "Goethe as Educator," *Opportunity*, pp. 152, 154–55, 175.

Chapter 5   Modernist Scholarship and Progressive Social Thought

1. Michael V. Gannon, "Before and After Modernism: The Intellectual Isolation of the American Priest," in *The Catholic Priest in the United*

States: Historical Investigations, ed. John Tracy Ellis (Collegeville, Minn., 1971), p. 327.

2. For an account of John Keane's recruitment of professors for the original faculty, see Patrick H. Ahern, *The Catholic University of America, 1887–1896: The Rectorship of John J. Keane* (Washington, D.C., 1949), pp. 5–8.

3. John K. Ryan, "Edward Aloysius Pace," *New Catholic Encyclopedia,* 15 vols. (New York, 1967), 10:850–51. [Henceforth *NCE.*]

4. C. Joseph Nuesse, "Thomas Joseph Bouquillon (1840–1902), Moral Theologian and Precursor of the Social Sciences in The Catholic University of America," *The Catholic Historical Review* 72 (October 1986):606–607.

5. Robert J. North, S.J., "The American Scripture Century," *American Ecclesiastical Review* 150 (May 1964):322–24 [henceforth *AER*]; John L. Murphy, "Seventy-Five Years of Fundamental Theology in America," *AER* 150 (June 1964):391–94.

6. Robert D. Cross, *The Emergence of Liberal Catholicism in America* (Chicago, 1968), p. 41.

7. Published in Boston.

8. John Hogan, *Les Études du clergy,* trans. Abbé A. Boudinhon (Paris, 1901); Jean Rivière, *Le modernisme dans l'église: étude d'histoire religieuse contemporaine* (Paris, 1929), p. 101.

9. Christopher J. Kauffman, *Tradition and Transformation in Catholic Culture: The Priests of Saint Sulpice in the United States from 1791 to the Present* (New York, 1988), p. 199; Magnien was close to Gibbons and Ireland.

10. Gannon, "Before and After Modernism," p. 330.

11. Kauffman, *Tradition and Transformation,* pp. 206–214.

12. Gannon, "Before and After Modernism," p. 330.

13. Kauffman, *Tradition and Transformation,* p. 211.

14. Michael J. De Vito, *The New York Review (1905–1908)* (New York, 1977), pp. 39–49. [Much of the following discussion on the *New York Review* is dependent on De Vito's work.]

15. Ibid., Appendix A, pp. 332–35, policy statement on p. 333.

16. Ibid., pp. 47, 121–123, 105–114, 314.

17. Ibid., pp. 210 n.36, 173–74 n.37; Articles appeared in the *New York Review* by George Tyrrell and Wilfred Ward, both of whom claimed Newman as their inspiration; George Tyrrell, "Consensus Fidelium," 1 (August–September 1905):133–38; idem, "The Dogmatic Reading of History," 1 (October–November 1905):269–76; Wilfred Ward, "The Function of Intransigence," 2 (July–August 1906):3–26.

18. Published in Paris by Picard.

19. René Marlé, ed., *Au coeur de la crise moderniste. Le dossier inédit d'une controverse* (Paris, 1960).

20. Mary Jo Weaver, "Wilfred Ward, George Tyrrell and the Meanings of Modernism," *The Downside Review* 96 (January 1978):28–29, 34; Weaver attributed Tyrrell's difficulties to an article "A Perverted Devotion," *The Weekly Register* (December 1899) in which he suggested that hell was not to be taken literally but that it was mysterious.

21. *Ernesto Buonauiti: Pilgrim of Rome: An Introduction into the Life and Work of Ernesto Buonauiti,* ed. N. Pittenger and C. Nelson (Welwyn, 1969).

22. Luigi Mezzardi, "Catholicity in Italy," in *History of the Church*, 10 vols., ed. Hubert Jedin and trans. Anselm Briggs (New York, 1981), 10:572.
23. Anne Freemantle, ed. *The Papal Encyclicals in Their Historical Context* (New York, 1963), pp. 202–205.
24. Joseph B. Lemius, *Catechism on Modernism: According to the Encyclical "Pascendi Dominici Gregis" of His Holiness, Pius X*, trans. John Fitzpatrick (New York, 1908), p. 117.
25. Cited in Émile Poulet, *Histoire, dogme et critique dans la crise moderniste* (Paris, 1960), 443. [Translation mine.]
26. For the issues involved, see De Vito, *New York Review*, pp. 197–203, 248–308.
27. Ryan Memorial Library Archives and Historical Collection at Saint Charles Borromeo Seminary in Philadelphia, Heuser Papers, TH 97, Tyrrell to Heuser, September 10, 1903, Richmond, York. Tyrrell gives this information to Heuser and regrets that he may put McSorley "on the spot." [Henceforth *RMLAHC*.]
28. De Vito, *New York Review*, pp. 264, 280–281, 303. It appeared in three installments in the second, third, and fourth issues of *NYR*, 1905–1906.
29. Ibid., pp. 267–268. The article fell into the hands of Père Alexis M. Lepicier, professor of dogmatic theology at the Urban College in Rome, who judged that many of the authors whom Hanna had cited were on the Index.
30. Ibid., pp. 269–70. One of Hanna's colleagues, Andrew Breen, delated him to Rome as lacking "firmness of orthodoxy." Breen, it seems, was insanely jealous of Hanna.
31. Ibid., pp. 289–90.
32. James Hennesey, S.J., "American History and the Theological Enterprise," *Proceedings of the CTSA* 26 (Bronx, N.Y., 1972):113f; Michel de Certeau, S.J., "Culture américaine et théologie catholique," *Etudes* November 1971, pp. 561–77; Margaret Mary Reher, "Americanism and Modernism—Continuity or Discontinuity?" *U.S. Catholic Historian* 1 (Summer 1981):87–103; Michael B. McGarry, "Modernism in the United States: William Laurence Sullivan, 1872–1935," *Records of the American Catholic Historical Society of Philadelphia* 90 (March–December 1979):33–52 [henceforth *RACHSP*]; R. Scott Appleby, "American Catholic Modernism at the Turn of the Century," (Ph.D. diss., Divinity School, University of Chicago, 1985); William L. Portier, "Modernism in the United States: The Case of John R. Slattery (1851–1926)," (unpublished, American Academy of Religion, Roman Catholic Modernism Working Papers, 1986). It should be noted that Albert Houtin, first historian of the Americanist crisis, saw it as a theological one. However, his *L'Américanisme* (Paris, 1904) was regarded with suspicion because Houtin later became a modernist.
33. De Vito, *New York Review*, p. 288 n.65; *NYR* 3, nos. 4-5 (January–February, March–April 1908):391–400.
34. Gannon, "Before and After Modernism," pp. 348–49, reports that an article Hanna had contributed to the Protestant periodical *American Journal of Theology* (1907), "Some Recent Books on Catholic Theology," was judged as tending toward modernism.
35. De Vito, *New York Review*, p. 301.

36. Gannon, "Before and After Modernism," p. 347.
37. Albert Houtin, *Histoire du modernisme catholique* 18 (Paris, 1913):242; idem, *The Life of a Priest: My Own Experiences*, trans. Winifred S. Whale (London, 1927), pp. 141–44. In this work the condemned modernist gossip claims that Driscoll had given up all theological belief before his death.
38. C. Harold Smith, "Recollections of the Aftermath," *Continuum* 3 (Summer 1965):235, 237. As a tribute to Duffy's chaplaincy, a statue of him overlooks Times Square in New York City.
39. Kauffman, *Tradition and Transformation*, pp. 212–20, 223, 313.
40. Gannon, "Before and After Modernism, pp. 349–50, gives a synopsis of the event; see also Colman J. Barry, O.S.B., *The Catholic University of America, 1903–1909: The Rectorship of Denis J. O'Connell* (Washington, D.C., 1950), pp. 177–81; details may be found in Gerald P. Fogarty, S.J., "Dissent at Catholic University: The Case of Henry Poels," *America* 156 (October 11, 1986):180–84. [The following discussion is based on Fogarty's account.]
41. Fogarty, "Dissent at C.U.," quotation on p. 182.
42. Ellis, "Formation of the American Priest," p. 69, states that only three American priests openly admitted their modernist views.
43. Portier, "Modernism in the United States," pp. 1, 4.
44. John R. Slattery, in his article entitled "How My Priesthood Dropped from Me," *The Independent* 61 (September 6, 1906):565–71, instructed the reader to consider the article an announcement of his defection.
45. William L. Sullivan, *Under Orders: The Autobiography of William Laurence Sullivan*, reprint (Boston, 1966), pp. 198–200, n.7.
46. Portier, "Modernism in the United States," p. 9, describes Slattery's growing doubts, and Slattery himself described 1901 as the unhappiest year of his life. He could no longer distinguish Catholicism from myth. Some years later Slattery engaged in polemics and stated that John Ireland, Denis O'Connell, and other ecclesiastics sacrificed intellectual honesty in the face of *Pascendi* in order to survive personally and promote their careers in the church. He claimed that Ireland and O'Connell shared with him unspecified radical religious ideas (ibid., pp. 6, 16). Sullivan requested to be relieved of his teaching post in Washington, D.C., in favor of parochial duties in 1908. He struggled for two more years; see Sullivan, *Under Orders*, pp. 198–200.
47. Houtin, *Histoire*, p. 229.
48. E. E. Y. Hales, "The Americanist Controversy," *The Month* 31 (January 1964):36, cited in Gannon, "Before and After Modernism," p. 348.
49. [Sullivan], "The Final Phase of Modernism," p. 3. Archives of the Harvard Divinity School Library, Sullivan Papers. Unsigned typescript with instructions that reader return it to William Sullivan, Kansas City.
50. John Tracy Ellis and Robert Trisco, *A Guide to American Catholic History*, 2nd ed. rev. (Santa Barbara, Calif., 1982), p. 10.
51. *Messenger* (June); Paul H. Linehan, "The Catholic Encyclopedia," *Catholic Builders of the Nation*, ed. Constantine E. McGuire, 5 vols. (Boston, 1923), 4:204.
52. *RMLAHC*, Shahan Papers, Box 2, newspaper clipping; Thomas F.

Meehan, "The Catholic Encylcopedia;" *Catholic Vigil* (November 17, 1920) [page number not included].

53. *The Catholic Encyclopedia and Its Makers* (New York, 1917), pp. vii–viii. [Henceforth called *Makers*.]

54. *RMLAHC*, Shahan Papers, Box 2, Wynne to Thomas J. Shahan, Catholic Encyclopedia, 23 East 41st St., New York, May 22, 1920. Pallen was obviously concerned about having his loan "secured." Wynne said that Pallen was "staling *[sic]* about at the C. E. office."

55. Linehan, "The Catholic Encyclopedia," pp. 206–208.

56. Roy J. Deferrari, "Thomas Joseph Shahan," NCE 13:156–57.

57. *Makers*, p. 159; *NCE* 13:156.

58. *RMLAHC*, Shahan Papers, Box 2, Editorial Department, *Catholic Standard and Times*, January 8, 1920. O'Shea expressed concern over the lack of support among the Catholic community for the "great Wynne encyclopedia."

59. Edmund G. Ryan, "John Joseph Wynne," *NCE* 14:1053.

60. M. Natalena Farrelly, S.S.J., *Thomas Francis Meehan, 1854–1942: A Memoir* (New York, 1944), p. 81.

61. *Makers*, pp. v, iv.

62. Linehan, "The Catholic Encyclopedia," p. 211. Of the American-born, two-thirds were educated in the United States.

63. *Makers*, *passim*.

64. Three women can be singled out. Florence Rudge McGraham contributed over eighty articles, a number of which were on religious orders; Marie Louise Handley wrote over thirty articles on art; Blanche Kelly authored more than thirty articles; *Makers*, pp. 72–73, 89, 107.

65. Linehan, "The Catholic Encyclopedia," pp. 213–214.

66. *Makers*, p. v.

67. Houtin, *Histoire*, p. 242.

68. *RMLAHC*, Shahan Papers, Box 2, Wynne to Thomas J. Shahan, Catholic Encyclopedia, 23 East 41st St., N.Y., August 16, 1918. Wynne reported that he had literally "slaved" to keep the operation afloat. Unlike Shahan, who was vacationing in Nova Scotia, Wynne said that he could not afford to "take a week off to make a retreat." Within a month Shahan sent Wynne a copy of an appeal from the board of editors to be sent to all Catholic, Protestant, and Jewish seminaries. Loc. cit., Wynne to Shahan, September 12, 1918.

69. *Catholic Encyclopedia*, 15 vols. (New York, 1907–1912), 4:491–97 [henceforth *CE*]; *Makers*, p. 143.

70. *CE* 4:497. Reid noted that the Pontifical Biblical Commission's decisions had the force of the acts of the Roman Congregation.

71. *CE* 10:415–21.

72. *Makers*, p. 178.

73. Hennesey, "Theological Enterprise," p. 99. Hennesey made this comment in the context of the nineteenth century, but it was equally true in the early part of the following one.

74. *CE* 10:418, 420–21, quotation on p. 420.

75. *CE* 14:250–54.

76. *CE* 3:744–61.

77. Linehan, "The Catholic Encyclopedia," p. 214; Meehan, "Catholic Encyclopedia," unpaginated.

78. *CE* 14:537–38.
79. Linehan, "Catholic Encyclopedia," p. 216, citing the *Dublin Review*, London, and *Etudes*, Paris.
80. *RMLAHC*, Shahan Papers, Box 2, W. C. J. Magee, Secretary, Encyclopedia Press to Shahan, November 16, 1920.
81. Meehan, "Catholic Encyclopedia," unpaginated.
82. Linehan, "Catholic Encyclopedia," p. 218. The decoration was awarded in 1914.
83. *CE* 15:687–94; Francis M. Mason, "The Newer Eve: The Catholic Women's Suffrage Society in England, 1911–1923," *The Catholic Historical Review* 72 (October 1986):628, citing the *Catholic Suffragist* (July 15, 1916):47.
84. Rössler was also sarcastic. In one place he said that there would be no fear that the academic professions would ever be "over-crowded" by women, who were naturally inferior mentally (*CE* 15:694).
85. *CE* 15:687.
86. Mason, "Newer Eve," p. 628 n.42.
87. *CE* 15:694–97.
88. James Kenneally, "It Seems to Me I've Heard That Tune Before: Catholic Women and the ERA, 1923–1945 and After" to be published in the *Catholic Historical Review*.
89. James Hennesey, S.J., *American Catholics* (New York, 1981), p. 233.
90. John A. Ryan, *Social Reconstruction* (New York, 1920), p. 226.
91. John A. Ryan, *Social Doctrine in Action: A Personal History* (New York, 1941), pp. 1–21.
92. Henry McDrewry, Thomas H. O'Connell, and Frank Freidel, eds., *America Is*, 2nd ed. (Columbus, Ohio, 1982), pp. 423–24.
93. Jay Dolan, *The American Catholic Experience* (New York, 1985), p. 148.
94. Joseph M. McShane, S.J., *"Sufficiently Radical": Catholicism, Progressivism, and the Bishop's Program of 1919* (Washington, D.C., 1986), pp. 3, 7–20.
95. Ryan, *Social Doctrine*, pp. 8–9, 41–50, quotation on pp. 49–50.
96. Francis L. Broderick, *Right Reverend New Dealer: John A. Ryan* (New York, 1963), p. 21.
97. Ryan, *Social Doctrine*, pp. 63–64.
98. McShane, *"Sufficiently Radical,"* pp. 7–11, 32–36.
99. See John J. Wynne, S.J., ed., *The Great Encyclical Letters of Pope Leo XIII* (New York, 1903); see "The Condition of the Working Classes," pp. 215, 230–35, for the circumstances in which Leo ceded state intervention.
100. McShane, *"Sufficiently Radical,"* pp. 32–36.
101. Published in New York City.
102. John A. Ryan, *A Living Wage: Its Ethical and Economic Aspects* (New York, 1906), pp. xii–xiii.
103. McShane, *"Sufficiently Radical,"* pp. 38–40.
104. Broderick, *New Dealer*, pp. 39–41, 44.
105. Ryan, *Living Wage*, p. 329.
106. McShane, *"Sufficiently Radical,"* pp. 43–44.
107. Broderick, *New Dealer*, p. 47, citing the negative judgment of the London *Pioneer*.
108. David O'Brien, "The American Priest and Social Action," in Ellis, ed., *Catholic Priest*, p. 442.

109. Broderick, *New Dealer*, pp. 55, 99.
110. Ryan, *Social Doctrine*, p. 105.
111. O'Brien, "American Priest," p. 442; Broderick, *New Dealer*, p. 83.
112. Hennesey, *American Catholics*, p. 212.
113. Philip Gleason, *The Conservative Reformers: German American Catholics and the Social Order* (Notre Dame, Ind., 1968), p. 90. [The following discussion of the *Central Verein* is dependent on Gleason.]
114. Broderick, *New Dealer* p. 60; Gleason, *Conservative Reformer*, pp. 3, 90–117.
115. Broderick, *New Dealer*, p. 75; Gleason, *Conservative Reformer*, p. 131. Pesch had written a five-volume work on "solidarism" entitled *Lehrbuch der National Ökonomie*, which Ryan considered the greatest single work on the subject.
116. Gleason, *Conservative Reformer*, pp. 105–115, 127–129, 132, 133–134, 136, 160–71, Hennesey, American Catholics, pp. 224–25.
117. John A. Ryan, *Distributive Justice* (New York, 1927), first published in 1916, pp. 1, 3, 73, 63–66, 180, 268–72, 281, 319–20, quotation on p. 66.
118. Steve Dawson, "Employee Ownership in the [19]80's," *Building Economic Alternatives* 2 (Fall 1986):10–11, 15. It is an adaptation of a speech by Dawson, executive director of Industrial Cooperative Association, Inc. He argued for "first class ownership" which included a share in profits and a share in ownership. He also cited the American Catholic Bishops' draft on the economy with approval.
119. Ryan, *Distributive Justice*, pp. 389–97.
120. McShane, *"Sufficiently Radical,"* pp. 76–77.
121. Ryan, *Social Reconstruction*, pp. 143, 217–24, 226, 234.
122. Henry J. Browne, "Catholicism in the United States," in *The Shaping of American Religion*, 2 vols., ed. James Ward Smith and A. Leland Jamison (Princeton, 1961), 1:105.
123. McShane, *"Sufficiently Radical,"* 192–200; 277–78.
124. Ryan, *Social Doctrine*, p. 13.
125. McShane, *"Sufficiently Radical,"* pp. 209–30.
126. O'Brien, "American Priest," p. 444.
127. Broderick, *New Dealer*, pp. 33, 45.
128. McShane, *"Sufficiently Radical,"* p. 281.
129. William M. Halsey, *The Survival of American Innocence in an Era of Disillusionment, 1920–1940* (Notre Dame, 1980), pp. 2, 8.
130. McShane, *"Sufficiently Radical,"* p. 84.
131. Hennesey, *American Catholics*, pp. 230–315.
132. Broderick, *New Dealer*, pp. 67–68.
133. Ryan, *Social Doctrine*, p. 224.
134. Broderick, *New Dealer*, pp. 63, 156–59.

Chapter 6   The Path to Pluralism

1. James Hennesey, S.J., *Catholics in the Promised Land of the Saints* (Marquette, Wisc., 1981), p. 29.
2. William M. Halsey, *The Survival of American Innocence in an Era of Disillusionment, 1920–1940* (Notre Dame, Ind., 1980), p. 2. [The following discussion is based on Halsey.]

3. Ibid., pp. 2–4, 53, 66, 169.
4. Patrick Carey, ed., *American Catholic Religious Thought* (New York, 1987), p. 51.
5. Monica Furlong, *Merton, A Biography* (San Francisco, 1980), p. 71.
6. Patrick W. Carey, "American Catholic Religious Thought: An Historical Review," *U.S. Catholic Historian* 4 (1985):137.
7. Halsey, *Survival*, pp. 162–63.
8. Steven M. Avella, "Thomistic Apogee: The Career of John T. McNicholas, O.P." (Paper presented to the American Catholic Historical Association at John Carroll University, April 1986), p. 2.
9. Steven M. Avella, "John T. McNicholas in the Age of Practical Thomism," *Records of the American Catholic Historical Society of Philadelphia* 97 (March–December 1986):17. [Henceforth *RACHSP*.]
10. Joseph M. White, "Archbishop John T. McNicholas and the Pontifical Commission of the Catholic University of America, 1934–1950" (Paper presented to the American Catholic Historical Association at John Carroll University, April 1986), p. 1. [The following is based on White.]
11. Ibid., pp. 2, 7, 11, 14–15. See also Christopher J. Kauffman, *Tradition and Transformation in Catholic Culture: the Priests of Saint Sulpice in the United States from 1791 to the Present* (New York, 1988), pp. 268–73.
12. Avella, "Thomistic Apogee," p. 15.
13. White, "McNicholas," pp. 15–16.
14. Kathleen R. Fields, "The Intellectual Stature of Fulton J. Sheen" (Lecture delivered to and printed by the Friends of Sheen at Saint Bernard's Institute, Rochester, N.Y., September 30, 1985). [The following is based on Fields.]
15. Halsey, *Survival*, p. 157.
16. Fields, "Intellectual Stature," p. 14.
17. Kathleen R. Fields, "Anti-Communism and Social Justice: The Double-Edged Sword of Fulton Sheen," *RACHSP* 96 (March–December 1985):84.
18. John Tracy Ellis, *Catholic Bishops: A Memoir* (Wilmington, Del., 1983), p. 83.
19. Halsey, *Survival*, p. 157.
20. Fields, "Intellectual Stature," p. 11.
21. Carey, "American Catholic Religious Thought," p. 138.
22. Archives of *The Thomist*, draft of Reginald Coffee, O.P., *Flight of the Eagle*, n.p.
23. Rodger Van Allen, *"The Commonweal" and American Catholicism: The Magazine, the Movement, the Meaning* (Philadelphia, 1974), pp. 5–9. [The following section is based on Van Allen.]
24. Ibid., pp. 27, 75, 17.
25. Halsey, *Survival*, p. 85.
26. Van Allen, *Commonweal*, p. 10.
27. Francis L. Broderick, *Right Reverend New Dealer: John A. Ryan* (New York, 1963), p. 172.
28. Published in New York City.
29. Henry J. Browne, "Catholicism in the United States," in *The Shaping of American Religion*, ed. James Ward Smith and A. Leland Jamison (Princeton, 1961), p. 116.
30. John A. Ryan and Moorhouse F. X. Miller, S. J., *The State and the Church* (New York, 1922), pp. 32, 39.

31. Broderick, *New Dealer*, p. 171.
32. Winifred Ernest Garrison, *Catholicism and the American Mind* (Chicago, 1928), p. 114.
33. Broderick, *New Dealer*, p. 185.
34. James Hennesey, S.J., *American Catholics* (New York, 1981), p. 253, citing *Catholic World* 128 (1928):357.
35. John A. Ryan, *Social Doctrine in Action: A Personal History* (New York, 1941), p. 242.
36. Arnold J. Sparr, "From Self-Congratulations to Self-Criticism: Main Currents in American Catholic Fiction, 1900–1960," *U.S. Catholic Historian* 6 (Spring/Summer 1987): 224–25.
37. Broderick, *New Dealer*, pp. 213, 225.
38. Van Allen, *Commonweal*, p. 55.
39. Broderick, *New Dealer*, p. 228.
40. Sheldon Marcus, *Father Coughlin: The Tumultuous Life of the Priest of the Little Flower* (Boston, 1973), pp. 45–47.
41. David H. Bennett, *Demagogues of the Depression: American Radicals and the Union Party, 1932–36* (New Brunswick, N.J., 1969), p. 68.
42. Hennesey, *American Catholics*, p. 275.
43. Van Allen, *Commonweal*, pp. 51–54.
44. José M. Sánchez, *The Spanish Civil War as a Religious Tragedy* (Notre Dame, Ind., 1987), pp. 184, 189. [The following is based on Sanchez.]
45. Ibid., 189, 199.
46. Van Allen, *Commonweal*, pp. 63–64, 69, quotation on p. 69.
47. Sánchez, *Spanish Civil War*, p. 196.
48. Van Allen, *Commonweal*, pp. 67, 69, 72–73.
49. Sánchez, *Spanish Civil War*, p. 196.
50. Sparr, "Main Currents," p. 222.
51. Paul R. Messbarger, "The Failed Promise of American Catholic Literature," *U.S. Catholic Historian* 4 (1985):153–58.
52. Halsey, *Survival*, p. 124.
53. Eugene Kennedy, "What Do Catholic Novelists Do?" *U.S. Catholic Historian* 6 (Spring/Summer 1987):249.
54. Halsey, *Survival*, 93–94, 97, 124.
55. Messbarger, "Failed Promise," pp. 153, 157.
56. Halsey, *Survival*, p. 135.
57. Messbarger, "Failed Promise," p. 155.
58. John Cogley, *Catholic America*, expanded and updated by Rodger Van Allen (Kansas City, Mo., 1986), pp. 149–50, 212.
59. Van Allen, *Commonweal*, p. 119.
60. Walter J. Ong, S.J., *Frontiers of American Catholicism: Essays on Ideology and Culture* (New York, 1957), p. 17.
61. Halsey, *Survival*, p. 120.
62. Van Allen, *Commonweal*, p. 119.
63. Joseph M. McShane, S.J., "Mirrors and Teachers: A Study of Catholic Periodical Fiction between 1930 and 1950," *U.S. Catholic Historian* 6 (Spring/Summer 1987):195.
64. Ibid., pp. 182, 189–90, 198. The total audience of five popular Catholic journals reached 610,000 subscribers.
65. Sparr, "Main Currents," pp. 223–24. [The following is based on Sparr.]
66. Ibid., pp. 223–25, 227, 229.

67. Bill Oliver, "Faith and Fiction in a Secular Age," *U.S. Catholic Historian* 6 (Spring/Summer 1987):118. [The following is based on Oliver.]

68. Ibid., pp. 120, 124.

69. Sparr, "Main Currents," p. 229.

70. J. F. Powers, "On Reading about My Faith and Fiction in a Secular Age," *U.S. Catholic Historian* 6 (Spring/Summer 1987):140–42.

71. *Wise Blood* (1952) and *The Violent Bear It Away* (1960).

72. *A Good Man Is Hard to Find* (1955) and *Everything That Rises Must Converge* (1965).

73. Oliver, "Faith and Fiction," p. 117, gives the quotation.

74. John B. Breslin, S.J., ed., *The Substance of Things Hoped For* (New York, 1987), p. 312, gives the quotation.

75. Quoted by Jay P. Dolan, *The American Catholic Experience* (New York, 1985), pp. 352, 388.

76. Walter J. Ong, "American Catholicism and America," *Thought* 27 (1952):528.

77. Paul Blanshard, *Communism, Democracy, and Catholic Power* (Boston, 1951), p. 173.

78. Ong, "American Catholicism," p. 535–36.

79. William A. Herr, *Catholic Thinkers in the Clear: Giants of Catholic Thought from Augustine to Rahner* (Chicago, 1985), pp. 236–41.

80. John Courtney Murray, "America's Four Conspiracies," in John Cogley, ed., *Religion in America* (New York, 1958), p. 39.

81. Van Allen, *Commonweal*, pp. 107–16.

82. Walter J. Ong, S.J., "The Religious-Secular Dialogue," in Cogley, ed., *Religion in America*, p. 207.

83. John Murray Cuddihy, *No Offense: Civil Religion and Protestant Tastes* (New York, 1978) makes this point.

84. Donald E. Pellotte, S.S.S., *John Courtney Murray: Theologian in Conflict* (New York/Ramsey/Toronto, 1976), p. x.

85. John Courtney Murray, *The Problem of Religious Freedom*, Woodstock Papers, no.7 (Westminster, Md., 1965), p. 12.

86. Pellotte, *John Courtney Murray*, p. 118.

87. Quoted in Philip Gleason, "In Search of Unity: American Catholic Thought, 1920–1960," *Catholic Historical Review* 65 (1979):199–201.

88. Lawrence P. Creedon and William D. Falcon, *United for Separation: An Analysis of P O A U Assaults on Catholicism* (Milwaukee, Wisc., 1959), p. 228.

89. Hennesey, *American Catholics*, p. 303.

90. Gustave Weigel, "The Present Embarrassment of the Church," in Cogley, ed., *Religion in America*, pp. 224–43.

91. Gustave Weigel, *Catholic Theology in Dialogue* (New York, 1965), pp. 69–82.

92. David Gannon, S.A., *Father Paul of Graymoor* (New York, 1951), pp. 256–83; Mary Celine Fleming, S.A., *A Woman of Unity* (New York, 1956), pp. 126–50.

93. Anne Freemantle, ed., *The Papal Encyclicals in Their Historical Context* (New York, 1963), p. 295.

94. Patrick W. Collins, "Gustave Weigel: An Uncompromising Ecumenist," *Journal of Ecumenical Studies* 15 (1978):684–85.

95. Gustave Weigel, S.J., *Faith and Understanding in America* (New York, 1962), pp. 1–13, 38, quotation on p. 13.

96. Collins, "Gustave Weigel," pp. 684, 690.
97. Quoted in George H. Tavard, *Two Centuries of Ecumenism: The Search for Unity*, trans. Royce W. Hughes (New York, 1962), p. 187.
98. E. E. Y. Hales, *Pope John and His Revolution* (New York, 1965), p. 82.
99. Van Allen, *Commonweal*, pp. 107, 130, 136.
100. William J. Parente, "Letters," *America* 154 (January 4–11, 1986):20.
101. Herr, *Catholic Thinkers*, pp. 241–44.
102. Thomas T. Love, "John Courtney Murray, S.J.," in Thomas E. Bird, ed., *Modern Theologians: Christians and Jews* (Notre Dame, Ind., 1967), pp. 32–38.
103. Herr, *Catholic Thinkers*, pp. 241–44.
104. Hennesey, *American Catholics*, p. 303.
105. John Tracy Ellis, *American Catholicism*, 2d ed. rev. (Chicago, 1969), p. 212.
106. Hennesey, *American Catholics*, p. 303.
107. Walter M. Abbott, S.J., ed., *The Documents of Vatican II* (New York, 1966), p. 675.
108. Quoted in Collins, "Gustave Weigel," p. 701.
109. Browne, "Catholicism in the United States," p. 120 n.50.
110. (Westminster, Md.), pp. 9–10.
111. Browne, "Catholicism in the United States," pp. 106, 111 n.43, 112–13.
112. Alden V. Brown, "The Grail Movement to 1962: Laywomen and a New Christendom," *U.S. Catholic Historian* 3 (Fall/Winter 1983):159. [The following is based on Brown.]
113. Ibid., pp. 149–66.
114. Charles A. Fracchia, *Second Spring: The Coming of Age of U.S. Catholicism* (New York/Toronto, 1980), pp. 40, 54–55.
115. Charles E. Curran, *Toward an American Catholic Moral Theology* (Notre Dame, Ind., 1987), p. 126.
116. Justus George Lawler, "The *Continuum* Generation," *U.S. Catholic Historian* 4 (1984):81.
117. Francine du Plessix Gray, *Divine Disobedience: Profiles in Catholic Radicalism* (New York, 1971), p. 86.
118. Published in Notre Dame, Ind., and London.
119. Van Allen, "Foreword," *Catholic America*, speaks of "creative inculturation."
120. (Washington, D.C., 1983), pp. 7, 36.
121. William A. Au, "American Catholics and the Dilemma of War, 1960–1980," *U.S. Catholic Historian* 4 (1984):53.
122. In a more restrained tone, James E. Dougherty's *The Bishops and Nuclear Weapons* (Hamden, Ct., 1984) reflects the first position; the pacifists' position is represented by Ronald G. Musto's *The Catholic Peace Tradition* (Maryknoll, N.Y., 1986). *Peace in a Nuclear Age*, ed. Charles J. Reid, Jr. (Washington, D.C., 1986) brings together a spectrum of perspectives on the bishops' pastoral letter.
123. Curran, *Toward an American Catholic Moral Theology*, pp. 174–92.
124. Gleason, "In Search of Unity," p. 186.
125. James Hitchcock, "Post Mortem on a Rebirth," *American Scholar* 49 (Spring 1980):211–25.
126. Mary Jo Weaver, "Feminist Perspectives and American Catholic History," *U.S. Catholic Historian* 5 (Summer/Fall 1986):402.

127. James Hennesey, S.J., "No More Than 'Footprints in Time'? Church History and Catholic Christianity," *Catholic Historical Review* 73 (April 1987):193–94.

128. Marie Augusta Neal, S.N.D. "American Sisters Now," in *Where We Are: American Catholics in the 1980's,* ed. Michael Glazier (Wilmington, Del., 1985), pp. 141–60, contains a good review of the literature on this transition; Jeannine Gramick adds her insights in "From Good Sisters to Prophetic Women," in Ann Patrick Ware, ed., *Midwives of the Future* (Kansas City, Mo., 1985), pp. 226–37.

129. Sydney Ahlstrom, *A Religious History of the American People* (New Haven/London, 1974), p. 1079.

130. Andrew M. Greeley, *The American Catholic: A Social Portrait* (New York, 1977), p. 37.

131. William J. Byron, S.J., "Credentialled, Commissioned and Free," *America* 155 (August 16–23, 1986):69–71.

132. Monika A. Hellwig, "American Catholic Theology Now," in Glazier, ed., *Where We Are,* pp. 89–101, makes this observation.

133. Curran, *American Catholic Moral Theology,* p. 163.

134. Hennesey, *American Catholics,* pp. 315–16, 326.

135. Robert McAfee Brown, "American Catholicism Now," in Glazier, ed., *Where We Are,* p. 12, describes his pleasure when being invited to contribute to the project.

136. Michael Glazier, "Introduction," in *Where We Are,* pp. 9–10.

137. Wilfred P. Schoenberg, S.J., *A History of the Catholic Church in the Pacific Northwest, 1743–1983* (Washington, D.C., 1987), p. 731.

138. Felician A. Foy, O.F.M., ed., and Rose M. Avato, asst. ed., *1986 Catholic Almanac* (Huntington, Ind., 1986), pp. 518, 525.

139. Neal, "American Sisters Now," p. 153.

140. Theodore M. Hesburgh, C.S.C., "Catholic Higher Education: A Personal Reflection," in Glazier, ed., *Where We Are,* pp. 192–99.

141. Dolores Liptak and Timothy Walch, *"American Catholics and the Intellectual Life:* An Interview with Monsignor John Tracy Ellis," *U.S. Catholic Historian* 4 (1985):191–92.

142. Ahlstrom, *Religious History,* p. 1094.

143. Liptak and Walch, "Ellis," p. 194.

Index